Practical Principles

to

Daily Devotion

JANICE T. PETERS

Order this book online at www.trafford.com
or email orders@trafford.com

Most Trafford titles are also available at major online book retailers.

Book: King James Bible

Printed in the United States of America.

ISBN: 978-1-4269-4886-2 (sc)
ISBN: 978-1-4269-4887-9 (e)

Trafford rev. 12/20/2010

Trafford
PUBLISHING® www.trafford.com

North America & international
toll-free: 1 888 232 4444 (USA & Canada)
phone: 250 383 6864 ♦ fax: 812 355 4082

God has given me a word without complexities or complication, purposed to further along the lives of the believers. You'll find that for everyday there's a new challenge to rise above what's customary and reach for extraordinary. Devotion doesn't consist of standing still; it's about taking what's distributed to you daily and applying it to your life, for this is the road paved with success, leading to new dimensions.

There are those who profess a warranted change then there are those who actually work at change; only one of these succeeds: the doer. Starting JANUARY 1st if you'll take the information shared daily through this devotional, when you arrive at DECEMBER 31,the odds of recognizing a noticeable change or pattern within your life are ten too none: i n short; it's destined to happen. Refuse to disallow another opportunity to enhance your knowledge by just reading what's prescribed, instead take what's being administered daily and ponder on it, meditate on it, for when the HOLY GHOST gave it to me He thought of you. Many believe Daily Devotion to be the express image of taking the time or the opportunity to sit and read what GOD has given one of his many servants; however I believe that to be only one of the many facets of true devotion.

In this book you'll find not only words that uplift and encourage, but it's filled with crucial information designed to lead and instruct along life's path. It's a prototype of how to practically live, honor and glorify GOD, while destined to enhance every area in your life. Some of these teachings are drawn from my personal experiences, nonetheless all of them are from GOD'S mouth to my heart ;to be distributed amongst those that hunger and thirst for righteousness ;so that they may be filled,(MT 5:6) Daily Devotion is more than an experience or ritual, it's a lifestyle that reflects the fullness o GODS glory! I pray that through "PRACTICAL PRINCIPALS TO DAILY DEVOTION" your life will be catapulted into a closer relationship with CHRIST as it strengthens and guide you.

BE BLESSED,

JANICE PETERS

JANUARY 1

"DO WHAT YOU SAY"

He also that is slothful in his work is brother to him that is a great waster (Pro 18:9)

Every year resolutions are made smokers decide that this is the year they'll quit, those who have the tendency to overeat or consume food contrary to their needs make a pact to exercise more, eat less or to become as physically fit as possible while others make declarations concerning work, paying more attention to a loved one and a host of other things which has the propensity to enhance their lives as a whole. However the reason so many believers are living below the bar or right outside of happiness on earth is because they inadvertently disqualify themselves by neglecting to "do what they say". You labor and toil over plans and purposes just to allow them to remain or go to the wayside. Solomon wrote in Pro 24:30-32) "I went by the field of the slothful, and by the vineyard of the man void of understanding; and lo it was all grown over with thorns, and nettles covered the face thereof, and the stone wall was broken down. Then I looked and considered it well; I looked upon it and received instruction". What does he describe? He describes the person who has good intentions; one with the resources to accomplish all that's needed in life, but one who has failed to follow through with their intended purpose. You don't have to become that person, within you lies the power to bind up and tear down, you've been handpicked by God to undertake all those things you've professed you'd do but have not carried out. Start now you don't have to be the slothful or the sluggard; your God doesn't want you on the other side of blessed. Begin to "do what you say" even to the slightest or minute point, carry it out by little and little so that can begin to visualize and enjoy the change you're striving for!

SCRIPTURE; Eccles 5:4

JANUARY 2

"MISTAKEN IDENTITY"

For I through the law am dead to the law: that I might live unto God (Gal 2:19)

A classic case of mistaken identity is described in John 18. In this chapter Jesus has gone before Pilate he's accused of numerous crimes by the Jews and the High Priest however Pilate now confirms that he has found no fault in him; he then inquires who should be released as per the custom and the angry crowd wants Barabbas and not Jesus (paraphrase John 18:40). They have been blinded by custom and religion which has caused them to mistaken the savior as a malefactor (John 18:30).

As Christians we can not forfeit a relationship with Christ for religion. Religion says when you should attend church, how you should pray; it restricts with customs and laws not allowing for a two way union. Relationship says "yes you made s mistake but I've made allowances and do forgive. I won't bind you with grievous burdens hard to bare; instead we'll come into agreement for I do talk back"!

Don't mistake a regular seat at your home church for a relationship; relationship says "yes Lord I want this but I trust that what you've given me is enough. Now ask yourself if the sinner can identify the Christ in you or if they would mistaken who you are for one of them; these results should show you where you are in life and allow for the necessary adjustments!

SCRIPTURE; Ps 103

JANUARY 3

"BACK AGAIN"

Restore unto me the joy of your salvation,: and uphold me with your free spirit (Ps 51:12)

In this Psalm David is requesting restoration from God, he has sinned before God and has now recognized the importance of being placed "back again" into his former position before the transgression. David understands that having all else without the presence and the pleasure of God meant nothing; for real pleasure in life is in knowing that he could come to God and hear well done my good and faithful servant.

After an initial place of restoration we are able to embrace the next level of enjoying and receiving "back again" that in which we have lost. The word says "in righteousness shalt thou be established: thou shalt be far from oppression" (Isa 54:14); fear not for I am with thee: I will bring thy seed from the east and gather thee from the west (Isa 43:5); blessed ye shall be in the city and blessed shall ye be in the field (Duet 28:3); you'll enjoy goodly cities which thou buildest not (Duet 6:11); he shall put out nations before thee by little and little (Duet 7:22). God bringing you "back again" entitles you to more than enough and not just barely enough; the only pre requisite is "thou shalt love the Lord thy God with all thine heart; and with all thine soul and with all thine strength" (Duet 6:5), plus love thy neighbor as thyself, in doing these you shall never cease to prosper and be blessed, you only need to know that the Lord delights to bless you. You can now expect to receive wholeness because the Lord has received you "back again"!

SCRIPTURE; Jer 31:16-17

JANUARY 4

"DON'T FORGET ABOUT CHRIST"

But I have prayed for thee, that thy faith fail not; and when thou art converted, strengthen thy brethren (Luke 22:32)

Religion (not religious, there's a difference) has become watered down. It's rare to hear the television evangelist (not all, but some) speak more on Christ than they do of all the many works that they've accomplished: tithes and accolades are tossed back and forth and the message of Christ is lost in the equation. Our jobs as fellow Christians is to "watch and pray that ye enter not into temptation" (Mt 26:41), Satan job is to "steal, kill, and destroy" (John 10:10), and he has infiltrated the church with his weapon of pride. Pride says "it's imperative that you be reminded or forewarned of every accomplishment I've attained, which takes the listener eyes off of Christ and places them on man.

Before the death of Christ the disciples argued among themselves who would be greatest (Luke 22:24); Jesus answered "it shall not be so, the greatest among you shall be as the youngest, the chief as he that doth serve" (Luke 22:26) exemplifying that no one is to be exalted above Christ for if any man be lifted up who will bare the ranks and lift up the name of Jesus? The word says" if I be lifted up I will draw all men unto me" (John 12:32), now that's our job!

Remember if anyone it was Jesus who earned bragging rites on every account, nevertheless he was content with being called Jesus; he kept it simple assuring he'd never forget his true intent and purpose, let us do likewise.

SCRIPTURE; Mt 7:13-14

JANUARY 5

"TRYING TO FIT A SQUARE INTO A PEG HOLE"

Wherefore also we pray always for you, that our God would count you worthy of this calling, and fulfill all the good pleasure of his goodness, and the work of faith with power (2Thes 1:11)

Think of the many people who've become comfortable with where they are currently stationed in life, now consider the ones who have been striving for years to go into dimensions where they have not been sent or called: these are examples of a class of people who are "trying to fit a square into a peg hole"; the reason nothing has threaded itself together is simple, they have either changed lanes or ventured into territory not designed for them.

During one of Jeremiah's many imprisonments as his heart began to fail him because of the reproach he endured for speaking the word of God he made a decision that "he wouldn't make mention of him (God), nor speak anymore in his name", however before the thought could complete itself in his heart he realized this "but the word was in mine heart as a burning fire shut up in my bones, therefore he was weary with forebearing and he could not stay (Jer 20:9 paraphrase). Jeremiah tried to deviate from his destiny and realized that it was like "trying to fit a square into a peg hole" it would never work, for God had ordained him a prophet while he was in the womb (Jer 1:5), there would be no element in his life or the next that would subvert what God had prepared before hand.

Being someplace other than where you should be has an adverse effect on more than just you. If you're endeavoring to make it work but it never really come together maybe it's time to double check the instruction manual, you could have missed a step. If all else fails go back to the beginning and contact the originator it's possible that you misunderstood or left out a detail. Don't waste anymore time on what hasn't shown growth or promise severe your ties and count your losses: the energy you spent trying to bring life to what wasn't promised will be doubled unto you while you make the change; it's in the word! (See Isaiah 61:7).

SCRIPTURE; 2Thes 3:3

JANUARY 6

"IT'S NOT THE PERSON"

Give and it shall be given unto you; good measure, pressed down, and shaken together, and running over shall men give unto thy bosom, for with the same measurement that ye mete withal it shall measured unto you again (Luke 6:38)

God hasn't given us spiritual weapons to fight a natural fight. Scripture says "we wrestle not against flesh and blood (Eph 6:12), in other words it's not the person; just as God uses man to operate in the earth Satan who has been a imposture from the beginning must also envelope and manifest himself through what is otherwise known as a willing unsuspecting victim.

Your strife or your complaint isn't actually for or about your fellow Christian. Let's take it one step further. Those who are called to be sons and daughters, but have not come into the knowledge of the truth or been conformed into the image of Christ are now fair game and it's possible that Satan has free reign in their lives which creates a clash in the spirit. It'll be unwise to conclude that you just don't like that person or they have somewhat against me but if you take the time to get to know the inner man and not the shell of a man you see this will close the invisible gap. We can't write off everyone who rubs us the wrong way; Heb 13:2 says "be not forgetful to entertain strangers: for thereby some have entertained angels unawares". A stranger doesn't have to be one who is considered unknown but they can also appear as one we have yet taken to know; someone we pass everyday on our way to work; that unruly neighbor who always take up two parking spaces.

The stranger could be that particular person who never has a kind word for you, the one Satan has manipulated and who is now living rent free in your head! Friend "it's not the person" who's posturing to make your life a living hell, it's the same spirit behind the person but just as penicillin became a cure for polio Jesus became a cure for demonic activity.

Don't mistaken your potential friend for a foe; Jesus said "give and it shall be given" (Luke 6:38) and he wasn't just speaking about monetary gain; longsuffering and grace falls into this category as well!

SCRIPTURE; Eph 6:12

JANUARY 7

"IDENTIFYING POTENTIAL CURSES"

Who shall lay anything to the charge of Gods elect? It is God that justifieth (Rom 8:33)

Growing up with the knowledge that your mother committed suicide isn't easy, but having the foreknowledge of how it was carried out has the propensity to cause a lasting effect on the child; this was my plight in life, I was that child; fortunately I never contemplated taking my own life and one day during an intense prayer session the Holy Spirit revealed to me tat Satan's weapon for my mother was a knife but the knife he chose for me was drugs: two different weapons with one common goal whenever used improperly!

David committed a sexual sin with Bathsheba (2Sam 11:3-4) which could be the reason their son Solomon found himself attracted to many strange women (1Kings 11:1), Rebekkah delved in deception which is why Esau was no match for Jacob her favorite whose name means deceiver (Gen 27:5-8).

Generally a generation curse is passed on from one generation to the next, it has the ability to strike in it's former form or that of its evil counterpart: be aware that unclean spirits dwell in tribes, an example is; if a perverse spirit is prevalent or abound it will partner with the spirit of homosexuality, sexual immorality, and a spirit of fornication and lesbianism abide there as well, the perverse spirit is connected with every other perverse form.

What you're battling with today was not established in your life time; it's bigger and older than you are naturally but it has to come under subjection of the word and power of God that has been transferred to you. Scripture declares "even the devils are subject unto us through thy name" (Luke 10:17b); comprehending that know that whenever you recognize potential curses you're not bound to rationalize or reason, your place as one who has been liberty is to send them packing: remember the process isn't all about you because whenever a unsuspecting soul comes along they depart to tackle new territory. You can't fail to do what you've been equipped to do even if you have to do it afraid or in discomfort, doing it anyway is what destroys the yoke, now think on those who are destined to come after you!

SCRIPTURE; Rom 10:8

JANUARY 8

"HEARING GOD"

And when the Lord saw that he turned aside to see, God called unto him out of the midst of the bush and said, Moses, Moses, and he said here am I (Exo 3:4)

One of the facets for a quality relationship with our creator is to be able to hear him. Your ears have to be spiritually in-tuned whereas regardless of the confusion or the chaos around your life, or the environment you reside in you will be able to hear God speak.

There was a period in my life when I wasn't afforded the opportunity to have my own private space and whenever I began to pray or praise and meditate one of my roommates would barge into our room; which would make me cry out to God and in my mind give credence as to why God needed to deliver me. One day after my temper tantrum I could hear god say "just keep praising me you have to be able to hear my voice amidst distraction, that's what I'm teaching you"!" This is to show you how to get a word from me while under intense situations or in duress". Remember the right atmosphere isn't one of the pre-requisite for hearing from God, the right heart and a willing and submissive spirit is all that's required.

God spoke to Abraham while subjected to the gods of his family and gave him a clear word to leave with the promise of making him a great nation. I believe God chose him because in spite of what was taking place around him he had a heart to hear from God (Gen 12:1-4). If you make that your position you will began to see God fill your desires.

SCRIPTURE; Ps 34:7

JANUARY 9

"THERE IS A SHEDDING PROCESS BEFORE YOU ADVANCE INTO YOUR DESTINY"

And when his brethren saw that their father loved him more than all his brethren, they hated him, and could not speak peaceable unto him (Gen 37:4)

Joseph understood the shedding process beyond his counterparts for he would have to undergo one extreme situation after the next before he would reach a place of maturity leading to his final destination. In the life of Joseph we see that he's shown favor with his father and with God nevertheless he would grow out of what he was to become established in who he is destined to become. His character defects would be the same as some of ours, Joseph had the tendency of talking too much, he is naïve in the way of dealing with people but God would use particular instances in his life to correct what has the potential to harm or keep him out of his glory place.

You may be dealing with issues in your life that you need to get rid of in order for you to grow. That issues may be that of a friend or a loved one, it maybe that you find yourself unable to clearly speak or do what thus saith the Lord, the thing that you need to be shedding can be something as simple as discarding the need to impress others with what the Lord has shown you: often times we don't understand that they could never appreciate what your saying because they're not heading in the same direction.

The process may seem painful but you must realize that "you must go through the shedding process before you can advance into your destiny": the good news is this "while you're going through the shedding process God has obligated himself to create a way for your dream to materialize and he does this by getting you around other dreamers. If you survey your surroundings and find that your inner circle consist of those who are busy visiting their yesterdays than it's apparent that you're out of place, therefore find your proper place, get in it and complete the process for at the end it shall bring forth a harvest to the full. Don't connect yourself with those that tolerate you find you someone who knows how to celebrate you instead!

SCRIPTURE; Pro 10:22

JANUARY 10

"ACCOUNTABILITY: THE KEY TO BREAKING SPIRITUAL BONDAGE"

For I have told him that I will judge his house for the iniquity which he knoweth; because his sons made themselves vile and he restrained them not (1Sam 3:13)

To grasp what God is saying in this hour we must take a journey in history and deal with the Levitical Priesthood. This priesthood was established by God and enacted specific rites that must be followed during the time of sacrifice which brings us to Eli and his sons who serve as priest. Eli is familiar with what his sons are doing but has decided to ignore and keep silent which places him in the position of being accountable, not because he indulge but that he refuse to correct.

That might be your plight today and something has been telling you to keep silent but what you must know is God has called you into "accountability". It's time to step away from the secret code of silence, you can't go through life acting as if you don't see what's taking place around you, he isn't calling you to be a busy body in other people matters but he has called you to be your brother's and sister's keeper. In John 21:16 Jesus ask Peter if he love him, Peter replies yes" and it is after this that he is told to feed his sheep, in other words; I need you to lift them up when they are spiraling down, I need you to advocate for them and stand up for what's right even if it hurt their feelings because you are "accountable" for those God has said will glean from your life, but how can they glean if you fail to open your mouth. This is your hour and God is waiting on you to take the reigns and become "accountable" so that he can break the spiritual bondages that have been holding you back!

SCRIPTURE; Gal 6:1

JANUARY 11

"BEHIND THE VEIL"

Heb 6:19-20

If you and I were born in the life and times of Moses, if would have been totally different. We would have needed the High priest, the only one allowed to enter into the inner court, to make intercession for you and I. Today that isn't our plight, because of what JESUS done at GOLGOTHA, place called CALVARY; we no longer have a particular place, at a particular time, under the supervision of a chosen person to enter into the holy of holies. When JESUS yielded up the ghost, the veil was rent in two (Mt 27:50-51) and we are now afforded the opportunity to come boldly too the throne of grace (Heb 4:16).

If your struggling with rather or not you are qualified to journey "behind the veil", first ask yourself, who on their own merit is qualified to go. No one is the answer, but if you have received JESUS CHRIST as your LORD and personal SAVOUR, than you are qualified and what's more important is, GOD is waiting to meet you there. You'll find safety behind the veil, joy is behind the veil, and peace awaits you there, along with love in abundance, to the full, until it overflows. Right now at this precise moment GOD has called you forth. He wants to take you where you've never been and deliver unto you the fruits of righteousness and the joy of salvation. Will you come? My father and I will meet you there.

(Study heb 10:17-24)

JANUARY 12

"UNANSWERED PRAYER" (PT 1)

Or what man is there of you whom if his son ask bread, will he give him a stone? Or if he asks a fish, will he give him a serpent? (Mt 7:9-10).

Because we are children of promise we oftentimes misconstrue our will for GOD'S will in our lives. Example: How many times have you made petitions before GOD, to receive access denied? What has happened is our flesh has told us in no uncertain terms that we must have or obtain this or that, for to do so would improve our portfolio as people. Therefore we pray attempting to convince GOD to provide this request would exalt us. However no consultation has been requested of by GOD, therefore we can never know that this very thing is the serpent or the stone. "We ask and receive not because we ask amiss" (JA 4:3), think about it, what appears to be bread has proven to be a stone. Have you been offering up prayers and it appears relief is no where on the horizon? Before you completely give up on this petition why not pray and ask your father if in fact you've been asking according to his will. Don't throw in the towel ,wait on a word from the LORD, it can be heard in a still small voice(1king19),for if in fact the fish is actually a fish you can look forward to it coming to pass, in GOD'S time and not ours!

(Read psalms 46)

JANUARY 13

"UNANSWERED PRAYER?"

But think on me when it shall be well with thee.... (Gen 40:14-15)

In today's scripture we see that after Joseph gave the interpretation of the butlers dream, he immediately went into a dialogue stating "think on me I've been stolen from my fathers' house". Here Joseph has misdirected his desires, from GOD, too man. He inadvertently request from a fellow servant that in which only GOD can provide.

Have your petitions become complaints in the ears of your brothers and sisters in Christ? Has your need for answered prayer become so desperate that you've taken your eyes off the only living entity able to produce the desired results you've been praying about? You may need to re-evaluate your position and ask GOD to forgive your impatience. Just as GOD reminded the butler about Joseph when pharaoh needed an answer, He has prepared you a butler who shall be reminded of the promise made to you that's destined to take you to your place of deliverance.

(Read psalms 41:1-2)

JANUARY 14

"WORK THE WORD"

For they have magnified thy word above all thy names. (Psalms 138:26)

Over two thousands years ago Jesus Christ of Nazareth walked the earth and performed more miracles than one can be accounted for. And in during all of this, he was merely working the word! When he healed the man with the withered hand, or stopped the flow of blood from a woman who had all her livehood tying to accomplish this feature. He was working the word. The word that says "He who fears my name, the son of righteousness shall arise with healing in his wings" (Mat 4:2). Some may believe working the word to repeat the word, or memorize the word, but that remains far from the truth. Working the word is considered putting God in remembrance of his word and declaring this word over and in your life. However, don't leave out the one antidote that propels it into action. You're FAITH! Of its healing you need. Find all the healing scriptures you can and decree them until you receive your healing. It works the same deliverance, restoration, financial breakthrough, generational curse and more.

Today is your day for renewal. Start right now and "work the word" you'll then see it begin to work for you. Remember, the will of God is the word of God

Scripture Is 59:1

JANUARY 15

"WHAT'S THAT IN YOUR MOUTH?"

Death and life is in the power of the tongue: and they that love it shall eat the fruit there of the tongue (Pro 18:21)

As we go through an average day we often use a lot of words haphazardly. Before my true confession I can recall always saying "This or that person makes me sick," it feels like I'm catching a cold and a bunch of other negative slogans too derogatory to mention. However, I believe you get my point. It was after accepting JESUS CHRIST in my life that I came into the knowledge of the truth which informs, "Life and death is in he power of the tongue and they that love it shall eat the fruit thereof (pro 18:21). What does this entail? It defines what we will or won't divide and conquer. The greatest power ever demonstrated on earth was performed through speech for when the almighty was ready to create ,He didn't cause a whirlwind or some other great feat he simply declared "Let there be"(Gen 1:3).making the principal of speaking so real that it's used for the saving of he race. (Rom 10:9-10)

Therefore if you are tired of getting what you have always gotten don't try a different street, using the same method. Think before you speak and only speak the things that edify.

Scripture: Job (21:28-29)

JANUARY 16

"THERE IS LIFE AFTER NO"

Not that I speak in respect of want: For I have learned in whatever state I am therewith to be content (Phil 4:11)

As we travel through the rugged roads of life we are either beginning a trail or in full combat in the middle of one. During these times we believe we need to hear from GOD the most but what isn't understood is this when GOD isn't talking to us he's busy taking us to where we can make it. The trail isn't there to kill you it's only there to purify you. During a particular trail in my life I got an answer and my answer was no. Initially this made me angry, the no made me ask GOD why. The no distracted me for 24 hours but right after this I realized that the no had given me the freedom I'd been seeking. My no released me too understand that I didn't actually need my prayer to go my way in order to excel. It took me to the next level.

So for that someone who's suffering through a no and the enemy is attempting to rage war in your mind God wants you to know that there is life after no Your life was birthed to create in you a new life a new hope an d a new direction so let your no set you free and not set you up because that isn't GOD'S best for you!

Philip 3:13-14

JANUARY 17

"HE CALLS ME FRIEND"

And the scripture was fulfilled which saith, Abraham believed GOD and it was imputed unto him for righteousness; and he was called the friend of GOD. (JA 2:23)

Have you ever been in a room full of people but yet you feel alone? Does the devil try to wreck havoc in your mind by bombarding you with thoughts of worthlessness or condemnation concerning a past failure or mistake? If so know that you are not alone. There are millions of Christians who have been where you are and have overcome this testament against themselves. I know; I too was once there. It's during these times that you must conjure up all of the stored up breakthroughs and miracles (great or small) and feed the spirit man who seems to be dwindling because of the lack of knowing just who you are in GOD through CHRIST JESUS. Don't become dismayed due to an intrusive feeling you are not alone. If it's a friend you need the word gives a description of friend. Proverbs 17:17 says a friend loves at all times who does this but GOD? Proverbs 18:24b says "and there is a friend that sticketh closer than a brother. The friend you've been looking for has been there all the time. Allow me to make the introductions reader meet JESUS; JESUS met your friend.

Scripture: Proverbs 22:23-24

JANUARY 18

"ONE SECOND IS TOO LONG"

Am I a GOD at hand; saith the Lord; and not a GOD afar off. (Jer 23:23)

Think about all the different chores you do in a day's time; now consider your method of travel. Rather or not we walk, run, use public transportation or private transportation we need Gods' presence to sustain us from every deadly situation that could befall us. This is why its' imperative for us to understand that one second out of the will of God is too long. Nothing should prove to be worth taking the risk of being out of God's divine will for your life; it's when we detour, that the enemy finds the pin hole needed to infiltrate the arsenal we've used to keep him at bay. Don't waste your day believing you can do what pleases you and not pay a penalty. Consider the parable of the ten virgins who took their lamps and went forth to meet the bridegroom, JESUS said 5 were wise& 5 were foolish (Mat 25:1-2) The wise took oil in their lamps and carried extra, but the foolish took no oil with them. They were out of the will for one second, and this second cost them eternity. Remember one second is too long.

Scripture (Mat 25:1-2)

JANUARY 19

"WHAT A DIFFERENCE A DAY MAKES!"

The Elisha said, hear ye the word of the Lord; thus saith the Lord, tomorrow about this time (II Kings7:1)

In this particular chapter God has given the prophet Elisha a clear word for relief and he has delivered it to the people of Samaria. The long awaited word declares" your problem shall no longer progress, for your help is on the way". As it was then, so shall it be in our time. There will be some who are skeptical just as the Lord on whose hand the king leaned (7:2) there are those who think of change as a process of evolving from one position to another, assuming an extended timetable is warranted to produce desired results. However, with God nothing shall be impossible (Luke 1:37) and there are such things as a 24 hour turn around as described here in our text.

What appears in your tomorrow can very well be that in which you've prayed for on today. So be steadfast, unmovable and run the race that's' set before you, tarry wait for it; because it will surely come, it will not tarry" (Heb 2:36)

Scripture Heb 12:1-3

JANUARY 20

"FOLLOW DIRECTIONS"

And the lord spoke unto me, saying, ye have compassed this mountain long enough: turn you northward (Duet 2:2-3)

Have you been traveling in a direction that God has spoken for you previously? Does it seem as if you're passing the same landmarks you passed, as you've traveled this route? Be not dismayed, God has ordained this also. This mountain isn't designed to kill you, its' here to prove you.

Often times God gives directions or instructions, but the purpose isn't completely given until sometime later. Its' during these assignments that we must strike out on pure faith. Scripture tells us "He who comes to God must believe that he is, and a rewarder of those who diligently seek him (Heb 11:6). Its' when you truthfully follow the directions of going around your mountain that God will intervene and give you another word that will release you from the first assignment and lead you into your next assignment, and your next level!

What are you doing as you travel your path? Have you remembered to thank God for the mountain "In all things give thanks (1Thess? 5:18) or are you real busy describing this mountain to God, through your attitude and complaints" Don't become one of the Israelites who journey in the wilderness 40 years because they could not follow simple directions. Don't be an Achan and touch the accursed thing (Jos 7:1) God has you where you are for divine purpose, don't kick against the bricks, and watch the power of God move you super naturally.

Scripture Joshua 6:12-16, Hag 2:9

JANUARY 21

"IMPRISONED"

Now when John had heard in the prison the works of Christ he sent two of his disciples (Mat 11:2-3)

When one thinks about being imprisoned or prison, the image of one who committed a crime comes to mind. If you have to conjure up an image of this so called prison You'd probably think of a place with cells instead of rooms, bars and the like. What doesn't come to mind is the innocent. The innocent in this case are those who have been afforded the opportunity to know Jesus Christ as their Lord and personal Savior, but fail to live at the level of blessing or expectancy God has ordained because of the prison they've placed their finance in, the prison of hopelessness and the prison of unbelief. The jail uniform is not implemented; no cells limit your degrees of mobility. However just as John allowed his circumstances to alter his confident in whom Jesus was. The enemy comes along to attack the innocent with doubt, to build the foundation of a prison in your life. Don't become imprison in your life. Don't become imprisoned in your thoughts or your soul. Know that God has made a way of escape for you. 2 Corn 3:17 says "where the spirit of the lord is there is liberty!" In this respect. Woman, man thou art loosed!

Scripture study John 1:29-34

JANUARY 22

"SUDDENLY"

For thus saith the Lord, Ye shall not see wind, neither shall ye see rain, yet that valley will be filled with water, that ye may drink, both ye and your cattle and be (2Kings 3:17)

Are you in a tight spot and it appears that no immediate relief in sight? Is this season in your life dry and you've been praying for rain? Good news rain is in the forecast, but you must make certain that you're residing in the designated location where this down pour is expected! We pray fast and make our supplications unto the Lord, but have we check our hearts, has anyone been out to monitor your faith meter lately? For these are elements needed or required of by the Lord. Jesus said in Mark 9:23 "If thou canst believe, all things are possible to him that believes." So you see, it take more than just the asking. You must stand in Faith, even when nothing is coming to pass, stand on the word when things are bleak and you feel like maybe the answer is not favorable. According to today's scripture

Elisha prophesied, "they would not feel it (see wind) neither would they see it (visualize it before manifestation) but the valley shall be filled! So be encouraged, and prophesy a sudden release of the power of God into your midst Remember, just because you can't see it doesn't mean it isn't there Isaiah 48:3.

JANUARY 23

"LET GOD BE GOD" (PART 1)

The Lord hear thee in the day of trouble; the name of the God of Jacob defend thee: (Psalms 20:1)

If your today appears to be as just as your yesterday, and it seems as if you haven't gained any ground; you're tried all you know to try and you've put forth your best effort, to no avail. Its' probably still complicated because, you under your own coalition have been busy trying to produce and won't "Let God be God."

The lord our God is a gentle man and he won't intervene on our own personal will or choices. However, if you would relinquish your problems to God, he will gladly pick them up, but not before you lay them down. Before the battle of Ziklag David inquired at the Lord, saying shell I pursue after this group, shall I over take them? And he answered pursue, thou shalt surely overtake them and without fail cover all. (ISam 30:8) To win your battle and recover all you must let go and let God.

Scripture Psalms 20

JANUARY 24

"LET GOD BE GOD" (PART 2)

And I will work among you, and will be your God, and ye shall be my people (Lev 26:12)

Letting God be God" means, freeing God' up to do as he please in your life, it dispels the idea that we can hold on to some of our own self will and it says, "Lord I don't quite understand how this will take place, but I trust that your word is true, when it tells me "you know the thoughts you think of me, thoughts of good and not equal, to give me an expected end (Jer. 29:11). So, Jesus take the wheel, I now relinquish all authority over to you. God, it's time for me to un-strap you from the hot seat; remove the gag I placed over your mouth, that wouldn't allow you to speak in my life, the things you had for my life. This means that I can no longer be the God of my decisions and look you as the God of my wants, needs, desires and miracles. I now relent, "God be God in my life!

Prayer: Father I'm often bombarded with thoughts and ideas that appeals to my senses and in acting without consulting my Father or hearing you and not obeying, I know I've sinned therefore, Forgive me father and restore me to the joy of my salvation in Jesus name.

Amen

Scripture I Cron 7:14

JANUARY 25

"DON'T GO BACK"

For it was charged me by the word of the Lord, Saying eat no bread nor drink no water nor turn again by the same way that thou camest (1 Kings 13:9)

In the scripture God gave the prophet an assignment and a directive following his mission, What wasn't discussed was the consequences for his disobedience .Oftentimes GOD will give you a charge but not fully disclose all the details however to be certain that you stay the course remember to follow the last directive for in doing so you can't fail.

If life is pulling at you and where you've come from or been delivered out of is appearing somewhat appealing, for a temporary fix too a permanent problem consider the delusion, for you can never solve a permanent problem with a temporary solution it patches but it never mends. Where GOD is taking you will far exceed where you've been, buckle down and enjoy the ride. Remember you will have valley lows but with them has to come the mountain top experiences.

(Study the outcome of the disobedient prophet) 1 kings 13:1-29

JANUARY 26

"WHY AM I THUS"

And the children struggled together within her: and she said, if it be so, why am I thus? And she went to inquire o f the lord. (Gen 25:22)

After being barren (not able to bare children) Isaac prayed to GOD for his wife and GOD answered their prayers and blessed them with not one but two children. It was during this pregnancy that Rebecca struggled with the unborn children and inquired of the Lord. This is oftentimes our plight. We pray for thus and so but once we receive it and experience the difficult times we question why am I thus: meaning, Lord I prayed for this business but it's driving me to distraction, Lord I wanted this child but they're now unruly, Lord you called me to be a prophet to the nations, why then am I still not traveling outside of my neighborhood.

Its simple Rebecca had two nations in her womb likewise, that business owner also has to experience perseverance, the parent must hone in on becoming a prayer warrior, while the prophet must began to utilize their gift right where they are. As it is with you, began to excel in spite of what you feel, for what you feel isn't or shouldn't be a real as what you know. The word of truth and the word said "it shall come to pass!

Scripture: Romans 8:28

JANUARY 27

"EMPTY VESSELS"

(2 Kings 4:3) Then he said, go, borrow thee vessels abroad of all thy neighbors, even empty vessels; borrow not a few.

When I think of the word empty what comes to mind is absolutely nothing nevertheless I'm fully persuaded that when we come to God in this condition, just as it was with widow woman, he began to pour into us all the strength, courage, endurance, stamina, wisdom, and truth we need to sustain us for every situation. If you are of the many people who believe that everything has to be put in place, that you must clean yourself up and make certain that you're full of the word of truth according to oneself before you step out on faith and come to the Lord know that you can never get yourself clean enough plus the word of GOD says "let no man deceive himself if any among you seemeth to be wise in this world let him become a fool , that he may become wise".(1 co 3:18) therefore your wisdom of this world is of no effect. To become vessels of honor we must put behind the elementary principal of already full and establish our position as empty so that we may obtain that in which GOD has prepared for us, in doing so those around you will become nourished from your overflow.

SCRIPTURE: Jer 18:1-6

JANUARY 28

"NEEDING A MIRACLE"

And he said to them go thy way thy faith has made thee whole ".
LUKE 17:19

JAN 28, 1986 my daughter Precious, who would have been 4 months in 4 days went home to be with the lord. When this happened ,I didn't know how I would make it ,but through my pain GOD birthed the miracle of my salvation . While I suffered though I almost missed it expecting the proverbial big bang, sky rocket, or this great audible voice. It was then that I realized , you can never look pass great or small miracles that's been performed in your life ,yes ,even those through pain ; you may actually have to piggy back on your small miracle until you get the big one you've been waiting for , lest you become discouraged.

When JESUS wanted to feed the multitude he took 2 small fish and 5 loaves, set the multitude down (which means; he prepared them too receive that in which they needed) blessed it brake it and gave it to his disciples, who distributed it, and they were fed (MT 14:17-20).   JESUS took what was available and created the miracle he needed. What's more important is he left you and I an example; remember he blessed it, brake it, but he passed it on. Are you a disciple, do you follow Christ, are you a part of the body of Christ? JESUS has done all the footwork and transferred all of the power over too you. Now is the time for your miracle however to obtain it you must remember to do your part.

SCRIPTURE: 2 Co 1:20

JANUARY 29

"NOT JUST ONE OF THE MULTITUDES "

And great multitudes were gathered together unto him so that he went into a ship and sat and the whole multitude stood on the shore .MT13:2

Some would think being one of the multitudes was an okay position because they were often fed, they witnessed many miracles, and they walked where JESUS walked, plus they were afforded the opportunity to be taught of the Lord. Needless to say none of these attributes brought them any further too the truth for they had not the ear to hear what the spirit was saying too the church. When JESUS spoke with them, he spoke in parables, and they were always separated from the truth due to them standing afar off. (MAT 13:2) As we follow the teachings of Christ we mustn't become one of those who hear the word and not do it. Or have a form of godliness but deny the power there with due to never coming into the knowledge of the truth.

The great news is you can never be just one of the multitudes if you're determined to become one of his disciples. Becoming a disciple takes you out of the ordinary and places you into the extraordinary, and gives you victory over every circumstance because according to (Rev 21:6) you've won because("it is done"). Remember, the disciple follows closely, walks as the savior walk, loves at all times shows himself friendly, pleases the father and takes control of the atmosphere around them. So "go into the entire world and make other disciples".

Scripture ST. John 15:17-18

JANUARY 30

"BORROWED TIME"

Take therefore no thought for the morrow: for the morrow shall take thought for the things of itself, sufficient unto the day is the evil thereof. (Ma 6:34)

Our lives can become so hurried at times that we often forget to sit back and reflect on where we are and how we arrived at this particular pinnacle in our lives. It's simple the grace and mercy of God has been following us around (Psalms 23). Consider how special you are too God, as you ponder on how many of your fellow country men were not afforded the opportunity to see this glorious day. How then do you diminish this prospect by lifting our voices to murmur and complain, if we find ourselves temporarily inconvinced? Lets not follow in the footsteps of our believed fore fathers who wandered in the wilderness 39 years and 354 days longer than necessary due to an ungrateful heart, who, suffering under the hand of cruel taskmasters prayed daily for a deliverer, and initially rejected their way of escape (Exo 6:9) Over I million people left Egypt all but two (Joshua and Caleb) perished before they entered the promised land. They died without receiving the promised, because they misappropriated the time granted to them. Time and choices work hand and hand. As you acquire time, you're left with the option of the most constructive decisions to utilize it. Therefore, use it wisely, knowing that you cheat your today by trying to borrow from you tomorrow.

Scripture Eph 3:14-17

JANUARY 31

"A MYRIAD OF EMOTIONS"

And he saith unto them, my soul is exceeding sorrowful unto death: tarry ye here and watch. And he went forward a little, and fell on the ground, and prayed that, if it were possible, the hour might pass from him (Mark 14:34-35)

In the garden of Gethsemane Jesus was faced with a torrid of emotions. While he knew his purpose and divine destiny; he had to compel his soul nature to make the adjustments necessary so that he could follow the course designed for him. It's apparent that this was no small feat for the scripture declares that he sought God 3 times to remove or change his course of destiny (Mark 14:40-41). We too, are likely to face dilemmas that will drive us to distraction or create havoc within our emotional capacity. However, Jesus has led by example by showing us how to bring every thought captive into the Obedience of Christ (2 CO 10:4-5). His message proves that the mirage lies within the things you feel however the truth will always remain in the word and the keeping of it. If you are one of the many people who are indecisive about a particular situation because you feel as if you might lose out unless you act now, or maybe it's an ex-companion you've gotten re-acquainted with and a myriad of emotions have begun to stir; remember whatever your plight maybe there is always an answer within the word of GOD.

Don't allow your emotions to rule your destiny as Eve did in the garden, you no longer live under the curse of the law but by grace. So hunker down and proceed too take back what the enemy stole from you! Since the day of John the Baptist until now the kingdom of heaven suffereth violence but the violent taketh by force.

SCRIPTURE: John 17:15-20

FEBRUARY 1

"A NEW SEASON"

Behold I will do a new thing now it shall spring forth, shall ye not know it? I will even make a way in the wilderness and rivers in the desert. (Isa 43:19)

A new season can be viewed in one or two fashions, either you're coming out of the bad into the good, or you're leaving the comfortable, entering into the grievous .Regardless of which we must be confident of this very fact "time and chance happens to us all" (Eccles .9:12), and in whatever state GOD deems it necessary we undertake, he has granted us the stamina to prevail over our circumstances.

If you're entering the good that means you've just battled some areas in your life which needed your utmost attention too shoot you into your new season, and you're now equipped to handle the new challenges you'll face in your new level, congratulations. For those who are seeing change in the opposite direction, it seems bad but the truth is, as GOD fine tune you into a vessel of honor you will gather the characteristics needed to keep you in a place of prominence. Remember anointing without character will take you places but it has no staying power, just don't forget to hold on for the same GOD who walked with you as you feasted, he shall also keep you in the lean times. Whatever you're going through isn't designed to hurt you it's purifying you.

Scripture Psalms 91

FEBRUARY 2

"RIGHT PLACE RIGHT TIME"

The woman saith unto him, sir give me this water that I thirst not, neither come hither to draw. (John 4:15)

The woman at the well knew not with whom she spoke with when she got up that morning. She probably had no inclination that day would be come an event in history too be read by billions, from one generation to the next; nonetheless this was to become her plight; not because there was no one else in the vicinity or even no one else in which JESUS could have made himself known to, this was her destiny, making her at the "right place at the right time", so to is it with us. To receive that in which has been predestined for us we must scrutinize all of our actions, and place ourselves in position to obtain a word of knowledge, and guidance that will ultimately lead us into the high places ordained by GOD. In us being positional placed we become conduits for those who have been speared to us by GOD to bring into fruition dreams and destiny.

If you think you're always one step behind or you're always a day late, you may need to consider rather or not GOD is still leading or if you've proceeded to try too lead GOD! Today is your right now moment and because you're devoting your time to the kingdom of GOD you are now said to be in the right place at the right time and in this place all blessings will flow

John 5:1-9

FEBRUARY 3

"SHIFTING"

For thus saith the lord of host; yet once it is a little while and I will shake the heavens and the earth , and the sea ,and the dry ; and I will shake all nations, and the desire of all nations shall come ; and I will fill this house with glory , saith the Lord of host.(Hag 2:6-7)

We live under a cloud of delusion if we believe we've reached a point in our lives where we've already obtained or arrived to that desired position, and I therefore need not go any further. It's imperative that we always realize that we shall never attain until we meet JESUS in the sky. To have the mindset of staying where we have arrived can only cripple, eventually everyone and everything will begin to move around us, subsequently passing us by. Let us be aware that life is always shifting and if we are not prepared for the shift than we can easily find ourselves on the downslide of a steadily progressing state of being.

Shifting is essential too everyday living to bring about the necessary fundamentals of livelihood. If you are encountering undue duress due to an unfriendly boss or co-worker, shift; if that unruly neighbor continues to taunt you with wayward antics; remember you have to shift. It's in your ability to shift, regardless of the situation; that you'll find that you are now that over comer you've always admired. JESUS left us an example of shifting in the garden. When he knew his time had fully come his soul was grieved therefore he prayed, "father if thou be willing remove this cup from me; nevertheless not my will but thine be done" (Luke 22:42). This was no small feat but he shifted and submitted himself unto death and we have been commissioned to do likewise.

SCRIPTURE: Phil 1:6

FEBRUARY 4

"IN RARE FORM"

And he dreamed and behold a ladder set up on the earth and the top of it reached to heaven: and behold the angels of GOD ascending and descending on it, and behold, the Lord stood above it and said.....Gen 28:12-13

The title for today's devotional always put me in mind of someone who is superseding expectations placed on them; they're outdoing themselves doing a phenomenal job at whatever task they've applied themselves too. Have you considered that this is always the position of our FATHER GOD? He was in rare form when he called the earth out of nothing (Gen 1:2) formed man from the dust of the ground (Gen 1:26), gave them dominion over the works of his hands (Gen 1:28), sent his son to die for us (John 3:16), and loves us in spite of ourselves. This is why we mustn't lose heart and give up. It doesn't matter what your circumstances are there will always be a word from the Lord to propel you in the right direction. The BIBLE tells us in PSALMS 91:7 "a thousand shall fall at thy side and ten thousand at thy right hand; but it shall not come nigh thee". This informs us that we shall see trouble but we shouldn't be moved by it, realizing that the trouble we see is not intended for us, it'll only affect those at our side and our right hand, for in the midst of a potential crisis we can count on help from ZION showing up "in rare form".

SCRIPTURE; Gen 43:5-6

FEBRUARY 5

"WATCHING OVER YOU"

And the Lord went before them by day in a pillar of a cloud, to lead them the way; and by night in a pillar of fire; to give them light; to go by day and night (Exo 13:21)

With all that's going on in the world today it seems safe to say we oftentimes, during our journey in life, suffer through the realization that we must be living on the brink of the last days. The word of GOD says "this know also that in the last days perilous times shall come. (2 Tim 3:1) With all that's happening right before our very eyes, wars and rumors of war, the love of many waxing cold, along with the census of those becoming victims of criminal acts on the rise we can conclude that the end draws near. Even as this fact becomes a stark reality, we can be assured that those that remain intact, those who walk and stay under the covering of the most high, shall not be effected eternally. We draw from the promise of GOD that he shall be a very present help in the time of trouble (Ps 46:1), and we know the word declare that "all the promises of GOD in him are yea and amen" (2 Co 1:20). Therefore if unemployment, sickness, or any other adversity comes too knock know that your help is near, for the spirit of the Lord is hovering above you and He's there to guide you through whatever.

SCRIPTURE; Is 59:1

FEBRUARY 6

"CONTAMINATION"

Be ye not unequally yoked together with unbelievers; for what fellowship hath righteousness with unrighteousness and what communion hath light with darkness.(2 Co 6:14)

During our everyday walk of life we can attest too coming in contact with a wide array of people. Oftentimes these are those we never give credence too, because to us they are mere passersby, not numbered among those in whom we believe to be an important part of our lives. It's easy to view those we have no knowledge of through the eyes of our standard and proclaim them as different counterparts, but how often do we critically evaluate those whom we find ourselves in close proximity with routinely? Not as critics but as fellow workers for the greater good. If you're delving into unchartered waters because you've chosen to hang onto that friendship that run perpendicular to the word of truth, or have you determined that it's okay for you to contaminate yourself all for the sake of what you consider love, with hopes that it will work itself out? "Be ye not deceived, when GOD said evil communication corrupt good manners he means it. (1 Co 15: 33) Remember Paul said a little leaven leavens the whole lump (1 Co 5:6). This is to say if you stay around corruption long enough you'll soon become corrupt. Don't allow the waywardness of another to determine your future; forsake any form or appearance of evil and watch the Lord take you places you've dared imagined.

SCRIPTURE: 1 Co 5: 11-13

FEBRUARY 7

"DO YOU BELIEVE"

BELIEVE IN THE LORD YOUR GOD, SO SHALL YE BE ESTABLISHED: BELIEVE HIS PROPHETS, SO SHALL YE PROSPER. (2CRON 20:20b)

If you took inventory would you find faith to move mountains or would you only see the things that you under your own strength are able to accomplish? Faith and belief are two totally different components, however I've found that they work hand in hand to bring into fruition, a dream, a vision or a destiny.

Again, belief in one's self is important nevertheless; one's self can't materialize the many miracles needed to fortify a day. You can't under your own right, Wake up and spring into action; it takes a powerful God to do this for us. Some believe it's their alarm clock that started their day however, I beg to differ. We lie down and rest, believing that we'll see the start of another day; we take this fact for granted when we kiss our children, good night and reply "See you in the morning." So for these we believe they have no faith, it's imperative that you know to believe such a statement, takes belief in itself. Therefore, it is high time for you to spring into action and start believing for the mountain top experience. Don't mender around with those things that are right at your finger tips. Start believing that God will do exceedingly, abundantly, above all that you can ask or think, according to the power that works in you. (Eph 3:20) and watch your life take off!

FEBRUARY 8

"REJOICE"

Rejoice in the Lord always: and again I say rejoice. Philip 4:4

When most people hear the word, rejoice or even as it's used to describe a particular situation we are left with the impression of one in a celebratory mood; someone delighting themselves in certain something or someone exuberantly excited, however this isn't or shouldn't always be your reality. The apostle Paul instructed the church in THESSELONICA to rejoice evermore (1 Thes 5:16). We can therefore attest that it's scriptural for us to give glory too the Lord for hardship and suffering we may endure. Let us not become of he mindset, just because we are joint Aires with Christ that we should cease from suffering, but let us take up the mantle which says, regardless of my life's posture, rather high or low, I will remember to rejoice in my pain, not because I have some but recalling, he who has begun a good work in me shall complete it until the day of Christ JESUS. It is therefore critical that you recall the good times while you're encountering the difficult and it's eminent that you believe; your ability to rejoice no matter the circumstance, will elevate you out of a slump sooner than later.

SCRIPTURE: Deut: 26:11

FEBRUARY 9

"BEING THANKFUL"

In everything give thanks for this is the will of GOD in CHRIST JESUS concerning you. (1Thes 5:18)

Whenever trouble is on the horizon and the immediate relief requested seems long coming our first response is often not again; why me; or maybe even Lord give me a break. We very seldom or if ever do as the scripture for today indicates; this could very well be because, so often we read a passage of scripture, believe we know it's contents and move on to the next without really getting it's total meaning. Our scripture declares "give thanks in all things for this is the will of GOD in Christ Jesus. What we must acknowledge is our giving thanks is the will of GOD for our lives. Therefore the offering up of thanks is not a request but a requirement. Don't allow only your complaints to fall upon the ears of our might GOD; let's on purpose find gratitude in whatever predicament we're faced with and lift our voices in thanksgiving for the rough waters in our lives and the calm currents; for GOD has ordained them both!

SCRIPTURE Ps: 100

FEBRUARY 10

"HE SENT A REPRESENTATIVE"

Therefore being justified by faith we have peace with GOD through our Lord and Savior Jesus Christ. (Rom 5:1)

If you are a person who has been living beneath your potential because you've failed too tap into the full knowledge of who you are in Christ it's far time for you to step out of your comfort zone and gather in the fruit of your labors. How is this possible? It's done by remembering that Jesus was hung up for your hang ups; and to establish an order in the earth which will allow us to flourish into our full potential; without a heart full of worry or fear.

We have many representatives presiding amongst us now. The bible declares that Angels are ministering Spirits and they are there for the saints. Yet there are other representatives also. They may appear in the form of a neighbor or an associate at work who always have a kind word when you're down; lend a hand when you're short or in need of a particular something; so don't overlook the small things knowing that without them a need would have gone un-met. Lastly the greatest representative sent on your behalf was Jesus Christ himself. The word says, "he is able also to save them to the uttermost that come unto him, seeing he ever liveth to make intercession for them (Heb 12:2). How? Because he's undefeated and therefore remains the greatest representative of all time, that's how.

(Word for the day; before GOD called Moses he sent a representative in the form of a burning bush, be encouraged your help is on the way.) SCRIPTURE (Exo 3:2)

FEBRUARY 11

"HELP IS ON THE WAY"

Thus saith the Lord GOD unto these bones; behold, I will cause breath to enter into you and ye shall live (Ezek 37:5)

If you're one of the many who happen to be under a financial strain and it appears no reprieve is coming your way; don't lose heart while undergoing this strain; this isn't the final decree for your life: God told the prophet Isaiah "no weapon that is formed against you shall prosper and every tongue that rise up against you in judgment he shall condemn, this is the heritage of the servants of the Lord (Is 54:17). God declares your victory over every weapon rather it be a weapon of finance, a weapon of divorce, a weapon of stigma; infidelity, fear or a host of other traumas; they will form but they will not prosper. Why? Because the Lord says it's your heritage; the weapons and the resource to overcome. Don't fret about that in which God has made provision for; your help is on the way. Your job is to stand in faith and follow the instructions given by the Holy Spirit, which will lead and guide you in all truth!

SCRIPTURE: Ruth 3:18

FEBRUARY 12

"WHEN THE SMOKE CLEARS"

But the fruit of the spirit is love, joy, peace, longsuffering, gentleness, goodness, faith, meekness, temperance: against such there is no law. (Gal 5:22-23)

Smoke can be defined as gaseous products of burning material, made visible by carrying small particles of carbons, which settles as soot. Even though we don't always encounter its degree of damage beforehand, the potential loss or damage it creates becomes fundamental as we process the cost. Rather it's with bad words spoken between two people or the selfish actions imposed on another; it's high time to realize that there is a penalty and or consequences. Let us not rely on our sense of reason to believe that the other person knows our heart or our true intentions, we should not assume that we are automatically excused if we have not taken the initiative too ask for forgiveness. In the interim feelings are hurt, ego's are bruised, relationships are torn, boundaries have been crossed and when the smoke clears you're left alone wondering how did it come to this. Simple, we have failed to follow the commandment Jesus gave in John 15:12, "To love one another as he has loved us". Paul encourages us to "Let nothing be done through strife, or vain glory, but in lowliness of mind let each esteem others better than themselves" (Phil 2:3). Let us therefore confess our faults one to another and embark on a journey of mending broken fences, as we begin to love not in word but in action and deed. (Scripture Philip 3:13-14).

FEBRUARY 13

"I SHALL RECOVER IT ALL"

And David inquired at the Lord saying, shall I pursue after this troop? Shall I overtake them? And he answered him, pursue: for thou shalt surely overtake them and without fail recover all. (1 Sam 30:8)

As we encounter an economic downturn and those around us lose their jobs, as they face a type of financial ruin, us , the saints of the most high God should be taking advantage of the opportunity to be that city which sits upon the hill (Mt 5:14). Now is our time to show to an un-repented world the love and the power of God through the abundance of our lives.

When there was a famine in the land Isaac, the son of promise, was instructed by God to sow in the land ; as he obeyed he reaped 100 fold in that very same year (Gen26 1&12). This is the time for   us to sow in obedience as those who have hope in Christ Jesus; knowing that the perilous times affecting those of the world shall not affect the child of promise. It's in our prospering (as the world experience a drought) that we lift up Christ, and in so doing, he'll draw all men unto him. Therefore rejoice today: for we shall recover it all. SCRIPTURE: (1 Kings 18:44)

FEBRUARY 14

"MY FIRST LOVE"

God so loved the world that he gave his only begotten son, so that whosoever believeth on him shall not perish, but have everlasting life. (John 3: 16)

So often we've quoted this particular passage of scripture and most "good Christians" have it taken to memory, but how many of us have taken the incentive to study it out or even meditate on the complexity of its truth?

As today is commemorated as a day we're to share with a significant other the depths of our feelings, let us take the time to realize who loves us; beyond all faults; beyond all failures; and even above and beyond each of our character defects. How do we know this: simple, the bible says that while we were yet sinners, the almighty God, the Lord Jehovah sent a portion of himself to redeem us from the law of sin and the curse of death?

SCRIPTURE; Col 2:12 (make him your first love, you'll find that it's worth it)

FEBRUARY 15

"CONSEQUENCES"

For the wages of sin is death; but the gift of God is eternal life through Jesus Christ our Lord (Rom 6:23).

Every day we're faced with choices; and even when we take the stance of choosing not to choose; we have made a choice. Are we fully aware that each choice we make in life bares consequences that our tomorrows' will reek of? The Apostle Paul declares to the church in Galatia "be ye not deceived God is not mocked withersoever a man soweth that shall he also reap" (Gal 6-7).

Does your today favor your yesterday? Are you investing the same investments produced in earlier years but miraculously expecting a different crop? This goes against the law established in the earth; it shall not happen. We must forsake the cloak of making spontaneous decisions without consulting God for instructions: in doing so we haphazardly create un-avoidable consequences, which require payment; oftentimes the cost is beyond that in which we are able to sustain. SCRIPTURE ;(Eph 4:22-27)

FEBRUARY 16

"ISSUES"

And behold, a woman which was diseased with an issue of blood twelve years came behind him and touched the hem of his garment (Mt 9:20-21)

There is a subject that each of us shares as a common ground; it matters not if you're rich or poor, black, white, Hispanic or of any other ethnic background; we all have issues: some small some not so small, nonetheless they remain issues. When the woman in our text faced an issue that proved to baffle even the finest of doctors in her time, she made a conscious decision to seek out the savior she'd heard so much about. The thing that separated her from the thong of people was her faith, her goals and pure determination.

Are you battling an issue that seems to linger without reprieve? Does an issue of lack, low self esteem, doubt and every other device used by the enemy continue to pop up like unwanted E-mail? If so consider the stance you've taken; are you playing pitty-pat with it? Are you sitting around tolerating your issue? Or have you grown accustom and or immune to it? In any event it's not until you press through your crowd, set your face like flint and proceed to touch the hem of his garment that you be made whole of whatsoever your issues are; which means you have something to do; don't hesitate do it today, he's waiting.

SCRIPTURE; Luke 8:45-48

FEBRUARY 17

"WHEN LORD WHEN, WHY LORD WHY"

Keep thou not silence, O God; hold not thy peace, and be not still, O God. Ps. 83:1

As you've journeyed the roads of life has there ever been a time you've felt that there has been an iron curtain blocking you and your prayer request? Have you been in an intense battle trying to understand why there has been no reprieve or when will God send the cavalry? I tell you as Peter declared in his first epistle(4:12)"beloved think it not strange concerning the fiery trail which is to try you as though some strange thing has happened unto you" for even if you've not come into the knowledge of the truth concerning your worth as a child of the King Satan has. He has launched an all out attack with hopes he'd get you to do what he declared Job would do,(see Job 1:11), but as God knew Jobs heart he knows yours as well. If you were not equipped for the battle God would not have enlisted you into the fight! Therefore endure hardship as a good solider of Jesus Christ (2 Tim 2:3) and gird up the lions of your mind (1 Pt 2:13) and realize, before the Lord allows your when to overtake you, or your why to engulf you he'll send the necessary resource determined by him; to alleviate and preserve.

SCRIPTURE; Js 1:2-3)

FEBRUARY 18

"DEPOSITS PROCEED WITHDRAWALS"

Give and it shall be given unto you; good measure, pressed down, and shaken together, and running over shall men give unto thy bosom. For with the same measure that ye mete withal it shall be measured to you again. (Lu 6:38)

It is often common practice for one to come and attempt to make withdrawals where there has been no form of deposit; so often this is done with those who never take the time out of their day to be an ear to a weary friend but always use them as a dumping ground for their concerns. It's ridiculous to believe that one can waltz into a bank, request a withdrawal without first having made the obligated deposit. We too must also understand that in every relationship, not withstanding who that person is too you, "Deposits will always proceed withdrawals" and to inflict one without the other leaves any relationship unbalanced. Balance remains an important factor to keep a thriving relationship healthy.

We must search our hearts, taking self inventory to reassure ourselves that when we go to the source God provides for us we are eligible to receive that in which we need; instead of the dreaded insufficient fund receipt because no imminent deposits were made in life.

SCRIPTURE; Pro 11:25

FEBRUARY 19

"NOT MY WILL, THY WILL"

Father, if thou be willing, remove this cup from me: nevertheless not my will, but thine be done" (Lu 22:42)

One of the hardest obstacles to overcome is the one which pertains to our self will. As we mature and grow in Christ there remain within us a battle of wills; for our carnal nature (which remains dead only through Jesus Christ) wars against the spirit man; and though we walk in the flesh we do not war after the flesh (2 Co 10:3). How do we then become victorious in this matter? The first step is submission. James instructs us to "submit yourselves unto God, resist the devil and he shall flee (Jam 4-7) which suggest that we surrender and humble ourselves under the mighty hand of God (1 Pet 5:6). The second step is to "die daily" (1 Co 15:31), which says you might feel like being rude to that rude driver, or give into the temptation to help God out since it seem as if it's taking too long to receive that in which you've been praying about, but because you've had a heart transformation you realize that Gods way is always best; realizing it's no longer about you, instead you can declare "not my will but thy will". Therefore pray: Father create in me a clean heart, cause me to know thy perfect will for my life and as I press my way pass second guessing you or being obstinate, please continue to be longsuffering toward me, while I die daily to your will.

SCRIPTURE; Luke 22:31-32

FEBRUARY 20

"FEAR NOT"

And the Lord said unto him, peace be unto thee fear not: thou shalt not die. Judges 6:23-24

With everything that's happening in the world or even right in own neighborhood it's sometimes difficult for us to not become a tad bit fearful. Looking back in history you'll find that it was during some of the most strenuous circumstances recorded in biblical history that God would send a representative to show up to make the proclamation "fear not". It wasn't because the Lord couldn't change the atmosphere around them quickly, or send a word and it be so, but this was done because God wants to relay to us, that even in stressful situations; when it feel like everything is falling apart and you're not sure the source needed to pull it together will come through that there is purpose in adversity and at the exact moment he'll strengthen you and bring you out, or he'll send re-enforcement. Gideon didn't see himself as a mighty man of valor (judges 6:12), but that's what God declared about him; so too is it with you!

Remember, if we harbor fear or allow the grip of fear to keep us in bondage we will never leave the port and we risk the chance of watching our golden moment pass us by. Fear is designed to keep you out of your promised land, enjoying your promised possessions, with your promised people. Therefore since God has warned fear not, begin to believe that there is nothing to fear and "fear not".

SCRIPTURE; Luke 1:11-13

FEBRUARY 21

"DESIRED"

Simon, Simon, behold Satan hath desired to have you, that he may sift you as wheat (Luke 22:31)

Most people are of the misconception that Satan has a plan for their lives and it's because of this falsehood that they live as though every mistake, every falling away or every bad decision is made because the devil made them and have constructed a plan for them that can not be detoured. However again this is a lie! Satan has no power to create nor can he pro-create. It's vital that you conceive this, "the thing Satan has for you is a deep down desire to see you as condemned as he himself is. Contrary to popular belief the only plans Satan has he power to create is a mirage designed to have you believing a lie instead of the truth. He dresses up sin, makes it appealing to the eye and the senses of man and dangles it before him for enticement sake. There is yet one flaw with these desires misconstrued as plans, God has made a way of escape for you (1Co 10:13), so then what has been instituted as a plan dwindles into a mere desire; one without authority or power to overtake or harm, unless you choose.

SCRIPTURE; Luke 10:19

FEBRUARY 22

"A BLANK PAGE"
Their sins and lawless deeds I shall remember no more. (Heb 10:17)

In Paul's' epistle to the Roman Church he reminds the Christians there "all have sinned and fallen short of the glory of God" (Rom 3:23). The great news is because of the love the son had for the father Jesus went to the cross and bore the sins of you and me so that we may have life and it so abundantly. It's due to this truth that we are afforded the proverbial "blank page" to re-write our futures. Before Calvary we were destined for hell; after Golgotha we were adopted into Christ's resurrection and given a clean slate. What you do with your life now after your conversion and repentance makes up how the father see you; all your past failures and disappointments are forgotten.

Now that your page is blank, what will you fill it up with? Will you reach back into the trash can of your memory delve into old hurts, rehash broken dreams or will you take the innovative approach and find out what the father has said about you and little by little begin to conquer the stumbling blocks placed before you until they are consumed (Deut 7:21-22). Remember the things you find on your page have been written with your ink, by your own hands.

SCRIPTURE; Isa 43:25

FEBRUARY 23

"RESTORATION"

And I will restore unto you the years that the locust hath eaten, the cankerworm, and the caterpillar, and the palmerworm, my great army which I sent among you (Joel 2:25)

If you or I were in the re-furbishing business we would take those items people consider worthwhile, exquisite, delicate or somewhat of a memoir, strip it of whatever covering it has then proceed to make it replicate it's once new or original state. To some this is considered refurbishing or restoring in either vain it's correct for it's the finished product which gives credence to its namesake.

When man fell and sin was introduced into the world God formulated a plan to restore us and all things that concerns us unto it's natural order; which was accomplished when Jesus gave up the ghost and declared it is finished (John 19:30). Knowing this it is imperative that we believe that God is still in the restoration business and he's orchestrated a plan that will (in due season) place us in a position of wholeness. Consider a chair in the hands of those assigned to restore it; there is a process that it must incur before it reaches the finished stage; while it's transitioning it may appear as junk, it may even feel like trash because the many nicks and splinters it has due to everyday wear and tear, however as it's positioned from step A to step Z it'll soon began to resemble the once favorite chair of it's proud owner and eventually begin to service them as well. Now consider you in the hand of your maker, restoration won't happen in a day, but if you'll allow the Lord to lead you through the process you'll look up and find that you're one step closer than you were on yesterday.

SCRIPTURE; Isa 45:2-3

FEBRUARY 24

"THE DOMINO EFFECT"

And because he loved thy fathers therefore he chose their seed after them and brought thee out in his sight with his mighty power out of Egypt: thou shalt keep therefore his statues and his commandments, which I command thee this day that it may go well with thee (Deut 4:37&40)

Some would probably disagree and even argue the fact that unbeknownst to them the choices they make in life effects not only those around them but those they will ultimately come in contact with. It's been said that you only love once; it's commercialized through television and radio; most often we hear of those who find it good sport to play life threatening games such as Russian roulette not actually considering the repercussion if the 1% becomes their fate. It's careless to make conscious decisions without first counting up the cost; which entails us delving into every consequence in the event bad decisions are made. We must then consider the" what if"! What if what you've analyzed before hand is incorrect? Do we then gamble with the futures of not only ourselves but those divinely connected to us well, if so the why? Is it because we have now become faltered between two opinions? Or do we take the address God gave Moses for the children of Israel as they were making their way through the wilderness (read Deut 5:9). In understanding and believing that it is the same God who commanded then, who also commands now, who exemplified that your actions or lack thereof always tinkle downward from one generation to the next.

SCRIPTURE; Isa 54:13

FEBRUARY 25

"GOD HAS A PLAN"

There is a way that seemeth right to a man, but the end thereof is the way of death (Pro 14:12)

If your life appears to be at standstill and regardless of all the effort you've put forth nothing seems to be materializing you probably need to come to terms with this fact "it's possible that your plan contradicts the plan God has for you and it's therefore time to abandon ship! Realizing that life isn't always cut and dried it becomes crucial for us to be flexible in our own plans: knowing that we are often limited in the ways of how God has purposed our lives to transpire fully.

We make arrangements and engagements feeling certain that this is the proper path to take, but when arrangements fall through and engagements are cancelled we become perplexed and often depressed or oppressed; instead we must be reminded that the lord thoughts are not our thoughts, neither are his ways our ways (Isa 55:8-9): Don't fret nor should you become dismayed for even when we think we know what is determined our best option God has one even better. It might hurt as you get there but once you walk into the fullness of what he has for you your soul will began to break forth in singing; The way to become recipients of what's fitting and graciously given is to "cast your care upon him for he careth for you" (1 Pet 5:7), as you walk by faith and not by sight (2 Co 5:7)

SCRIPTURE; Rom 8:28

FEBRUARY 26

"CONCERNS OR WORRIES?"

Which of you by taking thought can add a cubic unto his stature? Mt 6:27

This particular scripture is accounted to Jesus who has just completed a forty day fast where he has been tempted by Satan (Mt 4:1-10); it's illustrated in his sermon on the mount in Matthews account but its designed to show us how we as followers of Christ should live daily.

Often we're faced with difficulties and situations which command our undivided attention. It's during these bouts of indifferences that we understand that God is at work and to digress from concern to worry would only hinder the progress. Worry brings along its friend fear which has the propensity to cripple intent and purpose meant to cause your life to prosper completely. The Apostle Paul wrote to his young son Timothy from his prison cell declaring "God has not given us the spirit of fear; but of power and of love and of a sound mind" (2 Tim 1:7); Paul who was bound by chains could clearly make this declaration because he knew in whom he trusted: his circumstances were enough to cause worry but his belief in the Lord Jesus superseded all concerns for himself; he knew he had to trust God even when he couldn't trace him. We too must lay hold of the faith that is required to shoot us into our new levels. Let us not become so absorbed in the things around us that we miss what's been provided already; remember it's alright to be concerned but it's never right to worry!

SCRIPTURE; 1 John 5:14

FEBRUARY 27

"HARD PLACES"

And Jacob was left alone and there wrestled a man with him until the breaking of the day (Gen 32:24)

Life will always institute hard places in our lives for God has ordained it. The thing we mustn't do is respond to them as a people without hope! As we read and understand the will and the word of God it's often shown how God has used every hard place in the lives of his people to propel them into destiny. Jacobs hard place was designed to transform him into a new creation (Gen 39:28); Josephs hard place came in the form of a prison (Gen 39:21) designated to connect him with the king of Egypt; David hard place was in a cave (1 Sam 22:1) and while he was there God was vindicating him with his enemies.

Its expedient for us to know that where there are hard places, revelations awaits you there. God is attempting to show you what you'd otherwise miss if you were not there; your restoration has been decreed as you walk through your hard place because it is a refining process which will enable you to shed the old and walk in the new; don't curse your trails embrace them.

SCRIPTIRE; 1 Kings 19

FEBRUARY 28

"A VOICE FOR THE VOICELESS"

Say to them that are of a fearful heart, be strong fear not: behold your God will come with vengeance: he will come and save you. (Isaiah 35:4)

One of the hardest things for us to overcome even as believers in Christ is the need or desire to come to our own defense or that of a loved one. Too often we fail to hold our tongues when an uncomfortable position arise; in doing so we limit the voice of God who longs to step in and defend us. In Jesus Sermon on the Mount he declares "The meek shall inherit the earth" (Mt 5:5), inherit describes dominion and the liberty to enjoy all the abundance the earth shall produce. In qualifying for these we must be certain we remain teachable and meek; when the flesh cries out to speak recall what God declared to king Je-hosh-a-phat when the people of Moab and Ammon came up against him, (for the battle is not yours but Gods 2Cronicles 20:15b); he went on to say "you shall not need to fight in this battle; set yourselves, stand ye still and see the salvation of the Lord"2 Cron 20:17.

To put in practice what God has said releases the manifestation of the promise of Gods supernatural provision. We can not violate his principles or his decrees and expect his promises to materialize; from this moment on you've been released from defending yourself; no one can vindicate you like God can therefore when you're in the valley of decision recall that it's better to be swift to hear, slow to speak, slow to wrath (Ja 1:19)

SCRIPTURE; Pro 10:19

MARCH 1

"FLOURISH WHERE YOU ARE PLANTED"

And the keeper of the prison committed Josephs hand all the prisoners that were in the prison; and whatsoever they did there he was the doer of it (Gen 39:22).

To expect daisies to flourish and grow during the winter months, in adverse weather seems ludicrous but what isn't visible to the naked eye doesn't mean it isn't so; what isn't foreseen is the transition it takes to get the seed to bud. In the hard packed soil we believe there is no life but what has happened is it's being cultivated in the dark gloomy place and at the precise moment, after the incubation period it shall begin to bring forth life. The daisy has no say in whether or not the conditions are favorable it's thrust into a situation and expected to thrive and produce; the same rings true for us: life isn't always what we'd chose none the less we are required to flourish in whatever predicament we find ourselves in. Why? Because to do anything less says that our lives are dictated by our circumstances, which makes us powerless and contradict the word of God that says "we have been given dominion over every living thing (Gen 1:28), We are not to be distinguished by where we are but by who's we are and if" God be for us who than can be against us" (Rom 8:31)

SCRIPTURE; Ruth 1:16-17

MARCH 2

"RIGHT PLAN WRONG MOTIVE"

This people draweth nigh unto me with their mouth and honoreth me with their lips but their heart is far from me. (Mt15:8)

So often we see or hear of those who have labored and toiled in their calling; but it's because of their commitment and advancement (promotion comes from the Lord) that they reach a level of notoriety and acclaim; what was inspired by determination and a deep desire to serve or proclaim the goodness of God can become tainted when selfish ideals and monetary gain begin to dominate the reason for your achievement. Does it mean that motives were always impure, certainly not; however to realize the severity of such grave choices, refuse to repent and continue therein, leaves you accountable not only for your faults but for the faults of those lead astray. King Solomon wrote "remove far away from me vanity and lies: give me neither poverty nor riches: feed me with food convenient for me lest I be full and deny thee and say who is the Lord?> or lest I be poor and steal and take the name of my God in vain (Pro 30:8-9). Have your plans gone eschewed and your motive turned from selfless to selfish, are you a pillar in your community and what you now do can be misconstrued or defined as such: take note that a community can be in your household, at your workplace or in the grocery check out line; so you see it's imperative that we consistently take personal inventory to be certain no kinks are in our walk of life. If the occasion arise and some are uncovered or discovered there is an anecdote for it; John wrote, if we confess our sins he is faithful and just to forgive us our sins and to cleanse us from all unrighteousness(1John 1:9). Take time and examine yourself to see if you're in the household of faith.

SCRIPTURE; Ezekiel 33:13-16

MARCH 3

"RIGHT PLAN WRONG MOTIVES" (PT.2)

Many will say unto me that day Lord, Lord have we not prophesied in thy name? And in thy name have cast out devils? And in thy name done many wonderful works? And then I will profess unto them, I never knew you: depart from me ye that work iniquity. (Mt. 8:22-23)

Our scripture reading illustrate those who have been busy doing what they consider the kingdom business; but there's one flaw, they remain unrecognized by the Lord: not because they were without good merits, motives, good intentions or even a good heart, but because they failed to comply with all of the word. This is evident in the 23rd verse Jesus declares "I never knew you; depart from me ye that work iniquity (Mt 8:23). Some may say but didn't my kind words or my helping hand to the elderly account for anything? And declare" had that been too little I would have done more".

Don't fall prey to the illusion that just because you pay tithes and attend Sunday service that you've done all that's required of you. The scripture says" they cast out devils, prophesied and did wonderful things" which suggest that those spoken of were given the power to operate in this realm; so what then declares their default to the kingdom and eternal life? The iniquity that remained in their lives is the answer Jesus gives. Paul declares "and though I have the gift of prophesy, and understand all mysteries, and all knowledge; and though I have all faith so that I can remove mountains and have not charity(love) I am nothing, and though I give my body to be burned and have not charity, it profit me nothing(2 Co 13:2-3). Love is the essential element needed to produce fruitfulness; love covers a multitude of sins (Jam 5:20), it is our 1st and 2nd commandment, therefore whatever you find your hands too do, do it in love!

SCRIPTURE; 2Co 13:5-8

MARCH 4

"THE NORM"

And god blessed them and God said unto them, be fruitful and multiply, and replenish the earth and subdue it: and have dominion over the fish of the sea and the fowls of the air, and over every living thing that moveth upon the the earth. (Gen 1:28)

In society today we've been popularly addressed through the media and by those we account as noteworthy as to what is considered normal. Through the mere form of advertising we capture mental pictures of the things designed to enhance us as people and more often than not we take our cue from there: we emulate our counterparts and proceed to become the mirror image of the stereotypical family next door instead of looking back to our originator who made us in the similitude and likeness of himself and position ourselves as Enoch did in Gen 5:22. The bible declares "he walked with God", this means he found his place with God and regardless of the partying and carousing that went on around him he stayed there. He refused to identify himself with anything contrary to the norm according to thus said the Lord; he realized in whom he trusted and bonded with whom he believed.

Realizing then that the norm described how God intended (even before mans fall) has become unpopular let us forget about the popular and practice the original!

SCRIPTURE; Gen 6:9-13

MARCH 5

"COMMERCALIZED"

And whatsoever you do, do it heartily as unto the Lord and not unto men (Col 3:23)

Often we see those who proclaim the gospel of Jesus Christ and all he's done for them in terms of salvation but in the next instant a special offer of one kind or another or maybe even the registration for an event that's soon coming takes precedence; it's then that I'm left with the impression of an advertising or promotion company, instead of the spreading of the gospel.

When Jesus found the money changers doing business in the temple he became irate and threw them out of the temple declaring that they'd made the house of prayer a den of thieves (Mt 21:13). We must always consider the fine line which separates us from living Holy, as thus saith the Lord, as oppose to living semi-holy with a hidden agenda. God has declared that above all things he wants us to prosper and be in health even as our souls prosper (3 John 1:2), this is why it is expedient for us to remain steadfast and unmovable as we make the proclamation concerning the goodness of God: lets not be like that guy who's decided to give the word of God a ten minute clip instead of the 30 minute program designed to draw souls to the kingdom. As God propels you into our destiny recall that the same God who took you there will keep you there; let us not sell out to the commercialization of the kingdom of God, rather let us lay hold of Gods principle of purity!

SCRIPTURE; 1 Peter 1:14-17

MARCH 6

"FAMILIAR"

But Martha was cumbered with much serving and came to him and said, lord do thou not care that my sister have left me to serve alone, bid her therefore that she help me. Luke 10:38-42

When you've become accustomed to traveling in a particular pattern what happens is you forget to pay close attention to the particulars all round you, you take for granted the mental image you have projected previously is enough and you rely on it. What transpires now is we miss the small intricate thing all round us and sometimes we actually overlook the big things also. Have you become so comfortable with your pain that it's hardly recognizable? How about that little closet you've lived in for so long that you've almost forgotten that you've never intended to stay there for more than a few months?

To become familiar with a thing is always a positive experience; it's when we allow it to stagnate our growth that it becomes somewhat of a hindrance making what was initially determined a helpmate two materialize into a stumbling block. When King Saul was to do battle with the philistines he took it upon himself to do the duty of the prophet Samuel and offered burnt offerings unto God (1 Sam13:9-12). He was working out of the realm of the familiar but he missed it, and familiarity became the first event leading to his down fall as king. (1 Sam 13:13-14)

Don't become so familiar with anything that you fail to hear the new beckoning too you from where the familiar has always been.

SCRIPTURE; Eccles 12:13-14

MARCH 7

"WALK IT OUT"

And let us not be wary in well doing for in due season we shall reap if we faint not (Gal it 6:9).

When faced with opposition and you feel as if you're troubled on every side and no reprieve is in the forecast the first thing the carnal mind or this flesh we dwell in wants to do is give up; our emotions scream and moan under the weight of not being comfortable but you must not give in to the temptation to quit;

we must walk it out. King Solomon wrote" if you faint in the day of adversity thy strength is small" (Pro 24:10). Paul encourages us to consider Jesus who endured contradictions of sinners against himself, lest you be wearied and faint in your mind (Heb 12:3). You must understand that if the mind quit the body, and your will and your actions are soon to follow. We must endure hardship as the good soldier knowing that he who has entrusted us with the trial is also able to see us through it; for he who has begun a good work in you shall complete it until the day of Christ Jesus (Philip 1:6); therefore gird up for loins of your mind (1 Pet 1:13) and stand fast in the liberty in which Christ Jesus has made you free and be not entangled again with the yoke of bondage (Gal 5:1). You are to be the righteousness of God and you've been called with a holy calling. Your life won't excel from the no you receive, but it will flourish from the possibilities you create when you reject them.

SCRIPTURE; Heb 11

MARCH 8

"HIND SIGHT"

And thou shalt do that which is right and good in the sight of the Lord: that day in may be well with thee: and that thou mayest go in and possess the good land which the Lord Sware unto thy fathers (Deut 6:18)

There are millions of people who would like a heads up on what's to happen. They consult astrologers, fortune tellers and the like; they take for granted that what's been told to them is the truth and they base their existence upon this information; none the less they've been misinformed; the lines in your hands can't explain your lifeline and neither can any other gimmicks used to seduce the naïve regulate what is or what will be in ones life. We on the other hand can access whatever needed information desired to make one wise. God has left us an entire list of useable dialogue needed to give us the advantage as to how, what and why. The word clearly informs "all scripture is given by inspiration from God, and is profitable for reproof, for correction, for instruction in righteousness that the man of God may be perfect thoroughly furnished unto all good works (2 Tim 3:16-17); in short: every concern and desire has already been addressed for you, it's in the word!

Unless you are the inventor or the designer of a particular article that requires assembly you dare not attempt to construct the instrument without the instruction manual; how then do we intend to access the promises without complete knowledge of what they are and who's eligible to obtain them. Don't just utilize your bible as a matter of convenience or on Sundays; delve into the scriptures, pick your portion and proceed from there.

SCRIPTURE; Deut 7:22-24

MARCH 9

"COME"

Come now and let us reason together saith the Lord: though your sins be as scarlet they shall be white as snow; though they be red as crimson they shall be as wool (Isaiah 1:18)

There is something irresistible about the cry of God that the inner man, your spirit man gives heed to even when you don't want to; why, because spirit identify with spirit. Paul said the spirit itself beareth witness with our spirit, that we are the children of God (Rom 8:16); knowing this let us work to maintain a complete commitment to always obey when we hear God speak. His word says "behold, to obey is better than sacrifice and to harken than the fat of rams; for rebellion is as the sin of witch craft and stubbornness is as iniquity and idolatry (1 Sam 15:22b-23). How then do we justify procrastinating with whatever task God has entrusted us with? If father Abraham would not have listened to the voice of God and left when he was told he wouldn't have become the father of many nations (Gen 12:1-4). We must be mindful that any type of delay can detour the promise and re-appoint the purpose for that season. When God calls remember he has already equipped you for the journey, a journey that's guaranteed your victory in the end; move now!

SCRIPTURE; 1 Thes 5:24

MARCH 10

"DON'T TAKE THE BIRD"

But it is written, eye have not seen, nor ear heard, neither have entered into the heart of man the things God has prepared for them that Love him (1 Co 2:9)

In my early twenties I use to play cards and during this time I would make the proclamation "I'll take the bird, a bird in the hand beats two in the bush"; this meant I had a sure thing and to take my winnings now would disqualify me from receiving double later. Most of us took the bird so often I life because we were afraid of the unknown; we stayed locked up in bad relationships, dead end jobs and in financial stand stills thinking why chance losing what we have on the unseen; not realizing that faith without works is dead (Ja 2:20).

What this world has to offer is the lust of the flesh, and the lust of the eye, and the pride of life (1 John 2:16); these things have always been and shall forever remain temporal (it's the bird). You can't consume enough of those things to make you the winner God purposed you'd become; the word says "seek ye first the kingdom of God and his righteousness and all these things shall be added unto you (Mt 6:33). If you tally up the cost you'll find to abstain and to suffer a little while in Christ now is far better than enjoying sin for a season and forfeiting eternal life. Don't take the bird!

SCRIPTURE; JA 1:25

MARCH 11

"SECOND OPINION"

But the Jews did not believe concerning him, that he had been blind, and received his sight until they called the parents of him that had received his sight (John 9:18)

How often do we enlist that advice or opinion of another before making the calculated decision to not take heed and follow what we believe initially? In the story of the man who was blind it's clear that even when advised otherwise those who persisted in fault finding would not adhere to the miracle presented because of a hidden agenda. They weren't actually concerned about the truth they only desire to find some type of incriminating evidence to condemn the one they considered a threat.

Are you asking the same questions but demanding that answered coincide with your perspective? And when it doesn't do you take on the persona of victim? If so let us consider the stance we take lest we find that ulterior motives lurks on the surface of our yet unasked questions. As we recognize that it can become an essentially simple task two began to evaluate another from the standard of your personalized way of thinking let us consider the plank in our eye before we attempt to remove the beam out of our brothers eye. Scripture says in second Corinthians chapter two and Verse 11 that he will not have us ignorant of the enemy devices. It is deemed detrimental that we remember to keep the main thing the mainstay which eliminates veering off course; you don't need a second opinion if in fact you've known for certain that you heard God correctly the first time that. Take a leap of the faith and just do it.

Scripture; revelation 3:19-20

MARCH 12

"DIVISION"

Now I beseech you brethren by the name of the Lord Jesus Christ that you all speak the same thing, and that there be no divisions among you; but that you be perfectly joined together in the same mind and in the same judgment (1 Co 1:10)

When Jesus went about casting out demons some of the ones who refuse to believe he was who he said he was insisted that he was doing this work under the authority of to the devil; in return Jesus made known for every Kingdome divided against itself is brought to desolation; and every city or house divided against itself shall not stand (Mt 12:24-25).

In understanding the magnitude of his words we must take to heart that the same principals ring true today. We as the body of Christ are many members but one body. Paul admonishes the church in Corinth as he explains that the eye and cannot say unto the hand I have no need of thee (1 Co 12:21). It was god who declared" it is not good for man to be alone, and made him a help mate (Gen 2:18). How then as believers do we disengage ourselves from this simple concept? Have you been avoiding a particular seat at Sunday Service because of that sister who shout a little too loud? Or have you made a decision to not befriend others in the congregation due to a mishap with a previous member? Maybe neither of these scenarios is you but is there something weighing on you and it's caused you to shy away? Don't allow that enemy to get a foothold in your life by sitting on what's offended, hurt or harmed you. You must confess your faults one to another and pray one for another, that they may be healed. The effectual prayer of a righteous man availeth much (JA 5:16). In doing so your healing comes and you put to rest the spirit of division that's designed to divide and conquer; don't delay do it today!

Scripture; 1 Co 12:25-26

MARCH 13

"UNBELIEF"

And straight away the father of the child cried out, and said with tears, lord I believe help thou mine unbelief (MK 9:24)

In Mark 9:23 Jesus states if thou canst believe all things are possible to him that believes. This profound declaration describes the epitome or the essence of what every believer bases they're prayer request upon. But how many of us can be as open and honest as the father who harbored just a bit of doubt? Unbelief hinders the prayer, but as described in today's' scripture we see that the confession of such strong holds releases the grace and mercy and allows for answered prayer. Unbelief oftentimes goes undetected because it travels underneath the "religious radar"; the mouth utters words of belief but the mind question how. The lips rehearse the appropriate rhetoric while the heart inconspicuously distant itself from it's subject: your will declares and decree, while your actions prepare itself for plan b.

If you have a right now need recall that you serve a right now, on time God. While you're waiting and you find that your faith is wavering reach for your faith food; the bible says "so then faith cometh by hearing and hearing by the word of God (Rom 10:17); so make the necessary preparations to speak your declaration "Lord help thou mine unbelief"!

SCRIPTURE; Rom 3:3-4

MARCH 14

"TRANSPARANT"

For ye were sometimes darkness, but now are ye light in the Lord: walk as children of light: (Eph 5:8)

Scripture declares that in the last days perilous times will come (2 Tim 3:1); looking at our current position as a nation, as a people, in a world that appears to have gone mad it becomes a small feat to attest to the fact, the last days are swiftly arriving. Knowing this I find it more urgent for us to remain transparent; the word says to let not your good be evil spoken of.

One day while in prayer I could hear the Holy Ghost say, "take your pulpit everywhere you go" , which entails me working, living, displaying and being the persona of the one I preach and teach about: not just on Sundays or when assigned speaking engagements; this means in every area and at all times, I must remain transparent in my walk; to a dying world and to the saints alike so that I may (for Christ) win those who are perishing, as I continue to evangelize to the hungry the word of truth, the word of faith.

Transparency isn't always immediate, nor is it always easy, but to be the lights we've been called to become it is always necessary! In the infamous words of Christ he proclaims "let your light so shine before men, that they may see your good works, and glorify your father which is in heaven (Mt 5:16).Therefore let us mortify the members of our flesh and practice being that city that sit upon a hill.

SCRIPTURE; 1 John 1:4-7

MARCH 15

"TOTAL RECALL"

And Abraham lifted up his eyes, and looked, and behold behind him a ram caught in the thicket by his horns: and Abraham went and took the ram and offered him up for a burnt offering in the stead of his son (Gen 22:13-14)

In the old testament when one of the chosen people of God would receive a victory, miracle, a life changing experience or the like they would sometimes voluntarily or by the word of god erect a type of memorial or monument; this was done to exalt God for the blessing and to allow for a recall (Jos 4:6). God wants us to remain focused and in control as we deal with the hard places that's been designated to us. How? We must use our ability to recall the last miracle received and use it as a steeping stone too reach the one we now need.

Moses understood this principle and feared not when the Israelites came to a place where there was no water because God had previously proved himself able to make provision (via) a rock at an earlier date (Ex 17:5-6). Don't give in to the ability to quit; when Elijah sent his servant to check on the sea six times he saw nothing but on his last trip his report was altered, not because a drastic change had taken place but because of a little cloud (1 Kings 18:43-44). Therefore recall your last victory as you wait on the last report; for I hear the abundance of rain! (1 Kings 18:41)

SCRIPTURE; Ex 23:26-27

MARCH 16

"DIFFERENT"

Therefore is the name of it called Babel; because the Lord did there confound the language of the earth (Gen 11:9a)

Diversity is the trait of God and we must always acknowledge that when he made man he made him in the similitude and likeness of himself (Gen 1:26) which means: even though I might not look like you and you are not the same shade of another; on the inside we share the same spiritual DNA. What does that mean for the person suffering from physical illness? That says that it's possible for you to look to your fellow heir who works through the supernatural, the gift of healing and receive the resources you need to be healed (JA 5:14-15). Don't miss your window of opportunity to receive what you need because you looked for it through a familiar source or through those of the same nationality; different isn't always a bad thing; to be precise; different is what God demanded and the world needed to bring together a mass of originality too invoke creativity.

Today is your day to embrace your different; you have something that no one else has and it's your duty as a fellow Christian to show forth your love by displaying it to those around you. "Give and it shall be given to you good measure pressed down, shaken together, shall men give into your bosom, for with the same measure that you mete withal it shall be measured to you again (Luke 6:38)

SCRIPTURE; 1 Co 12:4-6

MARCH 17

"OFFENSE"

But whoso shall offend one of these little ones which believe in me, it were better for him if a milestone were hanged about his neck and that he were drowned in the depth of the sea (Mt 18:6)

Does occasion arise whereas you're doing everything to accommodate an individual and instead of them being appreciative they show annoyance? Which in turn create a spirit of offense because you're thinking how in the world; after all I've done; do they have the audacity too appear offended: you must first consider the source before you allow yourself to become bombarded with negative thoughts that allow for offense to fester and grow: now it becomes imperative for you to evaluate the circumstances and environment. If you're holed up in a place that entails you having contact with the person consistently you must take inventory of your spiritual growth as well as theirs; making Godly choices concerning the said relationship; the Holy Spirit will lead and guide you into all truth (JN 16:13). After evaluation you must now make the best decision based on biblical principles; it's hard to be offended or offend when you take the stance of the Good Samaritan: neither shall the atmosphere of offense take precedence over the spirit of love. For, love suffereth long, and is kind; love envieth not; love vaunteth not itself, is not puffed up, doth not behave itself unseemly, seeketh not her own, is not easily provoked, thinketh no evil: rejoiceth not in iniquity, but rejoiceth in truth: beareth all things, believeth all things, hopeth all things, endureth all things: love never fails (1 Co 13:4-8a)

Therefore if or when the opportunity of offense arise remember that we've been instructed to not give place to the devil (Eph 4:27), in doing you portray a portrait of Christ.

SCRIPTURE; Rom 14:19-23

MARCH 18

"THIS=THAT"

Be ye not deceived, God is not mocked, for whatsoever a man soweth that shall he also reap (Gal 6:7)

To make impulsive decisions without practical planning could lead to unchartered waters in terms of end results. King Solomon advises that there is a time and season for every purpose under the sun (Eccles 3:1), triggering the mind to acknowledge that "this leads to that"; so to have and obtain those things or the life we desired it's detrimental to begin every action conscious of the recourse.

What seeds have you sown lately too qualify you reap the harvest God has promised? You must intuitively use the resources you've been equipped with and position them into a place of fertility; to produce watermelons I must first plant the seed; to establish health healthy choices are imminent, if you want prosperity strong solid investments will deliver desired results. "I went by the field of the slothful, and by the vineyard of the man void of understanding and it was all grown over with thorns, and nettles had covered the face thereof, and the stone wall thereof was broken down"(Pro 24:30-31). Consider your choices, now consider your life; you have been given the authority to direct them both!

SCRIPTURE; Pro 28:19

MARCH 19

"FACING YOUR FEARS (PT 1)"

As Jacob lifted up his eyes, and looked, and behold, Esau came, and with him four hundred men (Gen 33:1)

Many people experience fear on one level or another but what do you do when you're face too face with that fear? In Jacob case he concocted a plan in which to deal with his situation according to thus saith Jacob, what he wasn't privy too was that the Lord had pre conceived his problem and turned the source of his fear into favor! Favor enough whereas the old grudge that stood between two brothers were dispelled and the once offended party could now embrace the sole proprietor of his long ago betrayal (Gen 333:4)

Fear is a force designed to cripple you, which comes directly from the pit of hell; for the word of the Lord declares that "God has not given us the spirit of fear, but of power and of love, and of a sound mind (2 Tim 1:7): so then let us lay hold of the truth and quash the deed of the enemy by facing those things that has always held us back, because we believed they've held more power than self. Your truth today is "you're more than a conqueror through him that loved you (Rom 8:37), and if God be for you who can be against you (Rom8:31)! Embrace your fears, get to know them personally, and once you do you shall begin to overcome them.

SCRIPTURE; Ps 27

MARCH 20

"FACING YOUR FEARS PT2"

...so that I may come again to my Fathers house again in peace; then shall the Lord be my God (Gen 28:20-21)

To get over a thing you must learn to navigate your life around it first; getting around it will take you pass it and once you get pass it you are at liberty to confront and ultimately conquer them.

Jacob had to leave home in a rush because he angered his twin who pledged to kill him after the death of his father (Gen 27:41). Approximately 20 years later Jacob would be on the road leading back to where he knew too be accusations, brokenness, a strained relationship and possibly murder (Gen 32:1-3). Could God have had him to detour and not travel backwards? Yes, however this would not be so; instead Jacob was met by the angel of the God and encouraged to take this path (Gen 32:1). Undoubtedly God who is all knowing knew that to continue forth and upward in life Jacob would have to "face his fears".

Is there something in your past haunting you, not allowing you to prevail? Have you hinged your life on the actions of another based on some grave error or some small insignificant injustice they've done or visa-versa? To excel where you've never been you must do what you have never done.

Before you can even attempt to meet this feat it's imperative that you nothing is left to chance, neither positioned too block you. Fear is an immobilizer used by Satan to keep you from your promise. When you face your fears you'll disarm your enemy; Saul didn't understand this concept but David did!

SCRIPTURE; 1Sam 17:37-40

MARCH 21

"HOW TOO BLESS GOD"

I will bless the Lord at all times his; his praise shall continually be in my mouth (Ps 34:1)

So often we petition our God with things we would love for him to do; more often than not you can hear the average Christian saying "lord bless me" but how often do we think of ways to bless God? God who made the heaven and earth, who's in need of nothing isn't actually twiddling his thumbs waiting on us to offer him up a blessing with our lips, scripture declares "when Jesus was riding atop a colt, the disciples began to rejoice (Lu 19:37) and praise God with a loud voice and the Pharisees asked him to rebuke them, Jesus replied" I tell you that if these should hold their peace the stones would immediately cry out (Lu 19:40) however God would rather hear from us; not because we're instructed to but because our hearts are so overloaded with the desire to always be in his presence; for in his presence is peace, in his presence awaits confidence and strength.

How do we then bless God? We bless him with the fruit of our lips, the work of our hands, by pursuing peace and following after it. God is blessed when we bless those less fortunate than us; the word tells us "he who has pity upon the poor lendeth unto the Lord (Pro 19:17). Why not sing unto him a new song and bless ye the Lord.

SCRIPTURE; Ps 149

MARCH 22

"ADVOCATE"

My little children these things I write unto you that you sin not. And if any man sin, we have an advocate with the father, Jesus Christ the righteous (1 JN 2:1)

Advocacy is an important facet of society today you can turn on the television to a news broadcast, or open up a news paper and find where some one is advocating for one cause or another; this is done because the person has a strong belief in what they proclaim, therefore they refuse to remain silent, and witness what they consider a type of injustice to the cause they represent: considering this when was the last time you took the stance and strongly advocated for the one who's always waiting to make intercession for you?

Does your life reek of the choices you've made to withdraw from the things of the world? If so I'm certain you're walking in the promises of God that's made available due to your obedience. If not, now's the time to monopolize the position made available too you through Christ Jesus, in turn always walking, talking and being the advocate this sin filled world needs to see the love of Jesus illuminating through you; which will or can lead too repentance for that wayward soul.

SCRIPTURE; Jam 5:20

MARCH 23

"STRONG HOLDS"

The weapons of our warfare are not carnal but mighty through God to the pulling down of strong holds: (2 Co 10:4)

During biblical times the terminology strong hold was used to describe a fortress like place in which one would defer too during a time of war. It was considered a non penetrated place designed to habitat the one while keeping the enemy at bay (1 Sam 23:29). However in today lingo we associate a strong hold with internal and not the external; now it's symbolizes as an act against ones will or person. Could it be that overtime the context of what God has so willingly provided for us has become diverted and twisted from its original intent? God provided a plan to insure safety when faced with distress but Satan has perverted what was designed to bless us and has used it to curse.

How can you know? Your life will project which strong hold is prevalent and dominate; you will either use your strong hold of defense or allow Satan strong hold to break down your wall of defense, remember the battle's not your but God (2 Cron 20:15b) and no weapon that is formed against you shall prosper...(Isa 54:17), so whose report will you believe? You must believe the report of the Lord!

SCRIPTURE; Ps 127:1

MARCH 24

"TODAY"

This is the day which the Lord hath made; we will rejoice and be glad in it (Ps 118:24)

One of the most difficult things to do and or accomplish is the ability to completely utilize your today oftentimes while it is called today we hustle here and there busily trying to create, plan for and orchestrate the things we count as prevalent to produce the tomorrows we want or expect. What's actually occurring is we are inadvertently despising and mishandling that in which God has already provided for us; Today! We cheat ourselves of completely monopolizing and enjoying a gift that's before us when we chose to overlook its importance.

Jesus advises us to take no thought for the morrow: for the morrow shall take thought for the things of itself (Mt 6:34). So while it is called today, make the most of it, don't despise it, enjoy it, learn from it, pay attention to it and most of all share love in it as you remember to not overlook your today, reaching for your tomorrow.

SCRIPTURE; JA 4:14

MARCH 25

"BITTER SWEET"

Then David arose and cut off the skirt of Saul robe privily, and it came to pass afterward that David's heart smote him because he had cut off Saul's skirt (1 Sam 24:4b-5)

In the story of David and Saul a bitter rivalry had begun in the heart of King Saul which led him to declare the death of David. It's during this period that King Saul comes to a place and makes himself vulnerable to David, who in turns spares the Kings life; not because he deserved it but because he realized that in spite of King Saul black heart he still remained the one anointed and appointed by

God to lead his people. The lesson to be learned here is, even when it's most convenient to get away from or do away with a particular problem it's not always considered best to do so. Many lessons are learned as we walk through the fire of affliction, and great character is developed while we suffer through the pruning process.

While the enemy was in hot pursuit of David life, instead of taking the first exit offered him he deemed it better to honor

God and continue the race for his life, believing that God would cause him to triumph. The test isn't pleasant but if you preserver it will yield the peaceable fruit of righteousness; it's often the worst thing that could happen but surely the best, for the end results are destined to position you where you would never go otherwise !

SCRIPTURE; Job 42:10

MARCH 26

"THIS IS ONLY A TEST"

Lay not thine hand upon the lad, neither do thou anything unto him: for now I know that thou feareth God, seeing that thou hast not withheld thy son, thou only son from me (Gen 22:12)

When things are drastic and everything around you seems as if it's going haywire you can be certain of this one fact, "God is not surprised concerning your immediate position. Test are orchestrated in our lives too elevate us too another degree and connect with those who've been designed to make certain we get there; test aren't always easy but you can be certain they are necessary.

When David was anointed King he didn't immediately go from little shepherd boy too King, he first had to go into the palace as Saul's armor bearer (1 Sam 16:21); during this time David stayed in the presence of the King, but there came a day when David had to return to his fathers house: there was no kingdom in his hand, no more sitting in the presence of the King and all other benefits were out; no longer was David playing for the King he had to go back and tend sheep (1 Sam 17:15). This was no coincidence, God was testing the heart of his servant, God wanted to make certain he would be the same in the palace as in the sheep fold, at the throne and at his home.

Every denial isn't about what you've inquired or petitioned God for, some are to see your response or reaction, good receptions and being adjustable can turn your test into triumph and your trails into testimonies of Gods unprecedented provision; remember it's only a test.

SCRIPTURE; JA 1:2-4

MARCH 27

"THIS IS A WARNNG"

And God said unto Noah, the end of all flesh is come before me: for the earth is filled with violence through them; and behold, I will destroy them with the earth (Gen 6:13)

There are often tell-tell signs before sudden destruction comes into our lives; we often miss it because we drown out the inner voice who's screaming to be recognized, the still small voice (1 Kings19:12) that's speaking volumes because it's sometimes more convenient not to respond, or it's more appealing and a little less complicated to just at as if we don't hear and do what we want. In doing so it's vital that you're able to completely deal with the full brunt of your choices.

In Noah's day no one wanted to believe nor listen to what they considered rhetoric; Noah was declaring a down pour while it had never rained previously (Gen 6). Life today seems as if it has repeated itself, much like then not a lot of people are considering the fact that Jesus is on his way back (1 Thes 4:17); riotous living is running rampant and it appears as if a great many people have had their hearts turned from God. Jesus said no one knows the day or the hour however we need to be ready. Consider the fall of Sodom and Gomorrah (Gen 19:24) don't become blinded by the glitz and glimmer of what's going on around you and fail to miss what has been proclaimed for thousands of years. God has sent a word so you have to be spiritually in-tuned to what the spirit is saying to the church (Rev 3:22); get familiar with spiritual prophesy, pay attention to the signs of the times, we must be ready for the coming of Jesus, not getting ready, this is a warning!

SCRIPTURE; Mt 24:4-13

MARCH 28

"CONFESSIONS"

Let people serve thee and the nations bow down to thee; be Lord over thy brethren, and let thy mother's sons bow down to thee: cursed be every one that curseth thee, and blessed be he that blesseth thee (Gen 27:29)

We read and study the scriptures but in doing so do we actually believe everything that's written? If asked, many if not all would reply they do. Why then are we living beneath the standards God has provided for us? I want to declare that if (and it was) the law of confession worked for Jacob and Esau why isn't it working for us? Or is it? Have we been misdirecting our blessings and those of our children because we've been saying the wrong thing?

It's no mistake that when Isaac blessed Jacob that the blessing came to pass, neither was it optional when Jacob called his sons together to tell them what would befall them in the last days (Gen 49:1). It's high time to take back the power we've handed over to the enemy; the word tells us that out of the same mouth proceed blessings and cursing, my brethren these things ought not to be (JA 3:10), how then do we reverse the curse that's been governing over our lives? We must become conscious of the words we speak and begin to speak not only the truth but those things that edify as well. Therefore as we grab a hold of our faith lets lay hold of the power of confession and begin to use what God has already used to get done what he desire.

SCRIPTURE; Job 22:28

MARCH 29

"ROME WASN'T BUILT IN ONE DAY"

But I have prayed for thee, that thy faith fail not; and when thou art converted, strengthen thy brethren (Luke 22:32)

Everything done today is done at a much quicker pace than when it was done twenty-five years ago; we've become the microwave generation and this creates the notion, it's unpopular to have to wait on anything. We sign up for instant credit and generate debt because we lust and have not (James 4:2). We sell out not really realizing that Rome wasn't built in one day. Why? Simple, the things that can be constructed in a short period usually have no relevant infrastructure, therefore taking little to no effort to cause demise.

The rings true also with our walk as Christians as well. God isn't expecting you to be an overnight success, however he does expect us to eventually become; We all come to God with baggage, but we are not judged because of these shortcomings or our mishaps. When he see's us, he see the blood of Jesus, and while we are walking this walk we must always consider that we are under construction. Yes, you may have missed the mark yesterday but thank God he's not through with you yet. He knows about your rough edges and has made provision for a specialist to step in and smooth them out. So don't become frazzled when you get to the fork in the road, you need that, it's a part of makeover. Consider Peter who walked with Jesus during his ministry but denied him during his time of persecution (Luke 22:56-60), God didn't throw him away because he failed, when Jesus rose from the grave he instructed Peter to feed his sheep (John 21:16). Meaning you denied me before but now that you have been converted and repented you can still be used.

Rome wasn't built in one day and neither shall you be, but as you humble yourself under the hand of God a beautiful finished project is expected.

SCRIPTURE; Jer 1:5

MARCH 30

"DESPERATE"

I love them that love me; and those that seek me early shall find me (Pro 8:17)

Has there ever been a time in your life when you've wanted something or someone so bad that you would do almost anything to have and or keep it or them? Have you been in a love relationship and regardless of how wrong things were becoming you just couldn't leave or let go? Is it safe to assume or say that you were in a somewhat vulnerable state and therefore a mere desperate? Now consider God's stance and his cleverly orchestrated design to put the work of his hands back into the original position designed for us. Can you imagine what God must have felt when he began to cultivate the plan of redemption or when he knew that we'd be utterly lost, he made the decision to send himself to become the slain lamb of salvation; he made the choice of desperate father destined to save his choice creation! He loved us so much where as he halted not at the decision to part with what was before we were (John 1:1-3). Let us therefore no longer consider ourselves, nor our situations in this present age, for in him we live and move and have our being (Acts 17:28); knowing this why not evaluate your place in the body of Christ. Are you as desperate for God and his righteousness as he was to redeem you from sin? Does your life prove your desperation to please the Lord? Is it witnessed to those around you without you speaking a word? Remember the eyes of the lord are in everyplace, beholding the evil and the good (Pro 15:3)

SCRIPTURE; Heb 11:6

MARCH 31

"A WORLD OF DARKNESS"

But if our gospel be hid, it is hid to those who are lost (2 Co 4:3)

I once had the pleasure of meeting and hearing a woman by the name of Ruth sing, Ruth could sing like a humming bird coupled with the anointing power of God, she sang this one particular song addressing the goodness of God and all he's done for her and been to her. Ruth is a small framed visually impaired woman, rather or not she was born blind or later in life became this way is not known to me. What stuck out most about Ruth to me is that even though she lives in a world of utter darkness her life speaks volumes; she radiates as a beacon of light. Why is this important incident? Because it seems as if the world is becoming a dark dismal place, and if God has chosen to use one who's without the resources to live with the illumination of physical light to be a light, how much more does he wait to utilize the gift that's embedded in us for the cause of illumination? It matter's not what the gift is what's vital is that you make use of it. Consider the steward who took the talent and hid it in the ground and produced no increase (Mt 25:25). In the end he was stripped of the talent given unto him and it was given to the one who had the most.

You and your gifts are significant to get a message across to a dying world that it is possible to come out of darkness into God's marvelous light (Acts 26:18)

SCRIPTURE; 1 JN 1:5-7

APRIL 1

"ONE WAY"

This is the testimony, God has given us eternal life, this life is in his son; he who has the son has life, he who does not have the son of God does not have life (1Jonh 5:11-12)

Life can be somewhat of a roller coaster ride; the twist and turns will often take you down roads you'd rather not travel and lead too heights often to hard to handle alone. In seeking refuge it's almost likely one will turn to a place of comfort without consciously weighing out the pros and cons; for your sole purpose is to stop the ride at whatever cost. When John was in prison and heard of the works of Christ he sent his disciples to inquire of Jesus" was he the one or should he look for another" (Mt 5:11-12). It wasn't that John didn't have first hand experience with Christ, for he baptized him (Mt 3:14-15), saw the spirit descend upon him (John 1:32) and heard God speak declaring who Jesus was (John 1:33), but somewhere during his time of trail, as his life began to spiral out of control past his comprehension, he suffered a crisis; a loss of confidence which was designed to bring and establish doubt and lead him on a path of darkness. Why, so that he would fumble around looking around for the savior when in essence he knew him from the beginning.

Jesus said I am the way, the truth and the life (John 14:6); don't become entangled in an emotional, physical or mental battle with the enemy, his purpose is to stop your purpose and he'll use whatever tactics necessary to bring this to pass. Contrary to popular belief (of those who are still lost) there is but one way to the father and that's through the son; there isn't and never has been any other portal designed to bring you into the presence of the living God.

Don't lose your confidence in whose you are; don't allow doubt too steal your commitment for you'll have need of these attributes as you travel the roads less likely traveled remember you're going someplace but your destiny is entirely dependent upon your choices.

SCRIPTURE; John 15:7

APRIL 2

"DON'T DOUBT THE WORD"

Verily I say unto you, if ye have faith, and doubt not, ye shall not only do this which is done to the fig tree, but also if ye shall say unto this mountain, be thou removed and be cast into the sea; it shall be done (Mt 21:21)

The most powerful weapon Satan has in his arsenal of weapons is the weapon of unbelief. Satan knows the word but if he can get the believer to dis-believe makes his job of deceiving that much easier. When Satan spoke to Eve in the garden he didn't use an array of wisely crafted words he simply persuaded her to discount what was previously disclosed to her (Gen 3:4-6): not only was disobedience and rejection in the garden but through these actions unbelief was birthed that day which created a cycle we as believers must contend with on purpose. How is this done? We overcome by the words of our testimony and the blood of the lamb (Rev 12:11b) as we learn the word for ourselves without allowing a type of antichrist to come in and pervert it. Most people declare "GOD said it I believe it so that settles it" when in essence even if you never believe it God said it so that settles it, to believe is a personal choice which works both ways!

Doubt hinders the process, prolongs the promise which in turn penetrate potential. The word of God has never ceased to work however we must alter our degree of understanding the principles that God has in place for obtaining what has been decreed; our faith. All the promises of God in him are yea and amen unto the glory of God by us (2Co 2:20) faith cometh by hearing and hearing by the word of God (Rom 10:17). Don't miss what God has for you because you doubt it's for you, it is for you, now obtain it!

SCRIPTURE; Num 23:19

APRIL 3

"WILDERNESS"

For in the wilderness shall the waters break out and streams in the desert (Isaiah 35:6)

As we read and understand the word of God we see that when God called great men out to do extraordinary work he did so by calling them forth after a wilderness experience. It seems the true patriots of faith had to go through a wilderness before embarking on their divine destinies.

Moses kept the flock of his father-in- law on the back side of the mountain when God called him forth (Exo 3:1): David kept the flock of Jesse when the Lord called him forth (1Sam 16:11); Jesus came out of the wilderness being tempted of by the devil and begun his ministry (Mt 4:17)

The wilderness gives off the persona of a dry and brittle place; it makes one think of tumbleweed and barren land; it depicts a picture of nothingness which belies Gods true intent for us. Your wilderness is designed too bring definition to ones life it's a derivative of life and death and implies strength and determination. When the children of Israel traveled through the wilderness they were not just traveling, life was being produced while they built and constructed a way of life for them and their children (ref; tribe of Manasseh). Are you in a proto type of wilderness due to the stresses in your life? Don't fret about it, consider the pioneers of the wilderness and their latter end; how God used the wilderness to try them and prove them; how they eventually walked into divine destinies that turned the world upside down. Now recall that Jesus Christ the same today, yesterday and forever more (Heb 13:8) is no respecter of person (Acts 10:34) and if you go through the process with humility you'll come out with victory.

SCRIPTURE; The story of David and Nabal 1 Sam 25

APRIL 4

"WARRIOR"

And the angel of the Lord appeared unto him and said unto him, the Lord is with thee, thou mighty man of valor (Judges 6:12)

It's vital to deal with how you see yourself because how you see yourself will help determine your altitude in this life! Many people are living with the scars of past hurts and failures due to what others have done or said inadvertently or even on purpose. It's because of these discrepancies that they view themselves far beneath the bar or the standard of who they really are. When God sent a word to Gideon he called him not as he saw himself but as God himself saw him (Judges 6:12-15).

Oftentimes when God comes speaking we assume he's talking to another because we expect God too see the brokenness when in essence what he see is the finished product. God called your end from the beginning (Gen 2:1), you're not the shell of a person you were before Christ; for in Christ you've been crucified and the life you now live you live it as unto God. You are a new creature in Christ Jesus (1Co 5:17) no longer are you a by product of the world; start calling yourself conqueror, healed, delivered, mighty man or woman of God! You are anointed, appointed and designed for greatness; you're the remnant that God has called out of the world to change the world therefore dispel the myth and begin to visualize yourself and your life as ordained and established by the Lord of Host, remember you shall have what you say, therefore make certain you're saying only the things you want!

SCRIPTURE; Pro 12:14

APRIL 5

"THE BLOOD"

And the blood shall be to you for a token upon the houses where you are: and when I see the blood I will pass over you... (Exo 12:13),

Are you covered under the blood? Are you more than convinced that due to what Jesus did as he shed his blood that you've been redeemed from the curse of the law? If this is you then you should be reassuring yourself that you will be spared, that you won't crash and burn as the world is faced with crippling decisions. Our scripture declares; because of whose you are when the financial death angel comes, they'll recognize the blood and pass you by. We must be reminded that the blood speaks, and whenever your life comes into question concerning your ability to stand against the signs of the times, you're not obligated to say anything because the blood continues too speak for you.

Its purity is designed to bring wholeness; nothing missing nothing broken, and to bring you into the fullness of God. You're now afforded the opportunity to live the life designed for you without fear; for God has not given you the spirit of fear, but of power and of love and a sound mind (2Tim 1:7), not because he doesn't believe you can't handle being afraid but because fear involves torment and God is the epitome of love and perfect love cast out fear (1John 4:18)

This is not the time too succumb to what's happening to your neighbor, co-worker or even a family member; for when the death angel comes down your street he'll see the blood and he's already instructed to pass you by.

SCRIPTURE; Rom 5:8-9

APRIL 6

"EGYPT"

And the Lord gave the people favor in the sight of the Egyptians so that they lent unto them such things as they required. And they spoiled the Egyptians (Exo12:36)

Egypt is considered a place of bondage because of the cruelty imposed upon the Israelites (Exo 3:7) however it's important for us to recognize that your place of bondage is also a place of prosperity; it's a place designed to take you from one level too the next. Take notice that he scripture declares "they spoiled them", which means they took all of their wealth, all of their riches and their substances (Exo12:36b). The Egypt you now find yourself in has all you need to get you into your promised land but you can't leave without spoiling it; that says, you must go through the rough spots too get to your dry land; you might have to go and get your own straw and still make the required bricks (Exo 5:11), but as you remain steadfast, as you press on, as you keep going you'll hear a word from heaven that will speak to your spirit declaring now is the appointed day go and spoil your Egypt! Take all of your experience, take your heartache; take up your assignment and prepare yourself for an overflow: I've already provided for you saith the Lord, look and behold there is a ram in the bush.

SCRIPTURE; 3 John 1:2

APRIL 7

"REFOCUS"

And it was so, when Elijah heard it that he wrapped his face in his mantle, and went out, and stood in the entering in of the cave, and behold there came a voice unto him, and said, what doest thou here Elijah........(1 Kings 19:14-15)

When the prophet Elijah killed the 450 prophets of Baal (1 Kings18:38-40) he became somewhat defocused and distracted after he received a message from Jezebel declaring the loss of his life (1 Kings 19:2); he temporarily forgot that the same God who consumed the sacrifice was the same God able to deliver him and keep him from falling (Jude 1:24). What happened to Elijah? I believe that Elijah had done so much work by himself that his natural resolve became torn down; he had a servant but the scripture makes no mention of him being utilized for any of the physical work, it states that afterwards he used him to go look as he prayed for rain (1 Kings 18:42-43): therefore being faced with his next task of believing God too resolve and intervene he failed to refocus and became defocused.

Now is not the time for you to go it alone, you must utilize the resources provided to you. The people placed in your path at your disposal are called there to be your helpmates: you can't purpose to do all of the strenuous tasks by yourself, failing to monopolize what God has provided; for in doing so can lead to a break down as it did for Elijah. Look pas the snares designed too impede your progress continue in faith and watch it come to pass.

SCRIPTURE; 1 Kings 19:19

APRIL 8

"DEEP WATERS"

And it shall come to pass, as soon as the soles of the feet of the priest that bare the ark of the Lord, the Lord of all the earth, shall rest in the waters of Jordan that the waters of Jordan shall be cut off from the waters that come down from above: and they shall stand upon a heap (Jos 2:13)

When faced with opposition with seemingly no place to go (the wilderness behind them and the promise directly in front) Joshua is left with the burden of leading the Israelites into Jericho; one problem remains, the river Jordan but as always there is a word from the Lord. As proven before when Pharaoh was in hot pursuit of Moses and the Israelites God parted the red sea, this time he calls for the leaders of each tribe to participate in the miracle too memorialize this great moment (Jos 4:2-6) as he dries up the river Jordan.

On the surface it appears Gods people are in deepwater once again but the thing that's always constant is our Fathers undeniable somewhat effortless ability to lead and direct you into constant victory. Have you come to the fork in the road and have not the slightest idea of what you should do next? Does it feel like your drowning in deep waters because nothing is coming together as you planned or hoped? Today is not the time to turn back and neither should you regress or throw in the towel, for thus saith the Lord "I will even make a way in the wilderness and rivers in the desert (Isa 43:19) and the great news is that he also decreed that "now it shall spring forth", there is a right now word for your right now need only be certain to take heed to the message and despise not the messenger!

SCRIPTURE; Mt 19:26

APRIL 9

"THE STUFF IN YOUR HAND"

And they came unto the brook of Eschol and cut down from thence a branch with one cluster of grapes and they bare it between two on a staff; and they brought of the pomegranates and of the figs (Num 13:23)

With the case of the twelve spies sent into Canaan to spy out the land (Num 13:17), they witnessed how the land flowed with milk and honey, they were even afforded an opportunity to taste the goodness, but they failed to make the connection with what God had placed in their hand; even while holding the evidence needed their actions proved that it's possible to be talked out of the promise or miracle in your hand!

Has God placed at your disposal deliverance, a testimony or a recourse too provide the resources needed too advance your stature and your work but you're mishandling it due to the size of the task or a critical word spoken by another? The stuff in your hand is a direct link to the promise; you mustn't allow doubt, worry or any type of fear to steal what God has deemed yours already: it's tangibly yours. No one can recall your deliverance but you can allow your circumstance dictate rather or not you will walk in your deliverance. Who can take back that in which you have visualized or experienced? Don't misappropriate the stuff in your hand by disbelieving it's truth an under estimating it's clarity; pinch yourself it really is real now use what God has meted out to you!

SCRIPTURE; James 2:26

APRIL 10

"KEEPING IT SIMPLE"

And God said unto Moses I AM THAT I AM; and he said, thus shalt thou say unto the children of Israel, I AM hath sent me unto you (Exo 3:14)

When God chose Moses to be the go between to deliver his chosen people a lot of unnecessary rhetoric didn't take place; even when Moses inquired "who shall I say sent me" our all knowing God used a seemingly simple term stating "I AM THAT I AM"(which being interpreted means the self existing one). How then do we as a people complicate most things consisting with life; including something none of us are ever wrong in doing, prayer? Jesus spoke of the heathens who prayed repetitiously, loudly and with many words (Mt 6:7) and gave instructions on how to pray. The enemy uses manipulation to keep you from entering the throne of grace, he feed lies and suggestions that you don't pray or sound like so and so therefore you shouldn't pray. The lie implicated is maybe you don't know how to pray and to dispel this theory Jesus gives us a format to follow, the Lords prayer (Mt6:9-13), he kept it simple.

Don't look for an answer where there is a bunch of chaos, for you won't find it there. When Elijah needed to hear from God "he was not in the wind, the earthquake nor was he in the fire but as soon as these great elements vanished God showed up in the still small voice (1Kings 19:11b-12). Your breakthrough is as simple as being still and knowing he's God (Ps 46:10) just as the blessing relies solely on you doing as thus saith the Lord.

SCRIPTURE; Lev 2

APRIL 11

"HOW YOU SEE YOURSELF"

And there we saw the giants, the sons of Anak, which come of the giants; and we were in our own sight as grasshoppers, and so we were in their sight (Num 13:33)

Out of the twelve spies sent to search out the land only two had a true knowledge of who they were in Christ. Unlike the ten spies who gave the bad report insisting that they were as grasshoppers Caleb and Joshua insisted that they were well able to take the land (Num13:30). In spite of what they perceived in the natural they had received a deeper revelation concerning the ability bestowed upon them to be victorious in this battle; this was not just head knowledge it entailed a spiritual connection between the creator and the created! What distinguished Joshua and Caleb from those around them was their ability to see past the circumstances which ventured on the horizon and see themselves as the God who had created miracles daily too sustain them as they journeyed proclaimed them to be.

The way you view yourself will determine your conscious consideration; your conscious consideration determines your actions, while every action alters your life! Don't perish in the wilderness with grasshopper mentality, instead rise to the challenge of conquering your giants knowing that how you see yourself determines your loses or your victories!

SCRIPTURE; Gal 2:20

APRIL 12

"KNOWING YOUR OPPONET"

For we are not ignorant of his devices (2 Co 2:11b)

James asks the question "from whench comes wars and fighting among you?"(JA 4:1). Is it because we always see the vessel as the cause of our discomfort and associate the vessel as the sole perpetrator instead of looking pass the obvious and focusing on the true culprit Satan. The word says that Satan himself is transformed into an angel of light; therefore it is no great thing if his ministers also be transformed as ministers of righteousness (2Co 11:14-15). This calls for us to understand that the person agitating or aggravating your sense of stability is not at fault; they happen to be the yielded vessel designated to break down your line of defense. Satan desire is to catch you in a vulnerable state and inflict pain. However if we take the mind set to always be one step ahead of him we won't easily become side tracked. How do we accomplish this, simple; understanding that we fight not against flesh and blood but against principalities... (Eph 6:12), use the weapons provided to us through the word (2Co 10:4) and remember that regardless of what you may think or feel nothing is more surer than Gods word.

Stop weighing those around you according to their mishaps or deeds. Don't allow a source of misinformation too keep you from embracing your fellow counterparts; these are the results of not fully understanding who actually waged war against you, know your opponent and refuse to fall prey to his wicked schemes, establishing that you have already overcome.

SCRIPTURE; 1Cron 21:1

APRIL 13

"HE'S NOT THERE"

He is not here: for he is risen as he said, come see the place where the Lord lay (Mt 28:6)

To fully understand what is meant by resurrection you must first come to terms with the fact that it was never about him; instead it has always been about you (us). With this selfless act Christ exemplifies, not only Gods uniquely devised plan to restore mankind back into its original position, but he also displays a standard in which one can emulate and have the life originated for them since the sixth day of creation (Gen 1:26).

He's not there is symbolic of how God makes us into new creations (2Co 5:17), allowing us too pass from a sin state into righteousness. It demonstrates how we have become established too fully enjoy life in every arena, rather it be mentally, physically, emotionally or financially, God declares "beloved I wish above all things that you would prosper and be in health even as thy soul prosper" (3John1:2). What then is the prescription needed to advance us into our destinies? The blood of Jesus and the new life you now live because of his resurrection.

SCRIPTURE; 1 Tim 2:11

APRIL 14

"LOOKING PASS THE OBVIOUS"

And Elisha sent a messenger unto him saying, go and wash in the Jordan seven times and thy flesh shall come again to thee, and thou shalt be clean (2Kings 5:10)

As life happens and we're forced into predicaments or situations we'd much rather avoid, taking a different stance and seeing pass what it entails for the precise moment will allow for the adjustment needed to properly process and recalculate your position. During a time of extreme famine a certain woman decided to take the last of her meal, bake a cake for herself and her son so that they could eat it and die (paraphrase) (1Kings 17:12), but when the man of God said unto her fear not; go and do as thou has saith, but make unto me a little cake first (1Kings 17:13). She looked pass the obvious which belied her situation and paid no attention to a need calling to her need too be fed first; instead she stepped out on faith and believed when instructed "if you'll do as required of by God you won't go lacking" (1Kings 17:14) (paraphrase).

Just as God allowed her meal barrel to replenish itself and the cruse of oil to fail not he's waiting on you to take the initiative to look pass the things meant too hamper or constrain and commit yourself to the cause of sowing into the kingdom so that you can reap a king or a queen reward. This is one of the avenues allotted to cause your barely enough too supersede into more than enough. Don't worry about qualifying resources for everyone is permitted to use what's in their hand!

SCRIPTURE; Job 5:19

APRIL 15

"IN THE MIDST"

....for he maketh the sun to rise on the evil and the good, and sendeth rain on the just as well as the unjust (Mt 5:45)

Today is the day for you to start looking for God in all of your situations. Often when we're dealing with a lot and it seems as if the weight has become intolerable we realize that we've come to the end of ourselves and we begin to look for answers elsewhere; needless to say, our first recourse should always lie within the Lord; knowing that he would never place on us more than we can bare.

When Joseph brothers sold him into slavery they ultimately ended up being saved because of this fact. Instead of Joseph being bitter he received a life changing revelation during the course of his highly orchestrated trail. He expressed his forgiveness of their folly by acknowledging to them "what they meant for evil, God meant it unto good (paraphrased) (Gen50:20). Instead of bitterly complaining why not decide to indulge in praise knowing that the word declares "in whatsoever state you find yourself in therewith be content (Philip 4:11b); for the same God who took you to the mountain top will also carry you through the valley; you need only to encourage yourself and recall that God is in the midst of all things.

SCRIPTURE; Mt 7:24

APRIL16

"YOU CAN FLY"

I can do all things through Christ which strengthens me (Philip 4:13)

Are you a little uncertain of yourself, and because of this fact instead of releasing your security blanket you tend to cling closer to it? Have you encountered a difficult period that has led you to the brink and left you staggering as you attempt to piece together your resolve? Whatever situation you face it's imperative that you refuse too knuckle under and or surrender to the spirit of co-dependency; for whatsoever God has called you to do he has also equipped you to do it. Chose to disbelieve that you are incapable of completing your task without the assistance of the crutch you've become accustomed too, God has not clipped your wings you can fly!

When Paul suffered persecutions and afflictions he understood that it was God who gave him keeping power and eventually delivered him from them all (2Tim3:11): he states "at my first trail no one stood with me " but thank God he rendered it unnecessary and proceeded in the will of God. Adopt a Paul mentality and refuse to allow any form of hang-up to keep you grounded never willing to leave the hanger and become the best you now, "you can fly"!

SCRIPTURE; 2Co 12:9

APRIL 17

"WATCHING YOUR GRAY SKIES TURN BLUE"

And thine ears shall hear a word behind thee, saying this is the way to go, walk ye in it, when ye turn to the right hand, and when ye turn to the left (Isaiah 30:21)

Not every test is as simple as being truthful as you have your taxes prepared or making certain that you're loving toward the unlovely; there are often the life changing test that comes along which makes one wish for the simple ones; but even as you deal with the difficult ones nothing is more rewarding than watching your gray skies turn blue. To visualize the manifestation of ones life transitioning from valley experiences to the mountain top position helps the tested to bond with the one generating the test; it allows us to appreciate not only the breakthrough, but the process even as it's sometimes bittersweet.

When the decree went forth Daniel learned that no one was authorized to ask a petition or pray to a God or any man for thirty days except the king, he hesitated not at the test before him and continued to pray as were his custom (Dan 6:7); as he was taken and placed in the lions den, his faith had to stand as he faced the lions all through the night (Dan 6:18-19). God could have delivered him before hand instead Daniel would be allotted the privilege of "watching his gray skies turn blue".

You may not be suffering through anything right now and all is well on the home front however, if or when the time arise rejoice knowing that you've been counted a worthy opponent and in spite of how it may look God has set you up to watch your gray skies turn blue!

SCRIPTURE; Ezek 34:22-25

APRIL 18

"THE LEAST TO THE GREATEST"

But many that are first shall be last; and the last shall be first (Mt 19:30)

Where you are today does not determine where you'll be tomorrow however what you do in today can and will affect the effectiveness of what your tomorrows entail. Every action in your today is deemed an investment for the future: worry not that you aren't positional placed where you'd prefer. The time will come for you to receive the fruit of your labor, and it's during this commencement that you'll hear the words "well done, good and faithful servant" (Mt 25:23) realizing that I've passed all the prestigious, but lost and crowned no longer least but greatest.

SCRIPTURE; Luke 21:1-4

APRIL 19

"TURNED YOUR CAPTIVITY"

And the Lord turned the captivity of Job when he prayed for his friends: also the Lord gave Job twice as much as he had before (Job 42:10)

Everyday combat is enough to drive the strong to distraction and it can easily cripple the very weak however just as God knew the stance of Job in his heart he also knows your limits. In Job 1:8 it appears that God has sort of thrown Job under the bus but what isn't explained is the all knowing, all seeing God knew that once Job made it through his place of captivity he'd never be the same. He knew that even as he was afflicted in his body, distraught in his heart and somewhat broken in spirit, that he would curse his birth but never his God (Job 3:1-3)

Let the day awake that you run out of yourself and run into the arms of your God; for it's when you reach your limits that he'll prove that he is able to see that you finish the course, in turn turning your captivity and enhancing your life. Thank God for the double portion!

SCRIPTURE; Ps 37:5-6

APRIL 20

"WHOS REPORT WILL YOU BELIEVE"

I will overturn, overturn, overturn it and it shall be no more (Ezek 21:27)

In every situation in life there is a word destined to help fight against the reality of fear it may cause. God told Moses to go in and take the land, he didn't tell him too address the giants (Num 13), so too is it with you. If you've received a bad report from the doctor have you forgotten that by his stripes we are healed (Isa 53:5). In a financial bind, does not the word declare "blessed thou shalt be in the city and the field" (Deut 28:3) (paraphrase). Child running rampant again the word says that you and your whole household shall be saved. Whatever situation you face you need not face it alone, find the report that best fit your circumstance and daily (as often as you think about it) and proclaim it over your life. Regardless of where you are you must remember that the word does work even when it takes longer than anticipated it is still working!

SCRIPTURE; Isa 55:11

APRIL 21

"THE VERY LAST MITE"

I tell thee, thou shall not depart thence till thou hast paid the very last mite (Luke 12:29)

Because we serve a loving God he deals with us in correction if or whenever we stray or begin to operate according to how we feel and think instead of what is scriptural. While going through a difficult period in my life constantly I prayed that God would intervene; God showed up, but when the answer came in a way I least expected I rejected it and in turn received (what was considered by me) the ultimate worse case scenario, I was sent to do a nine year prison sentence instead of the acquittal I expected! Our scripture pronounce that we are apt to pay complete penance for the mistakes we make if we fail to give diligence or conclude the matter before hand. I find that it's necessary to never overlook what is considered right, even when we think it's expedient to do so because of a dire need and commit offense. Under the law Moses gave the statues of God which declared an eye for an eye, tooth for tooth...(Exo 21:23), under grace we are bound by the commandment of love; let us then walk in the spirit of love ,for love knows no wrong and is kind. Remember your decisions create your consequences.

SCRIPTURE; Gal 6:7

APRIL 22

"YOU GOTTA BELIEVE"

And this is the confidence that we have in him, that if we ask anything according to his will, he heareth us (1John 5:14)

This particular scripture gives us an open door to have what's being prayed for; why then are we (the Christian) not seeing the manifestation of our prayers? Have we moved off our stance of God said into a place of false humility of "if it's the will of God", and positioned ourselves as spoke persons for God as we address every how, when and why nothing is materializing in our lives according to our prayers. Could it be that we've fallen prey to unbelief? So we put on the smiles, make excuses for God, pretend that everything is okay and continue walking in the sneaky spirit of unbelief.

One of Satan tactics is to get the believer to disbelieve but if you want to be numbered with those who'll receive the eyes have not seen nor ear heard....(1Co 2:9) "you gotta believe". Don't give up on your dream because of uncertainty, prepare yourself too stand amidst the adversity believing by faith that it's yours.

When Daniel fasted and prayed to God for three weeks concerning a vision he was shown at the end of his fast; an angel was sent to him and declared "fear not Daniel from the first day that thou did set thine heart... thy words were heard (Daniel 10:12-13), there was a delay not a denial. You are equally important to God therefore wait in faith believing that he'll bring it to pass; for he who has promised is faithful and will do it!

SCRIPTURE; John 16:23-24

APRIL 23

"THANK HIM FOR YOUR SOON"

Come unto me all ye that labor and are heavy laden and I will give you rest (Mt 11:28)

Constantly we wait on our God to deliver us from one thing or another even if it's not being in the natural sense but the spiritual journey we'll soon take into eternity. As you wait on the Lord; on purpose why not thank him for your soon; is when you can begin to thank him for what you're waiting on before its manifestation that you're allowed to enjoy where you are even if it is not where you prefer to be.

As the man Steven was being stoned the scriptures declares that he kneeled down and cried with a loud voice Lord, "lay not this sin to their charge" (Acts 7:60). I can believe that this had to be a very painful experience but what that it shows us is as Steven suffered he was able to thank God for his soon. Regardless of what's taking place in the natural always believe that God is working it out for your good (Rom 8:28). Refuse to disregard the present by borrowing from your tomorrow worry, doubt or fear instead lay a hold of the truth and remember to thank God for your soon!

SCRIPTURE; 2 Co 2:10

APRIL 24

"I WON'T COMPLAIN"

Death and life are in the power of the tongue: and they that love it shall eat the fruit thereof (Pro 18:21)

There is a thing that can become second nature to man; complaining, it's characteristics are so subtle that it eases up and can take you by surprise. What it fails to ascribe is its power to keep one from attaining and obtaining the promise. I once heard some one say "we can not expect to obtain the promises of God while violating his principles": it's also recorded in the word that "when the people complained it displeased the Lord: and the Lord heard it and his anger was kindled... (Num 11:1). Be not deceived the complaint isn't required to roll off our tongues; when a complaint is lodged in your heart or displayed within ones attitude, it remains a complaint. Consider the Israelites who perished in the wilderness and thoroughly re-examine your position; once done why not lift up praise, for it's praise which moves God, not complaints.

SCRIPTURE; Pro 3:1-4

APRIL 25

"I WON'T COMPLAIN PT2"

And when they begin to sing and praise, the Lord set ambushments against the children of Ammon, Moab, and Mount Seir, which came against Judah, and they were smitten (2Cron 20:22)

Personally I've been experiencing heart wrenching, difficult times as I'm currently incarcerated; have been for the last three years and six months. The days I'm at my lowest God always remind me that there are some who are worse off than I am. Yes it's uncomfortable, I'm lonely for family and friends, would love to eat a nutritious meal and have enough space to enjoy myself in the presence of God, but I'm certain of this very fact, my time will come soon. Some I've met her that will never leave; destined to perish while away from loved ones with hopes of someone coming to claim their remains: for me I know that there is a maturity date, therefore "I won't complain" especially in light of what others must endure.

1Peter 3:10 says "for he that will love life and see good days, let him refrain his tongue from evil and his lips that they speak no guile" what does this mean for us? It declares that the direction our lives will take is determined by what we allow to proceed out of our mouths. Those who died in the wilderness did so because of unbelief; unbelief that stemmed from the spirit of complaint; had they believed and trusted the Lord they would have failed to complain. Satan would have you to focus on what isn't right or the things that you're lacking, but if you'll take your mind off of the negative and thank God for the positive you'll release his hand to manifest the strength, the courage and the necessary conduit for provision. Wherever you are today god knows about it. He isn't surprised that your heart is heavy with concern. He is however waiting on you to turn your complaints into praise and give him the glory anyhow! A complaint may get his attention but praise will command his supernatural provision!!

SCRIPTURE; 2Cron 20:25-26

APRIL 26

"RIGHT BEFORE YOUR EYES"

And the Lord said unto him, what is that in thine hand? And he said a rod. And he said cast it on the ground. And he cast it on the ground and it became a serpent (Exo 4:2-3)

As you wait on your particular something from God it's critical that you fail not to see the things which are right before your eyes. Too often we miss what God has prepared for us because we expect it to be in a certain type of package, wrapped in a particular way or designed as we've pictured: not intuitively comprehending that if it were to appear dressed up as for seen by ones self it wouldn't be as God who knows what's best for us desires or will.

If you're looking for your husband or wife it's possible they've been there all the time. Pray that God will remove all distractions and allow you too clearly see what he has placed and prepared for you "right before your eyes", remember this isn't just about a soul mate but it's for every arena in life!

SCRIPTURE; Mt 9:28b-29

APRIL 27

"GOING BACK TOO INNOCENCE"

Verily I say unto you, whosoever shall not receive the kingdom of God as a little child shall in no wise enter therein (Luke 18:17)

When Jesus spoke of us becoming as little children we know that he spoke not of a natural matter, but rather spiritual. What's described is a necessity for us too return to our innocence. As you sit viewing life from the other side of the glass or just watching it at different angles start envisioning life as a child when everything was innocent; once this is done you'll be afforded the opportunity to receive the healing that's needed to overcome the drought your mind, body and soul has been in. You must (even though you can see what's transpiring in the natural) apply the spiritual anointing given unto you to see a lost people, a broken nation, a rebellious country, as delivered, as restored, as united and reformed. Take a mental picture of this innocence with your minds eye so that it take on form then you can begin to gravitate toward it becoming real, even if it only start with you; remember one day Rev. Martin Luther King Jr had a dream; it took a while but forty years later that dream came to pass (President Obama). God is no respecter of person. What about you, do you have a dream? Now is the time to live that dream, don't hesitate do it today!

SCRIPTURE; John 10:10

APRIL 28

"DON'T TAKE IT BACK"

There is a way that seemeth right to a man but the end thereof is death (Pro 14:12)

To often right after God has prevailed and delivered us from one set of afflictions or another, the enemy comes and attempts to hand us the very thing we've overcome. It doesn't matter where you are in life, if (and I'm certain that it's so) God has made provision for deliverance you are not obligated to take back any part of your old self or your old life; you've been given the right to refrain as you've already surrendered whatever has previously held you bound.

Before Jesus healed the man who had the infirmity 38 years he inquired "wilt thou be made whole" immediately the man began to explain his position, but Jesus overlooked his response because he spoke of everything except what was being offered (John 5:5-8). You don't have to forfeit your healing because you feel a little pain, don't re-own your financial instability because of a downturn in the economy; you don't have to take it back! The word declares "the wealth of the sinner is laid up for the righteous" (Pro 13:22b) and not just in a monetary sense for wealth is considered wholeness, nothing missing and nothing broken. You have a right to be free so don't take it back!

SCRIPTURE; Pro 30:5

APRIL 29

"WORSHIP"

The four and twenty elders fall down before him that sat on the throne, and worship him that liveth for ever and ever, and cast their crowns before the throne (Rev 4:10)

When King David moved the Ark of the Lord and it got positional placed he became so moved that the scriptures declares "David danced before the Lord with all his might; and David was girded with a linen ephod. In lay mans term "he danced out his clothes" (2 Sam 6:14). God had not required this; in fact, it was done because his spirit man longed to worship before and to his creator.

The praise and worship of our God can be seen in the wave of a tree, through the call of a bird, it's demonstrated in the billow of the ocean, regardless of it's temperament the call of nature continuously worship God. Is that you today, have you put aside those things you have need of and decided that, no matter what and regardless of my state, I will worship? Praise will get you into the presence of God but your worship will keep you there!

SCRIPTURE; Heb 11:21

APRIL 30

"SHOUTED"

...When the priest blew the with the trumpets, Joshua said unto the people, shout: for the Lord hath given you the city (Jos 6:16)

As Joshua took the chosen people over into the promise land I can imagine that he never pictured the enormous brick wall that would be placed before him; the amazing thing about his position is, God would not leave the giant wall before them too chance; to ensure the victory they were instructed to do what had never been done before. God instructed their strength out of the fight and told them to invoke their voices (Jos 6:16).

As you fight to put in practice what has been shown and delivered to you by the word of God, stumble not at the promise for what God has declared shall come to pass. Just like Joshua you must stop doing and relying on the obvious and situate yourself for the

Janice T. Peters

unsuspected; it's then that you'll be able to march around your Jericho and end with a shout of praise; your deliverance is in your mouth!

SCRIPTURE; Zep 3:14-17

MAY I

"DON'T FAIL TO AGREE"

Can two walk together except they agree (Amos 3:3)

During the time when Christ walked the earth he never failed to give perfect instructions on how one should live which would yield the peaceable fruit of righteousness. In the account of Matthew in the 18th chapter and the 19th verse Jesus said "if two of you shall agree on the earth as touching anything that they shall ask and it shall be done for them of my father which is in heaven". This gives us an open door policy to obtain the things we have need of. If you're not experiencing fullness of joy and you're lacking the wholeness in life that you desire why not find that someone who's excited about your future, that person who's living according to the word; that one individual who's willing to celebrate you and do what's essential to elevate you, and invite them to touch and agree with you: scripture affirms that it shall be done for you. You can't hesitate because your petition is waiting on your ability to obey!

SCRIPTURE; 1John 5:4

MAY 2

"REMEMBER THE SUNDIAL"

And Isaiah the prophet cried unto the Lord and he brought the shadow ten degrees backwards... (2 Kings 20:11)

106

The word of god says" put me in remembrance of my word (Isa 43:26) and concerning the work of my hands command ye me (Isa 45:11) however there is yet another very vital scripture that god has made available for those who have found themselves waylaid by disappointment and feeling forced into predicaments beyond their control. When God sent the prophet Isaiah to King Hezekiah during his time of sickness the report was "set thine house in order, for thou shalt die and not live (2Kings 20:1). Instead of becoming depressed or receiving this word in his spirit the King humbled himself and began to remind God of his faithfulness in serving him (2 Kings 20:3). God was so moved that he granted the King 15 years too his life, giving him a sign by turning the sundial backwards by ten degrees.

Has death or any other situation knocked at your door? If so consider your response to its call. Don't just invite the tragedy in and accept it began to cry unto the Lord your ways before God as Hezekiah did and receive the extension you need for your right now situation.

Food for thought: not only did God answer the Kings prayer he also gave him that in which he never inquired but needed!

SCRIPTURE; 2 Kings 20:4-6

MAY 3

"CLEANSED"

Then he went down, and dipped himself seven times in the Jordan, according to the sayings of the man of God: and his flesh came again like unto the flesh of a little child, and he was clean (2 Kings 5:14)

The story of Naaman depicts the picture of the unsavory or of one who was initially considered the unworthy, for he was not of the chosen people who God called for himself. The bible calls him a

Syrian or the captain of the host of the King of Syrian (2 Kings 5:1); none the less who he was made no difference in what he would receive.

At the prompting of a little maid who had been led captive Naaman would be allowed the opportunity of a life time. He would receive what no man before or during his time had been able to obtain. God would heal him of a disease that would forever change his life.

Your story may not be that of Naaman never the less you have one and it matters not what it is. The same God who administered everything needed to cleanse Naaman has made provision to do likewise in your life. Naaman was called to go where it appeared no help would meet him however in being obedient he obtained what God had placed there for him; so to must it be with you! The road may look blocked, the stream may look a little murky but if you take heed to the person of God who has presented you with your word of deliverance so shall you be cleansed, healed, set free and delivered.

SCRIPTURE; Pro 3:5-6

MAY 4

"OUT OF PLACE"

And it came to pass, after the year was expired, at the time when Kings go forth to battle... but David tarried still at Jerusalem (2 Sam 11:1)

The soul which believes it's impossible to find themselves out of place only fool themselves: for as the scripture declare "David tarried at Jerusalem during the time when Kings go forth to battle" and it was during his displacement that he would walk upon his roof top, see another mans wife bathing, desire her and eventually lay with her (2 Sam 11:2-4) (paraphrase). His slight change of plans would change the course of his life and destroy the lives of others (paraphrase) (2 Sam 11:15).

What God has shown us is plain, "it's crucial that you stay tuned to what the spirit of the Lord is saying and it could be devastating when we hear and disregard or know and not do. One of the many devises Satan uses to keep the Christian out of the divine order is the power of persuasion. A test come along and dictate it's time to do something, it's time to move and oftentimes we take flight without consulting rather this is God. Don't find yourself out of place because you've gotten in a hurry and become restless; pay attention to the tell- tell signs God has given you and always proceed with caution, realizing that a step made too soon or one that's taken one second short is a step out of place!

SCRIPTURE; Jonah 1&2

MAY 5

"DON'T PLAY WITH FIRE"

But continue thou in the things in which thou hast learned and hast been assured of knowing of whom thou hast learned them (2 Tim 3:14)

Which of us can take fire into our bosom and not suffer the consequences of its heat? How then do we find it possible to go around the old unsavory crowd, still date the person who refuses to make a total commitment or imagine that it's possible to delve into the unchartered water of bad personal choices and not experience the brunt of those decisions?

King Solomon who was recorded as wiser than all men (1 Kings 4:31) suffered from the habit of taking fire into his bosom because of his love for strange women (1 Kings 11:1). This obsession would prove to be the catalyst used to turn his heart from the living and true God (1 Kings 11:9) and result in him losing the kingdom to his servant (1 Kings 11:11).

Balk not a the decision too surrender it all and leaving it there for in doing so you can side step the repercussion of losing your own particular kingdom; rather that be your ministry, your gifts or talents and yes your prestige; whatever it is remember you have need of it.

SCRIPTURE; 1 Tim 1:9-10

MAY 6

"BEWARE OF THE JEZEBEL"

Unto the pure all things are pure; but unto them that are defiled and unbelieving is nothing pure; but even their mind and conscience is defiled. (Titus 1:15)

A mastermind of destruction is what the spirit of Jezebel is and does. In its wake it leaves chaos, division and confusion. What is a Jezebel spirit? It is the spirit of manipulation.

To the unlearned, Jezebel was thought of as a lady of the night, because of her painted eyes and flashy looks. However, scripture declares her as the daughter of king, a beautiful woman to behold. (1 Kings 16:31). It also says that she served Baal (1 Kings 16:32), killed the people of the Lord (1 Kings 18:4), conspired and had Naboth killed for his vineyard amongst other things (1 Kings21:8-13) It wasn't that the vessel was corrupt, for God made all things good in it's time, but being controlled by a spirit to dominate and manipulate, this is what defiled the woman.

The spirit of Jezebel is cunning, baffling and powerful. It can cripple the strong and demolish the weak. It disguises itself as friend, confident, business partner, and even family member.

Never prevent to prevent to take heed to what your spirit is speaking to you. You have been equipped with spiritual consciousness to guide you in every area of your life. Therefore, avoid the smooth talker, give no credence to that certain someone who always has to have their way. Pray for discernment and shun profane and vain babblings: (2 Tim 2:16)

Scripture Rev 3:21-22

MAY 7

"A FULL RETURN"

And I shall restore unto you the years that the locust hath eaten, the cankerworm, and the caterpillar, and the palmerworm, my great army which I sent among you (Joel 2:25)

In the midst of a storm it's somewhat difficult to adhere to what you know as your truth; which is "God has promised to restore unto you the years the locust....has eaten out of your life! During the turbulence it can become taxing as you attempt to forge ahead; focusing on the victory and not the immediate mess; none the less your full return comes with completing the course. Paul exhorts and says "and if a man also strive for masteries, yet he is not crowned unless he strive lawfully (2 Tim 2:2). How then do we obtain this full return? We must pray without ceasing, hold fast too our profession of faith and never waver at the promise; for he who has promised is faithful and will do it! Therefore regard not the day of adversity as a person without hope; for it's when you attain the victory that you can then enjoy a full return.

SCRIPTURE; Isa 65:22-24

MAY 8

"THE DANGER OF DOING WHAT WORKED BEFORE"

Behold I will stand before thee on the rock in Horeb, and thou shalt smite the rock, and there shall come water out of it... (Exo 17:6)

In Exodus 17:5-6 God commands Moses to smite the rock, and it shall bring forth water so that the people can drink (paraphrase). After this miracle the Israelites find themselves in another niche and in need of water again; as before Moses consulted God and is given instructions, never the less he ventures off course. In Numbers 20:8 God tells Moses to speak to the rock, instead as before Moses hits the rock (Num 20:11); his choice to divert and do what worked before would cost him his place in the promise land; he would miss out on what he traveled in the wilderness forty years to obtain.

You can never become so complacent in the way you operate that you defer to relent and or take heed and go different; what worked previously isn't guaranteed too always prove itself and go the distance, instead like Moses it can become a hindrance and stumbling block.

What you've always done may produce results but are you prepared to forfeit what you're entitled too because you refuse to change. Don't become boggled down with repetition now's your time to start thinking outside the box, remember every time God created or produced a miracle they never showed up as before!

SCRIPTURE; Exo 15:24-25

MAY 9

"HOW TO FIGHT YOUR BATTLE"

The weapons of our warfare are not carnal, but mighty through God to the pulling down of strong holds... (2 Co 10:4)

Before any professional boxer steps into the ring to fight there are preparations made to ensure they are up to par and equipped to fight the full battle. They began each fight believing and knowing that they are able to take out the opponent. They train and build up their stamina with hopes of taking home the prize. They never go into the ring ill equipped, to do so could mean a loss or worse, death; so to is it with Christians. Never prepare for a spiritual battle with fleshly weapons knowing that we fight not against flesh and blood (Eph 6:12) and neither is your ought with your brethren, it's with a defeated foe who lost his battle at Calvary.

Everyday when you rise remember to put on the whole armor of God; this will eliminate all gray areas and any open door opportunities for the enemy to get the upper hand, reminding yourself who you are in Christ and you are more than a conqueror, now go, divide and conquer!

SCRIPTURE; Ps 91:7

MAY 10

"A HIDING PLACE"

He that dwelleth in the secret place of the most high shall abide under the shadow of the all mighty (Ps 91:1)

There was a time when Moses; who was charged with leading the people of God out of the wilderness into the promise land inquired of God to see his glory (Ex 33:18); it was custom for Moses to speak to God as friend (Ex 33:11), so why then did Moses feel it eminent for God to show him his glory? Could it be that Moses felt himself to be given a task beyond what he could accomplish, and to make to the next leg of his journey he knew that it would take God showing him a different side to his glory? For this to be accomplished God knew that he would have to hide

Moses in a cleft of a rock and cover him with his hand (Ex 33:22). The seemingly insurmountable situations you face are not designed to destroy you; this is the atmosphere in which God has prepared a cleft and a rock to provide you the double anointing you need, not only will you get too visualize your father but the strength you need for completion awaits you there!

SCRIPTURE; Ps 139:7-13

MAY 11

"THE ANSWER WAS SENT"

...then said he unto me, fear not, Daniel for from the first day that thou did set thine heart to understand and to chasten thyself before God, thy words were heard, and I am come for thy words (Dan 10:12)

For every problem there is an answer, for every vision there is a maturity date, for every pain there is purpose and for all intents and purposes God is right there. When the people of God were carried away captives into the land of Babylon, Daniel a servant and prophet of the Lord was shown a vision; what he saw was so great that he set himself to fast and pray before God too seek out the divine answer (Dan 10:3). At the end of the 21 days Daniel was met by an angel Gabriel who assured him "on the onset of his prayer an answer was sent, but the Prince of Persia withstood him (Daniel 10:12-13); meaning a distraction held him back from delivering him the answer.

What oftentimes appear as no response is only meant to distract and discourage with hopes you'll give up and seek refuge elsewhere; however I encourage you today; as you stand in prayer and submit yourself unto fasting before our God, stand in faith. God exemplifies his word as he shows us through Daniel, even when you hear silence and nothing is transpiring as you hoped, delay don't mean denied, your answer was sent; for God heard you from the moment you set your face to pray: please know that whatever thing that's been withstanding it's delivery is destined to be defeated; wait again I say upon the Lord!

SCRIPTURE; 2 Pet 1:5-8

MAY 12

"MERCY SAID NO"

Let us therefore come boldly to the throne of grace that we may obtain mercy and find grace to help in the time of need (Heb 4:16)

Peter one of Jesus twelve disciple, one who was afforded the opportunity to share an up close and personal relationship with him did what he never imagined he'd do; he denied the Savior at a crucial time in his life (Luke 22:56-61). Peter no doubt believed he had blown it, but "mercy said no", I'm not going to let you go you made a grave error but this isn't the end, I know the thoughts I think toward you thoughts to give you a hope and a future (Jer 29:11).

Refuse to fret over past failures, instead make it an objective too recall all of the times, ways or events that God has miraculously made provision for you. When sin demanded a ransom God sent his only begotten son to pay its demand (John 3:16), this makes it possible too lead the life that has been pre-planned for you (refer to Jeremiah 1:5). Whenever you take the time to wrap your mind around the extent of Gods love for you and grab a hold of the concept that "mercy said no when Jesus paid the penalty" you will begin to walk in victory.

SCRIPTURE; Ps 51:1

MAY 13

"BE A NAME DROPPER"

At the name of Jesus every knee shall bow…. (Phil 2:10-11)

Are you attempting to close on a new house, get approved for that small business loan? Maybe you're striving to meet the everyday needs in life? Whatever predicament you're faced with can become obsolete once you begin to apply the healing balm of the word. Before Jesus sent the disciples out into the field he endowed them with power and authority over all the devils and to cure the diseases (Luke 9:1). John 14:12 declares "he that believeth on me the works that I do he shall do also; and greater works than these shall he do; because I go to my father. Jesus also declares that "whatever you ask the father in my name, he will give it you (John 16:23b).

If the things you believe God for appears to be long coming maybe you need to take into consideration your method of asking? Have you been dropping the wrong name? The name of a beloved relative or friend won't get a door to swing on its axel like the name of Jesus; I dare you to drop it and see!

SCRIPTURE; John 16:24

MAY 14

"OBSTACLES"

But he that endureth to the end shall be saved (Mt 10:22b)

One day as I began to run my customary 3 miles there were those who had taken to the path (to walk) that I ordinarily run. Instantly this made me realize that this would be somewhat difficult because for certain they would be in my way which would force me to leave the path and make my way around them. As I ran It increased from one person too four people and after only completing 28 laps I quit because I had become bothered. It was after I stopped that I could hear God say "life will often have obstacles and to become victorious in every arena of life you can not quit, you must find the recourse needed to always side step and get around those obstacles!

Reader if you're faced with obstacles don't allow them to steer you off course; find you a regiment which will permit you to get through the task even as the obstacle remain present; remember oftentimes it's the enemy who has established the barricade and since he has chosen a barricade he is attempting to steal what's right in front of you.

SCRIPTURE; Heb 12:1

MAY 15

"DO YOU SEE WHAT I SEE"

...And he answered, fear not: for they that be with us are more than they that be with them, and Elisha prayed, and said, Lord, I pray thee open his eyes that he may see... (2 Kings 6:16-17)

God has given your covering (the man or woman of God who pastors and instructs you) a vision, oftentimes you won't be privy to all the details and your input isn't necessary for them to cross every t or dot each I; you must consistently rely on the fact that God is still in control and your faith is in God and not man. The matured will often envision what the un-matured eye can not see. As your leader began to unfold the hidden truths and the path of least resistance essential for the obtaining of these truths trust that God has allowed them to see what has yet to be revealed to you and hesitate not to be of assistance.

As Elisha faced what some considered imminent danger he never wavered as he leaned and trusted in God because he was allowed to see what his servant could not "that there was more for them than against them (paraphrase) (2 Kings 6:16b), you are no different; if you believe your vision is too small, pray: if you can't see what those around you see, pray: in doing so God will open your eyes so that you may see that there's more for you than against you!

SCRIPTURE; Ps 37:3-6

MAY 16

"THE LANGUAGE OF THE LORD"

But it is written, eye hath not seen, nor ear heard, neither have entered into the heart of man the things which God hath prepared for them that love him (2 Co 2:9)

The language of the Lord is one of righteousness; even as God spoke of vengeance and damnation he was considered just. Psalms 53:2-3 declares "God looked down from heaven upon the children of men, to see if there were any that did understand, that did seek God. Every one of them is gone back: they are altogether become filthy; there is none that doeth good, no not one. How then do we assure ourselves of an audience with God? Heb 4:16 says we must come boldly to the throne of grace however you must be absolute that your speech remains one of righteousness; this is why he failed not to answer every prayer of Jesus and the men and women in whom he sent; they spoke the language required too receive that in which they requested. Balk not at the decision to speak what God has previously spoken, in doing so; things will begin to materialize right before your eyes, remember he's a righteous God who honors righteous prayers.

SCRIPTURE; 1 Co 4:20

MAY 17

"NO SLIGHT DEVIATIONS"

Set your affections on things above not on the things on the earth (Col 3:2)

It can be so tempting to want to give God a little nudge or push when it pertains to the things we feel are eminent or need our immediate attention; needless to say God requires no help being God. If your word is "be still and know that I'm God (Ps 46:10) be still, never become so antsy in your wait that you make any form of slight deviations, to do so can create a snowball effect of regrets.

When God told Jonah to go to Ninevah he boarded a boat for Tarshish instead assuming that he could run from the presence of the Lord (Jonah 1:3); this slight deviation would be the cause of a great tempest in the sea, almost the ruin of the boat he boarded, fear among the mariners, lots chosen and a great fish to swallow Jonah: ultimately when Jonah prayed with the sincerity to get back on course God had the fish to spit him upon the shore (Jonah 2:10). Refuse to be the recipient of a barrage of mishaps, stay your course, make no slight deviations; it's the insurance you need as you go from glory too glory.

SCRIPTURE; Acts 20:24

MAY 18

"TESTING YOUR HEART"

...for man looketh on the outward appearance, but the Lord looketh on the heart (1 Sam 16:7b)

After David was anointed King his first mission was not the kingdom; God allowed David to enter into the Kings palace, not as

King, but as an armor bearer (1Sam 16:21); shortly thereafter David would find himself returned home to watch over his fathers live stock.

Through study and revelation I find that David had to undergo tough scrutiny to reveal, not only to himself but to God and his family, who would ultimately watch his life that his heart was in the right place. God placed him in a place of esteem, had the rug pulled from under his feet and watched him continue to take pride in the work he would do outside of the palace, back in the field; because of this God could entrust him to do the work of the Lord.

If your life has taken a turn and you find yourself right back where you started it's not necessarily a bad thing; your seemingly set back is only a set up to give you more territory. God is at work testing your heart, making certain that you understand that it's not where God places you; it's what you do and who you represent once you get there.

SCRIPTURE; Pro 13:13

MAY 19

"PASSING THE TEST PROCEED GREAT DEFEATS'

...And David put his hand in his bag, and took thence a stone, and slang it and smote the Philistine in his forehead, that the stone sunk into his forehead; and he fell upon his face to the earth (1Sam 17:49)

In the story of David and Goliath what is oftentimes mentioned is David great defeat with just a sling and a smooth stone (1Sam 17:49). It usually isn't mentioned that before God allowed David to enter into this battle a test of his character would mark rather or not he could go. When God allowed him to go back to his fathers house to tend the flock unbeknown to him an inquest was being performed: if David would attend too and care for the small things as he did in the presence of the King; God knew that he would be ready to conquer his giant (see 1Sam 17:20-22).

What we face daily are subtle test of our characters, how you operate behind closed doors should never differ from the way you behave while in the eye of the public. It requires a right heart condition to propel you into your destiny, great gifting may take you there but great character is essential to keep you there. Pass your character test and you'll begin to defeat your giants!

SCRIPTURE; Mal 3:10

MAY 20

"THERE IS A BALM"

Is there no balm in Gilead; is there no physician there? (Jer 8:22)

During a time of extreme duress the prophet Jeremiah inquired "is there no balm in Gilead" and as we adapt to the economic downturn around us we can attest to those who may render that same cry. We however as the chosen elect people of God are not subject to the economic stresses caused by a failed market, for our source and keeper is God!

As bills become due and it's time to pick up the necessities to keep your household running, remember there is a balm and he came in the form of man to redeem you from the curse of sin and death so that you can have an abundant life: the word says he came that you may have life and that more abundant (John 10:10)

SCRIPTURE; Jer 24:6-7

MAY 21

"FREQUENT FLIER"

All the earth shall worship thee, and shall sing unto thee: they shall sing to thy name Selah (Ps 66:4)

A frequent flier in the content used for today devotional isn't one who frequents a certain airline taking flights. The frequent flier one should become is the one who frequents the presence of God through worship. Whenever one enters into worship you no longer hold fast to the cares of this era instead you recognize your need to kneel down in the humility and honor the presence of a loving God in your life.

Your flight doesn't have to emulate that of another because God knows that isn't what he placed in you to give back to him, never the less too revive and revitalize your spirit and soul you must become that frequent flier; in doing so you're able to fly pass worries, obstacles, fear, disappointment and every distraction designed too keep you from Gods promises.

In spite of what Daniel encountered he knew it took the hand of a loving God to soothe away the pain; this is why he failed not to lift up his voice in praise and psalms unto God. You don't have to emulate David however as you put in practice your plight of worship you'll discover that it's what you've needed all the time!

SCRIPTURE; Ps 63

MAY 22

"NO ONE CAN TELL"

Brethren, I count not myself to have apprehended: but this one thing I do, forgetting those things which are behind, and reaching forth unto those things which are before...(Phil 3:13)

For years I found myself bound by an addiction that refused to lie dormant or relinquish its hold on me; I was not alone, for there are millions who suffer from one addiction or another. Solomon was addicted too strange women (1Kings 11:1) and Lot enjoyed strong drink (Gen 9:21); the thing I find so compelling about the power and ability of God is "God can take the broken pieces of your life, piece them together again without there being any trace or residue pertaining too or attesting too the life you once lived. In short; no one will be able to tell for your life will not reek of any past failures.

To provide us with a witness God took Saul; conformed him, and created Paul (Acts 9:1-20). What Saul was previously couldn't hinder what Paul would become in his latter day. Further attesting to this principal is the victory of the three Hebrew boys as they exited the fiery furnace. The bible says "...they saw these men, upon whose bodies the fire had no power, nor was a hair on their head singed, neither were their coats changed, nor the smell of fire had passed on them (Dan 3:27b), in other words "no one could tell". As you emerge from your own personal dilemma remember this same rite is yours and what you once were can show up in the new you without your consent.

SCRIPTURE; Ro 12:2

MAY 23

"WILT THOU BE MADE WHOLE"

When Jesus saw him lie: and knew he had been now a long time in that case, he saith unto him, wilt thou be made whole? (John 5:6)

Concerning the lame man the scripture declares that Jesus knew that he had been a long time in that case; why then did the impotent man not immediately grab for the very thing he sat around the pool looking to receive? Could this be a testament too us, showing us that it's possible to become mentally tied to that which has kept you bound? Had he become accustomed to being passed over and no longer expected healing but stayed out of habit? Jesus asked wilt thou be made whole and instantly he began to dialogue as to why he was not whole. Today that no longer works for you; God I saying no more excuses, I'm looking pass what has happened and I'll make happen what you have given up on! Just as Jesus refused to address the excuse God has done likewise therefore "rise take up thy bed and walk" (John 5:8).

(Food for thought; the bed is identified as the thing that's been holding you back, so as you take it up and walk you will take control over that in which has been controlling you.)

SCRIPTURE; Eph 3:20

MAY 24

"STAND'

But they that wait upon the Lord shall renew their strength; they shall mount up on wings as eagles; they shall run, and not be weary; and they shall walk, and not faint (Isa 40:31)

The words but they in this scripture implies that there will be some who will chose to do the opposite of what God declares. It gives no indication as to why they would find it imperative to go in the opposite direction, neither does it conclude what would precisely become of the persons; it does however thoroughly explain the end results of those that wait; the implications are certain, for God has promised them." They shall renew their strength" entitles them to a fresh anointing and the power to stand," mount up with wings as eagles" declares a place way above your circumstance without struggle, why? Because you're able to glide as God has positioned you to have a fight less victory:" run and not be weary", places you in the race with the ability to compete and complete without being dominated: "walk and not faint" pronounces the victory that is absolute in God for your life as you "stand"!

SCRIPTURE; Phil 4:6-7

MAY 25

"CULTIVATION" Pt 1

But he that received seed into the good ground is he that heareth the word and understand it: which also beareth fruit and bring forth some a hundred fold, some sixty, some thirty (Mt 13:24)

When Jesus spoke concerning the kingdom of heaven he likened it unto a man who sowed good seed therefore it is expedient that you understand the concept of seed. A seed is necessary to produce any form of life however it remain just a seed unless it is placed in a position of death. As the seed dies it passes from the state of death into a place of becoming, which requires cultivation; much like our lives, when we are apart of the world we are cultivated through the world but now that we have passed from death to life in Christ we must also become cultivated in the word! Every dark season isn't about a wrong you've committed nor are the dry times you encounter: during cultivation you must go through the rainy season as well as the drought, however as you're being cared for by the tender touch of the Holy Spirit you're being groomed for the task which lies ahead. Even if it hurt know that God is cultivating you, making certain that all of the rough edges are being refined so that you will arise as an exceeding great army.

SCRIPTURE; 1 Peter 1:22-23

MAY 26

"PREPARATION" Pt 2

And Jesus said unto them, come ye after me and I will make you to be fishers of men (Mk 1:17)

Everyone isn't in the stage of cultivation some have reached maturity and now find themselves in the preparation phrase. Preparation is much like cultivation because it is a place of becoming, the thing which makes it uniquely different is the hands on period; this is the place you're allowed to get your feet wet and test the waters.

When the disciples began their journey with Christ they were not schooled in the way of Jesus ministry neither did they have any insight into what being a disciple of Jesus actually mean. It was through trail and error that Peter became the man God called him to be (see Acts 5:14-15), again this didn't transpire overnight. You must prepared for the glory God has for you and it will take dedicated preparation too ascend to the level of divine anointing deemed yours. Therefore even when it's uncomfortable know that it's necessary to stay where God places you because it's his desire to take you elsewhere, don't quit now you're almost there!

SCRIPTURE; Jer 12:5

MAY 27

"REVELATION" Pt 3

...and who knoweth whether thou art called to the kingdom for such a time as this (Ester 4:14b)

When God set the prophet Ezekiel as the watchman he was entrusted to deliver what thus saith the Lord at whatever cost, and if he failed to do so, God declared their blood to be on his hands (Ezek 33:7). In short; at the time of judgment he'd be judged for not doing or saying and would have to bare iniquities, for God had given him authority to make a difference and we are charged with the same charge.

As you've been groomed and prepared too venture off into the direction God is willing your life to take receive each new revelation bestowed upon you as a gift. What God is speaking to you in this hour is the very thing determined to add to your life and the lives of those within the body of Christ. When God commands hesitate not to speak even when if it means speaking it to self first!

SCRIPTURE; Ezek 33:1-8

MAY 28

"EXPECTATION"

And Jesus said unto the centurion, go thy way: and as thou hast believed, so be it unto thee (Mt 8:13)

You're armed with your revelation right so why doesn't it look as if anything is happening? Could it be that you've failed to wait in expectation. Expectation isn't a garment worn during a time of convenience it's a place where the believer abide in everyday of their lives regardless of what's happening in or around their lives.

Take the expectation of the centurion solider for instance he went to Jesus not because of what he knew first hand, but because of what he heard. What he heard was enough to convince him that if he went believing and expecting he'd have what was requested and expected (Mt 8:8-10).

How is your expectation meter? Has it fallen below the doubt gauge? Don't allow self doubt, fear or any other negative force steal what God wants to give you; if God has given you insight into what is or shall be start expecting it to happen while it is called today.

SCRIPTURE; Mk 2:3-5

MAY 29

"IN THE FULLNESS OF TIME"

...And thou shalt know that I am the Lord; for they shall not be ashamed that wait for me (Isa 49:23b)

At this precise moment I'm afforded the opportunity to bask upon the wonders of Gods love in the nature around me. It's during these tines that I'm amazed at what God speaks within the thumb print of his D.N.A, even without saying a word in his infinite wisdom He continues to guide and direct with the mere presence of how He allows the transition of nature and seasons to evolve.

In an observation I noticed that even as the leaves come into full bloom they have yet another step before completion, they must come into a complete color scale before they can become all that God has intended.

God spoke to me this day he said "in the fullness of time not only does this happen with nature, but it's the same design I've orchestrated for mankind". Moses had to stay on the backside of the desert 40 years but "in the fullness of time" God called him because it was then that he was ready (Exo 3:1). Look not at the unfinished product for as you race to do all that's expected of you know that your time draweth nigh!

SCRIPTURE; Isa 49:15-16

MAY 30

"BE A LIGHT"

You are the light of the world a city that is set on a hill can not be hid (Mt 5:14)

One of the toughest things to do as Christians is to always "be a light" however we've been commissioned by Jesus to let our lights so shine so that men may see your good works and glorify our father which is in heaven (Mt 5:16)

It's imperative for the Christian to recognize and acknowledge that we are never given a day off, we must always be that light; it matters not what type of day you're having nor does the altitude concerning your attitude give excuse to turn off or become dim. God is expecting you to be that city that sits upon a hill because those that sit in darkness will utterly fail if you decide to take a day off and refuse to illuminate the lives you come into contact with daily. This too is a part of your purpose don't relinquish your right to Live in continued victory because you find it easier to stop, the devil is a lie! "Be a light".

SCRIPTURE; Ps 1:1-3

MAY 31

"SPEAK"

And the Lord said unto Moses, wherefore criest thou unto me? Speak unto the children of Israel that

They go forward (Exo 14:15)

The simplest thing to do can oftentimes prove to be or considered the hardest when doubt sets in. When Moses the man of God was faced with opposition behind him and within the camp he decides to cry out to God, what he failed to comprehend was the same God who used him as the vessel to speak to Pharaoh, declare the plagues of the Lord and lead over 1million people out of Egypt would also give instructions on how to handle this crisis (Exo 10).

What God was saying to Moses He's also saying to us; "you've trusted me to lead you this far, don't stop keep moving, at your point of challenge stay focused and continue to proceed because I've incorporated the provision you need: I knew beforehand you would need it" therefore speak to your mountain and tell it to be thy removed (Mt 21:21) for you shall have what you say (Mk 11:23). Remember "one can put a thousand to flight and two can put ten thousand to flight!

SCRIPTURE; 2 Co 4:13

JUNE 1

"A SHIELD"

Be strong and of good courage, fear not, nor be afraid of them: for the Lord thy God, he it is that goeth with thee: he will not fail thee or forsake thee (Deut 31:6)

As the Israelites walked in the wilderness 40 years Duet 29:5 declares "their clothes were not waxen old upon them and their shoes was not waxen old upon their feet, neither did they eat bread or drink wine (paraphrase). In layman terms, "God was a shield for them", he fought their battles and fed them manna from heaven not only too sustain them but to prove to them his stature as almighty God.

Today is no different; you might be suffering through some economic difficulties but no one has come to place your belongings on the curb; you might not be able too purchase a new pair of shoes but you can still select a pair from the many pairs you already have. Even when nothing new by way of material gain is being added too your livelihood God is still providing; when He gave you the wisdom to store up He knew you would need it for the affront of a lean season. Nothing in isn't necessarily nothing gained for whenever there is a time of loss, a time of want or a time of need the spirit of God is always present; the bible calls him a very present help in a time of trouble!

SCRIPTURE; Pro 30:5

JUNE 2

"DO IT ANYWAY"

And he said cast it on the ground; and he cast it on the ground and it became a serpent: and Moses fled from before it (Exo 4: 3)

When God prepared to send Moses into Egypt to deliver the Israelites out of bondage Moses didn't believe that he qualified to fill the position. I can imagine that he felt what God was instructing him to do far exceeded his capabilities, and this could be why he feared "they would not believe him, nor harken unto his voice" (Exo 4:1). This would be where God would prove to him that He would use the ordinary to perform the extraordinary; God asked Moses "what is that in thine hand" (Exo4:2) and instructed him to cast it upon the ground, in turn, turning it into a serpent (Exo 4:3), had Moses refused to do as instructed as delegated he would have forfeited the ability to be used of by God.

As God instructs your life by way of revelation or in the form of a fellow servant falter not at the implication to do what seem ludicrous or even ridiculous at times. The most obvious thing to do when God has given directions is too "do it anyway", even when you don't understand and it makes complete (natural) sense to do the opposite "do it anyway"; it's at this juncture that God is trying to get to you the provision you need too advance; remember it doesn't have to make sense but it does make faith!

SCRIPTURE; Exo 4:6-7

JUNE 3

"ACCORDING TO YOU"

Now unto him that is able to do exceedingly abundantly above all that we ask or think, according to the power that is at work within us (Eph 3:20)

Many people fail to completely apply this scripture to their lives; more often than not they quote the scripture and wait on God to supply the abundance, forgetting that the promise comes into effect "according to the power that worketh in them", meaning there is something that you must do!

To experience above measure, even the very essence of a vivid imagination, stop relying on those around you to make you or too keep you happy; it's time to take the initiative and obtain it for yourself. True happiness isn't measured by the things you possess nor is it defined by how many zeros one has at the end of their annual earnings, it is however found when you find your place in Christ and remain there. In his presence there is fullness of joy and at his right hand there is pleasure evermore (Ps 16:11), are you ready for that? If so, recall that it's according to the power that's at work within you.

SCRIPTURE; Pro 10:22

JUNE 4

"NOT JUST AN EXPERIENCE"

And he trembling and astonished said, Lord what wilt thou have me to do? (Acts 9:6)

When most people consider the apostle Paul he's spoken of in the vain of the one who had the road to Damascus experience but I believe we clarity on this. What Paul had was not just another experience it became his life, the true conversion of a soul.

We experience a host of things in life and with these experiences comes an end for we either chose to continue or opt to quit, but if you'll commit and chose to be converted little by little day by day you'll find that what you believed to be an experience will become a lifestyle. Why should one just experience the love, grace, mercy and favor of God when the option to obtain it indefinitely remains within you; don't belittle the day you said yes to Jesus by counting it as if it were the same as the day you learned to drive. Your life in Christ should never be named as an experience, instead why not refer to it as it should be; the time of your becoming.

SCRIPTURE; Gal 2:20

JUNE 5

"STRAIGHT WAY"

And straightway he preached Christ in the synagogues, that he is the son of God (Acts 9:20)

When Saul was converted and renamed Paul immediately he began his ministry (Acts 9:20); he marveled not at the transformation for he knew in whom he believed; because of his strong conviction he refused to keep quite and continued to proclaim that Jesus was Christ, the son of God! The conversion we undergo today should be no different; God hasn't given us a prerequisite that we must follow, Paul didn't go to seminary school he followed the leading of the Holy Spirit and the Holy Spirit took him exactly where he was destined to go. The same rings true for you; God has called you to go straightway into the ministry that He has given you: if you've been called you've been equipped to make the journey.

When Adam ate of the tree and hid himself from the presence of God, God asked him "who told thee that thou was naked" (Gen 3:11a); you haven't eaten the forbidden fruit but he implications are the same! "Who told you that you had to wait before you can step into your calling? Who told you that now was not a good time? Right now is the appointed time, do it now!

SCRIPTURE; 1Peter 4:11

JUNE 6

"EXPECTING ALMS"

And a certain man lame from his mothers womb was carried, whom they laid daily at the gate of the temple which is called beautiful, to ask alms of them that entered the temple (Acts 3:2)

Even when expectations are low; those whom God has decreed will be healed, set free, delivered or just plain exalted; it will come to pass. The lame man laid at the gate expecting nothing more than alms this particular day, but God had wholeness in mind, he shot for a few pennies but received a Kings treasure.

Oftentimes what is meant and destined to be fall to the wayside because it remains unrequested. Had this beggar not taken the initiative to stop and solicit those that passed in front of him he would have missed his opportunity. Don't allow your miracle to walk pass due to no expectation or because they don't appear to have what you have need of. Ex: Peter or John had no silver or gold but what they gave far exceeded this mans expectations.

SCRIPTURE; Acts 3:6-8

JUNE 7

"IT'S CALLED SIFTING"

...And every branch that beareth fruit, he purgeth it, that it may bring forth more fruit (Luke 15:2b)

Those you come in contact with on a personal or even a professional level are meant to embellish your life and visa-versa; whenever times appear to be changing and those you consider of close relation seem to be fading away, don't consider it a loss, it's called sifting. We are like a great celestial garden and to totally represent our father He will and must reach down and sift the weeds along with other contaminants that rise to stunt our growth. Everyone who says goodbye isn't gone; oftentimes they're not considered necessary to enrich your life where you've been called; their not lost to you either, they will at some juncture return if the Lord is willing!

SCRIPTURE; Luke 15:5-7

JUNE 8

"NO EXCUSES"

If then I do that which I would not, I consent unto the law that it is good (Rom 7:16)

Yesterday I experienced somewhat of a firewall while at work, during this I sort of shunned my co-worker and if I must confess, I refused to be as friendly as I am normally. Not long thereafter I felt the Holy Spirit check me and say "no excuses" because it was then that I began to rationalize why it was okay to act untoward; so of course I repented and quickly apologized to this person.

People of God it's obvious how we should operate at all times for the word of God proclaim "we are to love thy neighbor as thyself" (Mt 19:19); there is no good time or acceptable time to walk in the spirit of strife and commit offense against one another. The god of truth didn't make provision for an excuse; he did however grant us the grace to walk through whatever situation we face. In the word it says "where sin abound, grace did much more abound" (Rom 5:20) therefore we have no excuse for as He is Holy we too must be Holy (Lev 11:25).

SCRIPTURE; Rom6:1-4

JUNE 9

"A LONG WAY OFF"

Declaring the end from the beginning and from ancient times the things that are not yet done... (Isa 46:10)

In the story of the prodigal son it's often spoken of how he took an inheritance that was not yet his, and went to come into his own but squandered it away however there's another facet to the story that is really quite necessary. Luke 15:20 says "and he arose and came to his father, but when he was yet a great ways off, his father saw him" God wants you to know that he is that father; He's that father that's able to recognize you even when you're enveloped in the stench of sin and past failures; He see you as you're making your way; you might be walking a bit unsteady, your footing isn't sure and you're uncertain about your reunion but because you're heading toward the father He has spotted you, even from a long way off.

This means: you might not be where you want to be but God will honor the progress; you're a little worse than when you went left but that has been over looked because he see you in your finished state. When He look at you He see the blood of Jesus not the sins of your past!

SCRIPTURE; Luke 15: 20-24

JUNE 10

"THE POWER OF TWO"

After these things the Lord appointed other seventy also, and sent them two and two... (Luke 10:1)

Scripture declares that "one can put a thousand to flight, two ten thousand" (paraphrase); God in his infinite wisdom wants us to understand the power of unity. We sometimes assume that we are capable of tackling our situations alone, but according to the word that isn't always the course we should take. When Jesus was prepared to send the disciples out to heal, set free, deliver and rebuke demons He sent them out by two and two; there's no spoken word that one alone wouldn't have been able to accomplish the task: it is however my opinion (through revelation) that Jesus sent re- enforcement so that they could keep one another encouraged and if a problem arise they would have the confidant needed to give sound advice. He sent another with the same capabilities to help carry the load so hang on to your counterparts with them you'll get double the work done in half the time!

SCRIPYURE; Pro 27:17

JUNE 11

"CALLED TOO OVERCOME"

… In the world ye shall have tribulation: but be of good cheer; I have overcome the world (John 16:33b)

Everyone has or will face difficult aspects in their lives; what one calls tragedy will appear in different stages, to those who are struggling to maintain and row pass the storm what they're encountering seems to be the tempest designed to overtake them; this is far from the truth God has called you to overcome!

Regardless of what you're facing right now there is a resolved placed on the inside of you to help you in your hour of need; the word says" that he would not leave you comfortless" (John 14:18), the spirit of truth has come to lead you so when you feel weak pull at the strength that's placed inside of you V.I.A the Holy Ghost for you have been called to overcome. Weeping may endure for a night but joy cometh with the morning!

SCRIPTURE; John 14:26

JUNE 12

"GOD CONNECTIONS"

Wisdom is the principal thing: therefore get wisdom: and with all your getting get understanding (Pro 4:7)

There is no meeting that should not be considered as a God connection our lives are predestined and orchestrated by God himself, we however play out which road we'll travel and ultimately choosing those we'll come in contact with. You have a say so in the connections that you'll allow to influence your life; some are designed to build up whereas others are meant to pull down.

What connections have you made that will edify the person God has called you to be? Are you evaluating those you come in contact with on a case by case? Or are you allowing bad connections to infiltrate the headquarters of your person causing you to miss what has been decreed yours? Re-evaluate your connections and begin too weed out those going in the opposite direction of where you want your life to ultimately arrive!

SCRIPTURE; Eccles 3:1-8

JUNE 13

"ADMIRATION OR IMITATION"

Wherefore my beloved as you have always obeyed not in my presence only, but much more in my absence, work out your own salvation with fear and trembling (Phil 2:12)

Everyone has been called and expected to grow, especially in grace, therefore it is utterly important that you shy away from an excessive amount of admiration of anyone other than Christ. There is a very thin line between admiration and imitation; once crossed you'll find that those who does so can never truly develop into the mature person they've been called to be: not because of a desire not too but as they imitate another they leave out a true quality of oneself.

God created only one you and the distinct attributes that make you unique are detrimental to the rounding and grounding of those closely knitted around you; don't allow admiration to cross over into imitation for I'm certain you'll make for a poor double as oppose to being a uniquely profound you!

SCRIPTURE; 1 Co 3:6-8

JUNE 14

"NO IDLE WORD"

Believe in the Lord your God so shall you be established, believe his prophets so shall ye prosper (2 Cron 2:20)

Every word that God, Jesus and the Holy Ghost (who now abides within us) has ever spoken can never be construed as idle; as you search the scriptures you'll find that whenever Jesus spoke It came to pass immediately. When He spoke of crossing over unto the other side in Mt 4:22 He never disclosed that they would encounter a massive storm, he only spoke of the end; a bunch of unnecessary rhetoric wasn't used because He knows the every word spoken has the propensity too evolve into life.

Your words will frame your life therefore make it personal to say and repeat the things you want to materialize in your life "death and life is in the power of the tongue and they that love it shall eat the fruit thereof" (Pro 18:21).

SCRIPTURE; Pro 10:31

JUNE 15

"IN THE MIDDLE"

And God remembered Noah, and every living thing, and all the cattle that was with him in the ark, and God made a wind to pass over the earth and the waters assuaged (Gen 8:1)

In the account of Noah it's written how God gave Noah specific instructions concerning the erecting of the ark (Gen 6:16), how to orchestrate housing in the ark and lastly his intent to make it rain upon the earth for forty days and forty nights (Gen 7:4). Noah was inclusive with the plan of God however he probably didn't take into account the length of his stay in the ark and God being God chose not to foretell what was in the middle. Noah trusted God enough to follow through on what He instructed not knowing that his real test would be" in the middle", the middle would be a faith walk!

When the rain stopped and the ark kept moving he had to believe that God was leading the ark and would perform what he promised! Are you in a full battle? You've made it past the starting point, you're to far out to turn around but the finish line appears to be away off still? My friend you're in the middle and in the middle is where your faith must kick into overdrive; you might not be able to see it but you must believe that it's there; it's not tangible, but it's coming, it still hurt but it's healing. Remember when you act as if you can't you must rely on the fact that God can!

SCRIPTURE; Gen 8:6-16

JUNE 16

"BUT IF NOT"

But if not be it known unto thee O King, that we will not serve thy gods, nor worship the golden image which thou hast set up (Dan 3:18)

In the book of Daniel in the 3rd chapter there's a remarkable miracle mentioned as Shadrach, Meshach, and Abednego comes face to face with a choice of worshipping the one and only true God or the god of Nebuchadnezzar. The decree is worship my image or be thrown into the fiery furnace, their response is one of faith "our God whom we serve is able to deliver us from the burning fiery furnace and he will deliver us out of thy hand O King, but if not.. (Dan 3:17-18a), they were confident in whom they believed and wavered not in the face of death, instead they trusted that either way it was Gods decision and deliverance comes from God.

Your situation may not be as drastic as the three Hebrew boys; you may even believe that you know the course you'll take however you live on the brink of a partial reward until you reach maturity and cry out "but if not", Your complete surrender shoots you into your destiny and allow you to reap a complete harvest.

SCRIPTURE; Dan 3

JUNE 17

"CAN'T FIX WHAT ISN'T BROKEN"

For as a man thinketh in his heart so is he (Pro 23:7)

As we're born into the kingdom of God one of the most important things we must understand is "God can't fix what isn't broken". He isn't calling you to be broke financially or fundamentally he does however expect you to come empty. To come in arrogance believing that you're okay as you are; thinking I need to stop thus and so but God knows my heart therefore I'm okay is a grave error for any true believer. Yes God knows your heart and Jer 17:9 says "the heart is desperately wicked; who can know it. This is why David prayed that God would create in him a clean heart (Ps 51:10); He also knows that we were conceived in sin and in need of repairing therefore to repair us we must come broken because He can't fix what isn't broken!

SCRIPTURE; Jer 18:1-4

JUNE 18

"INGRAINED"

For man looketh on the outward appearance but the Lord looketh on the heart (1Sam 16:7b)

Habits good or bad are hard too break, well not hard they do however require consistent determination; also through perseverance they are either formed or broken.

David being a man of war understood this principal, if God did not give him consent he did not go (1Sam 30:8), even when it appeared that it would be his life or that of his enemy he knew that it would be better to allow his then enemy a reprieve than to touch or kill the previously anointed of God (1Sam 24:4-6). David had the love of God and the fear of the Lord ingrained in his heart and this is what kept him grounded in God. I believe it came through him taking the initiative to know God on a personal level.

Are you taking the time out to meditate on the word of God? Reading it is fine but if you want to expand your boundaries or enlarge the place of your tents you must take every necessary effort to make certain that the things of God are deeply embedded and ingrained in all of who you are!

SCRIPTURE; 2Tim2:15

JUNE 19

"LIFE AFTER DEATH"

Therefore if any man be in Christ, he is a new creature: old things have passed away: behold, all things are become new (2 Co 5:17)

Many consider life after death as an event which takes place after one passes from this life into our Heavenly realm; this too is factual however there is a new exciting life waiting for the converted soul even before we cross over into the Heavenly. We can begin to enjoy what God has declared our as we die to the old man who is guided by the sinful nature and become resurrected in Christ Jesus.

Don't miss what God has decreed because you're kicking against the goads, surrender the remainder of your broken life, die to yourself and begin to live as unto God for it's in the release of your desires that God will step in and grant them to you.

SCRIPTURE; 2 Co 10:3

JUNE 20

"SILENT PRAISE"

An above all things have fervent charity among yourselves; for charity shall cover the multitude of sins (2Pet 4:8)

Praise is generally thought of as waving or the clapping of the hands, singing unto the Lord and maybe even dancing before the Lord; however there is a type of praise that the Christian can bring forth to honor who God is in their lives and it's called silent praise.

Silent Praise is initiated whenever our lives reek of who God is; when those who comes within our circle of influence becomes persuaded too want to know more of the God we serve: not because of the rhetoric we use but they want what we have due to what is being materialized in our lives, stemming from our silent praise. Peter instructs the church in how wives should win their husbands he says "if any obey not the word, they also without the word (silent praise) be won by the conversation (mannerism) of the wives (1Pet 3:1), this isn't only applicable for married couples it's directions for us all.

FOOD FOR THOUGHT: Now is the perfect time to allow your silent praise too not only reach Heaven, but those you meet daily as well.

SCRIPTURE; Jam 4:17

JUNE 21

"NONE LOST"

And I give unto them eternal life; and they shall never perish, neither shall any man pluck them out of my hand (John 10:28)

Scripture says "for many are called, but few are chosen (Mt 20:16), this implies plus informs us that there will be many who will hear the cry for salvation; many will even answer to this call but only a few will answer the call "turn from your wicked ways and allow God to heal your land" (1Cron 7:14).

By no means does "none lost" imply that we'll be exempt from trouble, trails or tribulations; it does however guarantee us that as we are faithful in holding on to our confession, the God in whom we believe shall administer the grace we need to get through them: it also grant unto us the privilege of being called "the planted of the Lord".

FOOD FOR THOUGHT: Scripture declares that no man can pluck you out of his hand, you can however, by action and deed chose to leave, the choice is always yours!

SCRIPTURE; Joshua 24:14-15

JUNE 22

"THE LORD PASSES BY"

...to give unto them beauty for ashes, the oil of joy for mourning, the garment of praise for the spirit of heaviness... Isa 61:3

In the Holy Scriptures it gives us only two accounts when the Lord passes by. During a time when Moses is feeling distressed and pressured by those God has given him charge over he inquired of the Lord to "shew me thy glory" (Exo 33:16), the Lord places him in a cleft covers him with his hand and passes by.

The prophet Elijah has just called down fire from heaven which consumed the offering unto the Lord on the altar, killed 450 prophets of Baal and turned the heart of the people unto God by proving that God was God. As he finished his work Jezebel sent him a word that his life would be as one of the prophets of Baal (1Kings 19:2); these mere words become the catalyst that would send the prophet into a tail spin of depression. God saw his position, sent him food and drink, gave him instructions and placed him in a rock that he would pass by him.

When the men and women of God are under duress, when the spirit of heaviness creeps in and threaten to cloud your vision or judgment to make you quit, recall what the Lord has done for Moses and Elijah and what He has already done for you. It's the same God who showed these great men of faith another facet of his glory who will pass by you and strengthen you for the next leg of your journey; for strength is made perfect in weakness (2Co 12:9).

SCRIPTURE; Isa 61:1

JUNE 23

"WRONGED NO ONE"

And their sins and iniquities I will remember no more (Heb 10:17)

The Apostle Paul wrote to the church in Corinth and boldly exclaimed "we have wronged no man" (2Co 7:2). Before Paul conversion he was known as a terror, he stood at the feet of Steven as he was being stoned for naming the name of Christ (Acts 8:1) and sought out dutifully that he may bring any man or woman bound in chains to Jerusalem to stand trail before the high priest (Acts 9:1-2). How then does one who has done so much boldly declare "I've wronged no man? He could boldly make this declaration knowing that the man who made those bad decisions did so in ignorance, and the person he now was, through grace, had received complete forgiveness, not only from God but from oneself as well.

Don't waste another moment living in past failures, what you've done knowingly and unknowingly has already been forgotten by whom it matters most. The word declares "as far as the east is to the west, so far hath He removed our transgressions from us" (Ps 103:12). This means that there is no meeting place, for the east and the west meets not! So start living today knowing that you have wronged no one.

SCRIPTURE; Mt 6:12

JUNE 24

"THAT'S MUSIC"

Evil pursueth sinners; but to the righteous good shall be repaid (Pro 13:21)

What one tend to take for granted is often the wish or desire of another. The sound of children playing would be considered answered prayer to the barren womb. Just as being afforded the opportunity to gaze upon the wonders of Gods creation in nature; to one it's looked upon as ordinary too another it becomes the music needed to embrace the void due a different type of disability.

Refuse to half heartedly enjoy what you've been blessed with thus far. Always consider that there's one person whose situation is just a tad bit worst than your own. Think about it, what you believe to be average to someone else "that's music".

SCRIPTURE; Phil 4:12

JUNE 25

"PURE"

...And who shall stand when he appeareth? For he is like a refiner's fire and like fullers soap (Mal 3:2b)

If you're someone who's concerned about how you look or what your life look like when you appear before God, allow me to enlighten the eyes of your understanding. When we come before God, even in our prayer life, all that's on our lives because of impurity is automatically destroyed due to the great glory and the presence of God. The word calls him a consuming fire and sin can't stand in the presence of God.

When Moses appeared before God he was drastically changed, so much so that those God had given him charge over were unable to look upon his face and he was made to wear a veil (Exo 34:30). That's what the presence of God does in ones life, it takes the corruptible and makes it incorruptible, the old and make it new; the un -pure and cause it to be pure; therefore as you come before God come naked for you already are!

SCRIPTURE; Mt 5:8

JUNE 26

"A GOOD IDEA OR A GOD IDEA"

There is a way that seemeth right unto a man but the end thereof is death (Pro 16:25)

Being able to decipher between your will and Gods will for your life is the key element needed to sustain a good life here on earth. I once heard someone say "when you do things Gods way, you'll receive God results" this word can and will revolutionalize your life.

Many will experience what appears to be good ideas, but if God isn't in the midst it can't work. Some of my best thinking took me places I never intended to go and required more of my time than I ever thought I'd give. Don't sit around fretting over rather or not your vision will produce fruit; if it's a God idea you already know that "all things work together for good to them that love the Lord and called according to his purpose (Rom 8:28): if it's a good idea the word also proclaim "I am the vine, ye are the branches: he that abideth in me, and I in him, the same shall bring forth much fruit; for without me ye can do nothing (John 15:5). You consider, is it a good idea or a God idea?

SCRIPTURE; John 16:13

JUNE 27

"A SEGMENT OF TIME"

For my thoughts are not your thoughts, neither are your ways my ways, saith the Lord (Isa 55:8)

In the course of becoming God will often use odd situations and or unpleasant circumstances too help you evolve into the person He's called you to become. Don't consider it strange if it appears that you're in a place or sitting under a minister that seem somewhat unbearable at times, it's for your good.

As I found myself contending with this particular episode God spoke to my heart and assured me that "the hardest part was not in being there but what I would allow myself to think as I was there. I could torture myself with thoughts of "how I wish this was over, why did I have to sit and listen to this or that person speak, beat myself up by concentrating on the time they had left or I could recognize that the "segment of time " used to sit there would become apart of my refining process.

My brother, my sister, God will instill in you the patience you need by taking small segments of time too rain upon you what you would otherwise miss if you were not where He placed you, don't despise your small beginnings!

SCRIPTURE; Isa 58:14

JUNE 28

"IF HE CAN DISTRACT YOU HE CAN STOP YOU"

Take us the foxes, the little foxes that spoil the vine: for our vine have tender grapes (Songs of Sol 2:15)

We usually look for the enemy presence in our lives when were faced with what appears to be insurmountable problems; what we oftentimes misjudge is he'll (Satan) will interrupt our live by sending small, miscellaneous or frivolous problems our way; he deals with the big but he'll side track with the small.

As distractions become more than a fleeting thought, it's time to consider our stance in God. If we takes the initiative to address those things that's meant to drive us to distraction; we leave our post delaying our progress, in essence we stop!

The author of Hebrews warns us "fear lest a promise being left us of entering into his rest, any of you should seem to come short of it" (Heb 4:1). Whenever we walk in stress, worry, fear, anxiety or even focus on life distractions we leave the rest of God; walk from under the covering that he has so graciously granted and leave ourselves vulnerable for the possibility of failure. Consider the work allotted to you, turn away from all distractions and full speed ahead; in doing so you put the devil where he belongs "under your feet"!

SCRIPTURE; Heb 4:10-11

JUNE 29

"A GOODTHING TURNS INTO A BAD THING"

Seek ye the Lord while he may be found, call ye upon him while he is near... (Isa 55:6)

In the course of a day we have to consistently make choices and sound decisions but what happens when what you thought was a good thing turns bad? For it sometimes will if we are not careful. During the week as I prepared for my assignment or work, if you will, the Holy Spirit quickened in my spirit a grave deviation which had slipped in unaware. During my preparation I would automatically turn on the news, which is a good thing, for it's only a source of information however my good thing turned bad because it so distracted me whereas for two days I had to run off to work without opening up the word. Of course the word should be in you but why do we expect a new Rhema word from God when we fail to open up the word to receive it.

Your good thing can easily become bad if it detours your life from the ways and things of God. We can't build up our Holy temples if our lives are pointed in the opposite direction so take time every morning as you rise and start your day with God for its God who's needed to direct and fulfill it.

SCRIPTURE; Isa 58:8-9

JUNE 30

"UNFOUNDED FEARS"

There is no fear in love; but perfect love castest out fear; because fear involves torment. He that feareth is not made perfect in love (1John 4:18)

There is a tool that God has given us that will easily work against us. This is our ability to over analyze, over think or to rationalize our situation. As one plays a scenario around the mind it has the tendency to swell or diminish as carnality is doubled or coupled with what is being prayed about. However it lies within the grasp of the believer to bring into captivity any unwanted thoughts or expressions that so easily beset us. How? By casting them down (2Co 10:5), the mind either works for us or against us; it is us however who decides. Everything that is not found in the word, revealed by divine revelation or exposed by the Holy Spirit should be considered as "unfounded fears".

God has not given us the spirit of fear (2Tim 1:7), he has however equipped us with everything needed to assure us that what's needed, what's desired and those things that remain important to our stay here on earth and in heaven are provided.

SCRIPTURE; 2John 2:8

JULY 1

"THE BIG PICTURE"

But seek ye first the Kingdom of God and his righteousness: and all these things shall be added unto you (Mt 6:33)

Everyday is a day of challenge; you face nay Sayers among a host of other obstacles that requires your undivided attention. It is imperative to not fall prey, focusing only on the task at hand or the confusion which lies around you minimizes what's actually important.

Yes we want to be comfortable now but we must defocus from the lust the eye and the pride of life and refocus on the "big picture" which will allow us to embrace this truth "God shall supply all of our needs according to his riches in glory". The things we attain in this life are only tangible and useful during this era, for we can not take anything with us. We can however store up riches in glory," where your treasures are there shall your heart be also" (Mt 6:21).

SCRIPTURE; Mt 6:19-20

JULY 2

"A LIFE WITHOUT GOD"

Not everyone who says unto me Lord, Lord shall enter into the kingdom of heaven; but hr that doeth the will of the Father which is in Heaven

Would it not be a travesty to do all that you do here on he earth and still miss the mark, leading to a "life without God", this is possible. The scripture declares that "many will say to me in that day, Lord, Lord have we not prophesied in thy name? And in thy name have cast out devils? And in thy name done many wonderful work and I will profess unto them, I never knew you, depart from me, ye that work iniquity (Mt 7:22-23). These this scripture speak of are those who were seemingly busy doing what they considered the fathers work, what failed to qualify them was the sin that remained in their lives; the sin that was made manifest through knowledge but overlooked because of status or no desire to stop.

There is a great life in which the one we now attain proceed; one that speaks of joy un-foretold and perfect peace. Don't disqualify yourself and risk living a "life without God", you'll live forever where you reside is totally decided upon by you.

SCRIPTURE; Mt 25:1-12

JULY 3

"NEVER WITHOUT COST"

The curse of the Lord is in the house of the wicked, but he blesseth the habitation of the just (Pro 3:33)

There are those who have always had it good or easy; those who were born with what some would call a silver spoon in their mouth: then there are some (like myself) who have had to work extremely hard to obtain what others so easily inherit. Does that make us any less important in the eyes of God? Certainly not!

In Luke 16:20-31 Jesus teaches a parable concerning the rich man and Lazarus the beggar. In verse 25 it explains that Abraham spoke to the rich man calling him son (which demonstrates this man knew God and he ways of God) but goes on to say "remember thy in thy life time receiveth thy good things and likewise Lazarus evil things but now he is comforted. Scripture doesn't say but I'd like to suggest to you that maybe the rich man obtained his riches without cost causing him to have no regard for the poor; making his heart calloused concerning those of a lowly state. But Lazarus, he who God allowed to suffer in this lifetime would go on and inherit the blessing, which didn't come without cost.

Easy isn't always expedient, neither is it wise to compare oneself too another, remember what Paul said "if a man don't work neither will he eat"!

SCRIPTURE; Pro 11:21

JULY 4

"HEART CHECK UP"

As in water face answereth to face, so the heart of man to man (Pro 27:19)

From time to time if not daily it's in the opinion of self that it would be wise to take spiritual inventory of ones life because of those we come in contact with or those within our circle of influence: for this reason we must have our spiritual monitors checked for infiltration and or any type of deficits. This requires only that you sit down and seriously view where you are in your walk in Christ. Have you been a little lippy lately? Has your patience meter dropped below freezing and you find yourself becoming short with those around you? Is that someone who never really gives you trouble seems to be doing just that? It's time for an evaluation it probably isn't them you can very well be the culprit working against yourself.

Peter never imagined that he would in any form betray Jesus however when faced with opposition he did so (Luke 22:54-60), this wasn't done maliciously, peter didn't know his own heart. Don't fall into anything similar too what Peter experienced, sit down and evaluate your heart, not with condemnation, but with clarity and truth.

SCRIPTURE; PRO 4:23

JULY 5

"THANK GOD FOR THORNS"

...there was given to me a thorn in the flesh, the messenger of Satan to buffet me (2Co 12:7b)

One of the simplest things to do is to thank God for the good in our lives. It's an easy feat to rejoice when everything around us is at the top of the charts; no real mishaps are springing up and it's as though Satan has gone on vacation or taken a leave of absence in your life; can you however "thank God for the thorns or the thorny places in your life"? This can be a difficult task to adhere but it's necessary. You must realize that life could not produce a rainbow in your life unless you suffer through the rain. Instead of wallowing in what's not right, "thank God for the thorns" and concentrate on what's good; realizing that thorns are manifested for character building and advancement!

SCRIPTURE; 2Co 4:8-9

JULY 6

"IN TOTALITY"

For all the promises of God in him are ye, and in him amen, unto the glory of God by us (2Co 1:20)

God has given each of us a promise. Some he has even spoken with directly by way of the Holy Ghost; He has given instructions, pronounced decrees, and painted mental images designed too steer the believer lives into a permanent place of growth. How then have some managed to fall below the bar of what's expected? Simple, through trails and what's considered tribulations they stop living their lives according to the totality of what God has spoken. Once the mind has become assaulted with drama it goes into auto pilot as it engage in constructing a line of defense which steers the life off course creating an illusion of wholeness when in essence, you can never attain what's been foretold because you're out of sync. To resurrect the dream you must go back to the beginning and begin to live according too the totality of what God has spoken.

SCRIPTURE; Acts 26:16-18

JULY 7

"ALWAYS ANOTHER TEMIKA"

For if ye love them which love you, what reward have ye? Do not even the publicans the same? (Mt 5:46)

Maybe you're one of the million of people who is experiencing grief by way of another who is being deathly inconsiderate; you know that person who isn't on purpose being rude, but they are not on purpose not trying to be considerate! Well that's my plight for this precise moment and her name is Tameka. As I began to ponder and pray concerning my attitude on how to deal with this situation I heard the Holy Spirit say, "There will always be another Tameka". It was then that I realized that God uses these types of instances as sandpaper to smooth out the rough edges in our lives and to push you over the hump you've been treading. How do you deal with these particular situations? You approach them in love, leaving nothing out; remembering that at some juncture in life you were someone Tameka!

SCRIPTURE; Mt 5:44-45

JULY 8

"SALT AND LIGHT"

Let your light so shine before men, that they may see your good works, and glorify your father which is in Heaven (Mt 5:16)

Consider the divine purpose of salt; could it not be defined as the preservative needed too ensure and preserve the item it has been added to? The ingredient needed to sustain life. What about light, one could consider light as a powerful force designed to lead, penetrate and guide for it does each of these actions.

Placing each of these nouns within the lives of the believer is what the word call for. In the word of Jesus "we are the salt and light of the earth" (Mt 5:13-14), which calls us to a very high standard. We've been commissioned to preserve the church and light the way for those who are lost in darkness. You must look pass that hurt, disappointment or anything designed to stifle your progress; the person next to you has need of your salt and light; go ahead preserve, produce and lead, in doing so the father smiles down thinking well done thou good and faithful servant.

SCRIPTURE; Mt 5:13-15

JULY 9

"FACT V.S TRUTH

Verily I say unto you, whatsoever ye shall bind on earth shall be bound in Heaven: and whatsoever ye shall loose on the earth shall be loosed in Heaven (Mt 18:18)

In life faced with struggles, disappointments, hardship and even death, not necessarily death in the natural but the death of a dream, a vision, or a secret desire we often cling to the fact and fail to confess our truths.

The truth in the word is the one thing that remains unchangeable. What appears to be factual is always inadmissible under the scrutiny of the truth, for it's the truth that has the power too change fact. A fact maybe that your bank account has gone negative but the truth is "my God shall supply all my needs according too his riches in glory". The fact is your marriage has taken a down hill turn but Gods truth says "he that findeth a wife findeth a good thing and obtaineth favor from the Lord" (Pro 18:22). Fact, you've been given a bad report from the doctor; truth, "by his stripes we are healed" (Isa 53:5). Fact, your enemies are positional placed over you; your truth is, "the Lord shall make you the head and not the tail, above only and not beneath" (Deut 28:13).

If you want to change your facts you must start to apply the word of truth to your situation and confess it out of your mouth, "you shall have what you say" (Mk 11:23).

SCRIPTURE; Mt 7:7-8

JULY 10

"LAST CHANCE"

...and while they went to buy, the bride groom came, and they that were ready went in with him to the marriage: and the door was shut (Mt25:10)

In the parable of the fig tree, the one in which the Lord planted and it produced no fruit for three years (Luke 13:6-7), Jesus depicts a picture of those whom he's called, who belies their purpose and live unproductive lives (Luke 13:6-9). It also describe the unproductive, speaks of its latter end; tells us of the longsuffering of Christ while it remain stagnant in life and ultimately a decision is made. It will be fertilized and given a last chance to bring forth or suffer the consequences.

Have you been in sort of a funk lately, unable to push pass yourself and reach your full potential? Has your delay progressed from year to year and you are no closer to reaching the goal you know God has given you? This is your season; God has not turned you over, he's granted you a reprieve and given you an adequate amount of time to produce. Take what God has already provided you with and capitalize off of it. Do it now, and if you're confused about your next move relate back to the last thing you were instructed to do and do that!

SCRIPTURE; Luke 13:6-9

JULY 11

"PURPOSE"

By faith Enoch was translated that he should not see death, and was not found, because God had translated him: for before his translation he had this testimony, that he pleased God (Heb 11:5)

There are countless of Christians who still has no clue as to their purpose here in the earth. Some wait on God to pierce the eyes of their understanding, relating to them what they as Christians should be accomplishing in the name of the Lord; this mystery is no mystery at all. The bible declares in Rev 4:11b "for thou hast created all things, and for thy pleasure they are and were created". In short: your purpose is to always please God. We've been commissioned to do other work here on earth, what that is will be revealed in due season, but your number one purpose is to please God.

There was a time when Jesus was hungered and saw a fig tree from afar off but when he got to this tree, it had leaves and no fruit therefore he cursed the tree and it withered away (paraphrase) (Mt 21:19-20). Many believe it's because the tree was fruitless that Jesus cursed it however the Holy Spirit showed me that even though the tree could still provide for others; for it provided shade and it gave the birds a place to rest their feet, but the only time it was required to make a mark in the earth and please God it was unable to, therefore it was cursed. What's your story? Let not your living be in vain. Good works won't get you there; having a good heart or being a good person isn't enough: get involved in what's needed and get intense with pleasing God, that's your true purpose.

SCRIPTURE; 2Tim 2:4

JULY 12

"TWO ARE BETTER THAN ONE"

Two are better than one for they have a good reward for their labor (Eccles 4:5)

Our scripture declares "two are better than one; because they have a good reward for their labor; for if they fall, the one will lift up his fellow (Eccles 4:5-6a). god is speaking out to that independent person, that person who calls themselves self sufficient ; for those who rely on the strength of self will soon come to naught and the person who believes they need no one only fool themselves, for two are better than one.

In the garden God realized this important truth and declared "it is not good that man should be alone, I will make him a helpmate" (Gen 2:18). Don't go through life, here on earth neglecting yourself of the freedom in which God has made available to you: the freedom to touch and agree; freedom to come in agreement with and the freedom to bind and loose. The word says "where two or more are gathered together in my name, there am I in the midst". Two really are better than one; find you a prayer partner who's as adamant about the kingdom of God as you are and in doing so some of those stored up prayers will begin to materialize; they've been waiting on you to hook up with the other half so that can become answered prayers!

SCRIPTURE; Eccles 4:9-12

JULY 13

"REAR VIEW MIRROR"

The heart is deceitful above all things; and desperately wicked who can know it (Jer 17:9)

The duty of a rear view mirror is to give the driver a sneak peek at those things that are taking place behind them. It allows one to get glimpse of the things previously passed; and it act as buffer between the things that has the potential to cause harm or danger.

What happens when one becomes overly involved in what the rear view mirror has to offer? Simple, you leave yourself open too forfeit what's in front of you: looking back has its place but it isn't always expedient; take Lots wife for example. When Lot and his family were being spared death during the destruction of Sodom and Gomorrah; after being forewarned Lots wife neglected the charge and looked back; for this she was turned into a pillar of salt (Gen 19:26); the look back required her life.

We must be wise as serpents but gentle as doves, knowing when and how long we should even venture the look back, especially in our hearts!

SCRIPTURE; Isa 55:6-7

JULY 14

"IN THE PROCESS OF TIME"

Blessed is the man that trusteth in the Lord and whose hope the Lord is (Jer 17:7)

When God called Abram forth and revealed to him how he would bless him, he also unfolded another truth to him. He told him how his descendants would undergo and suffer through a period of bondage, but afterwards they would come out with great substance (Gen 15:13-14); they would inherit the blessing but not until they incurred the bondage.

It's only natural for the person who's under the pressure of a financial strain to want to be released of the burden. Just as it's sufficient for that one who is suffering from a type of illness too want to be healed immediately; however we are reminded that Gods ways are not our ways and it is in "the process of time " that you'll step into the fullness of what is intended for you. A grape isn't developed into a raisin overnight; it must be sundried and processed before it reaches its full maturity. As God has promised and come into covenant relationship with you hold fast to your confession, for when the hour is right; "in the process of time" he who has promised, is faithful and will do it!

SCRIPTURE; Jer 17:14

JULY 15

"YES YOU"

The lord God hath given me the tongue of he learned, that I should know how to speak a word in season to him that is weary: he wakeneth morning by morning, he wakeneth mine ear to hear as he learned (Isa 50:4)

1Peter 4:12 tells us think it not strange concerning the fiery trail which is to try you, as though some strange thing happened unto you. I'd also like to suggest to you not to balk at the instructions or the direction in which God is taking you.

Lack of experience will cry out not me, fear can leak and sing a tune of what if, but know that rebellion is as the sin of witch craft (1Sam 15:23a) and to obey is better than sacrifice (1Sam 15:22b). In the book of Numbers God used a very unlikely subject to speak a word in due season, which in turn would save the prophets Balaam life (Num 22:28).

If you're assuming that God would rather use someone with an incredible diction; who's more out going; someone everyone seems to enjoy, I ask you to think again. As God has relayed to you what need to be done or said he has also prepared the heart of the people for reception. "Yes you", you are capable of being and doing whatever task needed too enhance those God has genetically connected to you. When fear show up recall how God used the donkey to speak and save, and become determined to not allow it to out shine you, just do it!

SCRIPTURE; Num 22:23-31

JULY 16

"FAR REMOVED"

And the Lord thy God will put out those nations before thee by little and little... (Duet 7:22)

The other day I began to meditate on where my life use to be and from what God has delivered me out of and as I began to realize the severity of where my life was before Gods distinct transformation; my soul, and my spirit begin to thank God that I'd been "far removed" from that place.

Taking that scenario to heart lets apply what the blood of Jesus has done for our lives and the sin which did so easily beset us. Due to the selfless act of Christ we are far removed from eternal death; that one act has set us at liberty to proclaim the life Adam turned his back on when he ate of the forbidden fruit (Gen 3:6). Every hang up, bad deed, callous decision and former mistakes has been forgiven; the debt was paid in a way whereas it contained the power to pay in advance for every delayed sin. The incredulous love of the father has "far removed" you from that thing destined to destroy you. Celebrate today knowing that you are no longer tied too the past but bound by your future! Amen.

SCRIPTURE; Duet 7:14-15

JULY 17

"BOTH RUINED"

Neither do men put new wine into old bottles else the bottles break, and the new wine runneth out, and the bottles perish: but they put new wine into new bottles, and both are preserved (Mt 9:17)

During the time of Jesus ministry among all of the profound and prophetic statements he made he ask or state this "what shall it profit a man to gain the whole world and lose his own soul (Mt 16:26)? This implies that they both shall be ruined; for in the final moment when the Christian believers are caught up with Jesus the word says "corruption shall be raised in incorruption (1Co 15:42), implying that the things we've acquired here in the earth shall pass away. Why then does there seem to be a struggle within when choosing what is profitable? How is it that the intelligent, the wise and the knowledgeable fail to distinguish that the corruption of this world can't and will never fit into the new life we have in Christ?

By no means am I suggesting that you shouldn't have riches and wealth for the word tells us that "every good and perfect gift is from above and comes down from the father of light... (Jam 1:17, it also tells us that "it is God who gives us the power to get wealth (Duet 8:18): however I am suggesting that we not take the old baggage of what our lives were and attempt to incorporate it into what our lives entail in Christ now, for they both shall be ruined, a little leaven, leavens the whole lump.

SCRIPTURE; Mt 4:4

JULY 18

"LEFT ALL"

The woman then left her water pot, and went her way into the city, and saith unto the men... (John 4:28)

In the story of the Samaritan woman who Jesus spoke with at the well; he depicts a picture of the lost; those who were not the first born, but those he was sent too for scripture says "he must need go through Samaria (John 4:3). We're revealed an amazing truth in this scripture, "that if we ask he would give us living water" (paraphrase John 4:10). The living water is a representation of the word of God; it's hidden truth: its divine power and the revelation knowledge within it that will cause the unjust become just, the unrighteous, righteous and the sinner, sinless. How can we be assured of this truth? The word declares that after she's exposed too Jesus she left her water pot. Her water pot was tied to her livelihood it represented substance and life and now she no longer needed what she'd always required because she had received what she'd always been looking for; therefore she left all that she was to become all that she could be.

After coming into the knowledge of the truth are you still carrying your water pot? Is there no fire under your feet which makes you want to run and tell it as the Samaritan woman? Are you no longer as excited as you were when you were first saved? Perhaps you've picked your water pot back up and can't seem to put it down, remember the water pot is your adversary, it gave the woman an excuse to be where she shouldn't have been during that time of day and it'll keep you going back to draw from broken wells which profit little or nothing. Therefore leave all so that you can be counted among those who would love life and see good days (1Pet 3:10)

SCRIPTURE; Eph 3:17-19

JULY 19

"IF YOU WOULD HAVE ASKED"

If thou knewest the gift of God, and who it is that saith to thee give me to drink, thou wouldest have asked of him, and he would have given thee living water (John 4:10)

Jesus terms the phrase "if you would have asked, I would have given" (John 4:10) but it's easy for the believer to miss what's needed due to no diligence in asking. James says "you ask and receive not because you ask amiss (Jam 4:3). Have you asked amiss, praying about that which is carnal or fleshly, and when the answer fails to show up you deduced that God didn't hear you? The devil is a liar; James also tells us that "you have not because you ask not" (4:2b), Jesus said until now you have asked for nothing in my name, ask and you shall receive and your joy shall be complete (John 16:24)

Don't adopt the mindset that you don't need to ask because "he knows what you need of before you pray", the elected word is pray: You must make your petitions known unto God by prayer, supplication and thanksgiving (Phil 4:6)

To count yourself as unworthy leaves you at a great disadvantage; for this cause many fail to see answered prayer because of unbelief. Refuse to be that person who attained only a portion of what God intended; ask for it even when it seems too big, those are the things God desires to bless you with.

SCRIPTURE; Phil 1:6

JULY 20

"BEND DON'T BREAK"

And the earth brought forth grass, and herb yielding seed after his kind, and the tree yielding fruit, whose seed was in itself, after his kind, and God said that it was good (Gen 1:12)

When God began creation he instituted an example of his awesomeness when He caused the earth to bring forth (Gen 1:11). I'm certain we were left an unspoken truth or message within the characteristics of these creations. God designed them in a way that allows them to stand up under an enormous amount of weight; the desired are at liberty too come and be fed, and through the intricate design of God they are refreshed supernaturally.

You who are designed and crafted in the image of God himself, that chosen vessel appointed to carry around the Holy Spirit of God; we're also crafted, on purpose to "bend and not break". God who called your end from the beginning understands your pressure points and whatsoever light affliction you're faced with is only for a season. When the burden feel to heavy, begin to bend; even if you only bend over and leave it at the foot of he cross: just don't break!

SCRIPTURE; Eph 6:10-12

JULY 21

"OUT OF ORDER"

...And Adam said this is now bone of my bones and flesh of my flesh: she shall be called woman because she was taken out of man (Gen 2:23)

When Satan began his attack on Gods greatest creation (man kind), he used his craftiness to take the order God set precedent in the earth and dis-aligned it. In his attempt to undermine God he bypassed the headship (man) and began a courtship with what Peter calls "the weaker vessel" (1Pet 3:7) the woman. This set in motion not only the fall of mankind but the redemptive plan of God as well!

God has placed a divine order in the earth and whenever that order is interrupted we become displaced. Some of us have missed many opportunities because we have either walked from under or side stepped the order God has structured for our complete wholeness; this is the reason some get close to the finish line then all falls through, and what has been worked to achieve becomes elusive. If you want final results, lasting results you must get in order for this is when the puzzle becomes a complete picture.

SCRIPTURE; Heb 5:8-14

JULY 22

"FIND YOUR ELIZABETH"

And it came to pass, that when Elisabeth heard the salutation of Mary, the babe leaped in her womb; and Elisabeth was filled with the Holy Ghost (Luke 1:41)

The right connections play a pertinent role in ones life. Take the life of Mary and Elisabeth for example; before the Holy Ghost came upon Mary and endowed her with the savor child, six months prior her cousin Elisabeth, who was barren; had been prophesied too and impregnated with the forerunner of our Christ. However there would come a time when the two would have to meet, to make the spiritual connection orchestrated too empower the babe Elisabeth carried with the Holy Ghost (Luke 1:44). This planned meeting would be the catalyst designed for a Supernatural transference.

The implication is simple; you are spiritually connected too a certain someone in such a way that once the acquaintance is made it will take your life into areas you would otherwise never travel: this won't be a chance meeting for it has been ordained even before you were. Warning, don't become hurried and attempt to create you an Elisabeth; wait on God and "find your Elisabeth".

SCRIPTURE; Eccles 11:1

JULY 23

"SOUL TIES"

But his wife looked back from behind him, and she became a pillar of salt (Gen 19:26)

Because we are spiritual beings in earthly bodies we have been equipped with senses, emotions, unction of what's good or bad and right or wrong. When used correctly and cohesively with what thus saith the Lord we can easily expect a life full of fertility and fruitfulness. How ever if the occasion arises and the emotional becomes attached to the unfruitful or the ungodly problems will persist and arise.

We're given an example of this within the life of Lot and his wife. Lots wife is mentioned only twice and it's during the second mention that we're informed of her demise (Gen 19:26); an occurrence that proceeds because of the soul ties she establishes within a place of ill repute. The bible doesn't tell us why she looked back we're only informed that she does. Maybe it was her possessions that she wanted to retain or valuables and acquaintances she felt connected with; it could have been something as frivolous as curiosity; one can never really know. However it's a certainty that she inquired ungodly soul ties for when it was time to disentangle herself from it or them and follow the instructions of God she could not, for her heart was back within the chaos!

What attachments are you making? Have you allowed what you feel overcome what you know to be right? Are you finding yourself connecting too others or things which divert or misdirect? Soul connections aren't easily broken this is why it is imperative to understand and know what the will of God is for your life. Wrong connections can be costly even unto death, but when you make the right connections they'll bring forth and bud into life long commitments with a production rate of 100 fold!

SCRIPTURE; 1Co 15:33

JULY 24

"ONE TRACK MIND"

Only let your conversation be as it becometh the gospel of Christ, that whether I come and see you, or else be absent, I may hear of your affairs, that ye stand fast in one spirit, with one mind, striving together for the faith of the gospel (Phil 1:27)

Recently I met some individuals that caused me to stutter step and take a look back at what can happen if we become lax or even begin to operate in the vain of a one track mind. Quietly I've studied their behavior and what I've surmised is this: oftentimes they're not being rude or even inconsiderate; what has happened is quite simple. They've become completely engrossed in what they've conditioned themselves to attain or ministrate in their lives that they've inadvertently disregarded you and your presence, not because they don't care, they just don't care enough pass what's being focused on; they have a one track mind.

When it came to the ways and things of God our covenant father Abraham shared this same attribute. The bible says that Abraham believed God and it was counted unto him for righteous. There came a time when God called him to offer Isaac as a sacrifice and because Abraham had a mind set to please God he hesitated not at the request and proved himself faithful (see Gen 22:2-9). You don't have to be Abraham to make the correct impression with God. If you set your affection on the things which are above and not sensual you'll find that as your mind is stayed on the Kingdom of God you'll begin to experience the "in earth as it is in Heaven" (Mt 6:10) type of life!

SCRIPTURE; Phil 4:8

JULY 25

"JUST BECAUSE YOU CAN'T SEE IT DOESN'T MEAN IT ISN'T THERE"

And now I exhort you to be of good cheer; for there shall be no loss of any mans life among you, but of the ship (Acts 27:22)

There was a time when Paul and those along side him at sea was faced with travesty. A great tumultuous storm was wrecking the ship and it appeared the crew and all of the cargo would be lost (Acts 27:14) but in the midst of this trouble God sent forth a word saying "fear not" (Acts 27:24). As trouble beckoned on every side and the hope of survival became minimal peace was introduced into this situation because God spoke! They saw no way out of their immediate situation, surely they feared they would never make it out alive, but Paul trusting in whom he believed understood this principle "just because you can't see it doesn't mean it isn't there". He learned this reality as he traveled on the road to Damascus when he heard a voice but saw only light (Acts 9:3-4)

What previous trails have you faced and realized later that you couldn't see your way out or through it but thanks be to God the answer showed up? The same principle applies now! You have not been called and not provided for; God has not blessed you with the desires of your heart to allow another enjoy what you've worked with your own hands to obtain; neither has he forgotten you. When help doesn't look as if it's coming you should consider looking past the natural and tapping into the spiritual for that is where the provision remain!

SCRIPTURE; Acts 27:41-44

JULY 26

"PRAY YOUR WAY THROUGH IT"

And at midnight Paul and Silas prayed and sang praises unto God... (Acts 16:25-26)

At 6:00 am I get up to exercise and run two miles. There came a morning when I got up, began my regiment and shortly into the run my left knee began to ache. I thought about stopping instead I began to defocus on my pain; I went into the Spirit of prayer and as entered into my final laps I realized that the pain had subsided, plus I would finish my course.

What is being suggested here? I'm simply implying that while prayer may not (in some instances) change your position instantaneously; the atmosphere of prayer will internally and externally take you through what you're facing. Whatever plight you're withstanding today "pray your way through it" remembering that prayer produces need, and needs will also produce prayer!

SCRIPTURE; Acts 5:19-20

JULY 27

"DISQUALIFIED"

And if a man also strive for masteries, yet he is not crowned, except he strive lawfully (2Tim 2:5)

In sports or even in the everyday activities we encounter on a personal level there will be rules to follow: to obtain the prize or reach a place of maturity instructions are necessary.

Paul wrote to young Timothy and divulged a necessary word of advice; a complete word that would give a broader sense of instruction to not only Timothy but to those who would, during the existence of time would read Gods word of truth. He states "and if a man, (person) also strive for masteries, yet he is not crowned except he strive lawfully". What is being purposed here? Paul is admonishing the church on what is expedient as a life is being lived; he explains that the short cut can and will disqualify you. Would it not be a travesty to have lived life believing that I've done what's right and pleasing to God and later find out that you've disqualified yourself, not because you didn't know, but because you failed too completely comply. Therefore don't drop out of the race, remember he who endures to the end shall be saved (Mt 10:22).

SCRIPTURE; 2Tim 2:11-13

JULY 28

"PULL ON HIM"

And Jesus said, somebody hath touched me: for I have perceived that virtue is gone out of me (Luke 8:46)

As the woman with the issue of blood searched here and there, going from one physician to the next, to have her need meet, she finally realized, what she needed was not within the power of a man to provide (Luke 8:43)

At the right time, during a time of transformation, a new season would come to birth in this woman the wholeness she spent 12 years seeking. What happened? She mustered up all of the stamina, courage and faith needed and "pulled on him." The bible says she "came behind him and touched the border of his garment" (Luke 8:44), and was immediately healed. Are you pulling on Jesus to meet that in which you have need of. Have you spent all you've had, have you tried one thing after another has no effective door opened for you? Why not pull on him?! Jesus was passing through when her issue was healed. However, he now stands at the door, and if any man (person) will open the door, he will come in and sup with them. In short: He's available to you. Remember, a resource remains data until you utilize it!

SCRIPTURE; Nahum 1

JULY 29

"IN YOUR HEART"

......Singing with grace in your hearts to the Lord (Col 3:16b)

Occasions will arise when you can't find a quite moment, and just when you believe you have, someone intervenes on your private time; and you find yourself somewhat boxed out again. As I entered a season of little or no privacy, I heard God speak to me and say "Praise me in your heart; when you can't find a quite space, pray to me "in your heart", if noise and confusion attempts to prevail, begin to worship me "in your heart".

Some believe the altar is where they'll receive a fresh touch from the Lord, others may think it necessary to be on bended knee, or in a prostate position to clearly hear or effectively communicate with our Father. That's far from truth. While driving to work you can speak to him in your heart, as you travel on the subway, walking through the grocery store, in the midst of what could become an altercation God will give you guidance in your heart. There is no format which reveals how to hear, pray, praise or worship God, the secret is to "just do it".

SCRIPTURE; (EPH 5:19-20)

JULY 30

"ADDED MEANS TO MULTIPLY"

And Elisha said unto her, what shall I do for thee? Tell me, what hast thou in thine house? And she said, there handmaid hath not anything in the house, save a pot of oil (2 Kings 4:2)

In Matthew 6:33 Jesus admonish the multitude in the way of righteousness and its fruit. He advises to "but seek ye first the kingdom of God and his righteousness; and all these things shall be added unto you". The watermelon is produced from a seed. The seed was first and then the fruit showed up. When God called forth fruit, he called the seed first. (Gen 1:11) How then do we or can we expect a harvest without first having what is vital in producing increase. Jesus states that "all these things shall be added unto you", he doesn't suggest given, but added. In this context added is representation of multiplication. Meaning he'll use your take your little and make it a lot, he'll take your barely enough and produce an overflow, he'll use your meager substance to promote not only your life, but the lives of those who are around or in your circle of influence. What are the requirements, the word says to "seek ye first the kingdom of God and his righteousness", that's step one, and it's also imperative that you have the necessary vehicles in which God can add unto.

SCRIPTURE: (2 KINGS 4:3-7)

JULY 31

"THE BREAKING OF DAY"

And, he said, let me go, for the day breaketh. And he said, I will not let thee go, except thou bless me. (Gen 32:26)

As Jacob wrestled with the Angel of God, (the Bible says he wrestled with him until the breaking of the day (Gen 32:24) it's apparent that he fought for change and refused to give in to defeat. What isn't disclosed is his mental or emotional state. However I'd like to suggest to you that during this intense fight for his life, Jacob was renewed, during "the breaking of the day", the breaking of a new day, on doubt, breaths of newness. As the call of mature begins to sing a new song, I believe this encouraged Jacob to fight a bit harder, and to build on his resolve. Hearing life begin allowed him to honestly know that he as not ready to quit; that he had a whole lot of living to do, therefore he must fight to win. If you're one of a host of people who's been sort of wondering through life, not consciously putting forth the fight to obtain the blessing. Consider Jacob, who, for all intents and purposes, refused to knuckle under, and forfeit life. This isn't the time to be beaten by life, but to wrestle with what's designed to hold you back; and prevail. When you do, you'll see that the thing standing between you and your victory was only doing what it was purposed to do, but God who is all knowing; had pre-prepared you too win during the "breaking of the day".

SCRIPTURE; (Heb 10:35)

AUGUST 1

"WHEN IT'S RIGHT THERE"

He shall deliver thee in six troubles: yea in seven there shall no evil touch thee (Job 5:19)

As Job faced a very difficult time in his life; he lost all that he owned; his servants and his children were killed, plus he was afflicted in his body (Job 1:13-19, 2:7) yet he could boldly make this declaration "though he slay me, yet will I trust him" for he clearly understood his one concept, even in he midst of personal dilemmas God was right there!

As you face difficulties, dilemmas or even turmoil you must be encouraged enough to know "when it's right there". What? Your breakthroughs, your petitions before God; your hearts desire for "when it's right there" the enemy will come up against you like a flood, he'll attempt to inflict fear, doubt or worry, but as he's working against you God is raising a standard for it's right there!

SCRIPTURE; Isa 26:3

AUGUST 2

"V IS FOR VICTORY"

Behold I give unto you power to tread on serpents and scorpions, and over all the power of the enemy; and nothing shall by any means hurt you. Luke 10:19

In the scheme of what we call life, we will always face challenges. We either overcome them with a victory mentality, or we succumb to the victim mentality and skirt the problem or challenge, time and again.

Caleb understood this principle when it was appointed to him and eleven others to go into Canaan and spy out the land, (Num 13:2) those that went with him on this assigned mission, because of their lack of self confidence, saw themselves as grasshoppers adopting the victim mentality. However young Caleb who envisioned the same territory and saw the same people refused to be a victim (V For Victory): I'm certain he recalled manna from heaven, the quail that blew in with the wind, or maybe he deemed the fact that his clothes never wore out or his shoes and understood the same god who provided through all his other perils would prevail in this instance also.

Don't allow the V in your life to cry out victim, vagabond, vulgar, villain, or void. "V is for virtue, visionary, vivacious, viable, and victory".

SCRIPTURE; LUKE 11:9-10

AUGUST 3

"A LEARNED BEHAVIOR"

Thou he were a son, yet he learned obedience by the things which he suffer (Heb 5:8)

By the breath of God ice is given (Job 37:10a) and it's during the process of time that we acquire "a learned behavior". The bible tells us clearly that even though Jesus was and is the son of God "that he learned obedience from the things he suffered", both the obedience and the suffering was the will of the father.

The things you learn in what is called today will either be stepping stones or dungeon steps, which leads to the future of the generation behind you, a generation which includes your children and your children's, children. You will pass on to others detriment or confidence which derives from a pattern of "learned behavior". Jesus learned from the things he suffered in our time we call it wisdom and experience. If you are looking for different results start applying other methods; don't wait until your internal clock has almost run it's course before you realize you are the mirror image of the person you promised you'd never become; I can assure you it didn't happen overnight, instead it's the summation of a "learned behavior".

SCRIPTURE; 1Tim 4:11-16

AUGUST 4

"AT WHAT COST"

Now the spirit speaks expressly, that in the latter times some shall depart from the faith, giving heed to seducing spirits and doctrines of devils (1Tim 4:1)

Being analytical has its ups and downs; the downs need to be far and few in between as the ups will always motivate you to continue to trust in the Holy Spirit who shall lea and guide you into all truth. Because we're human we oftentimes view what is transpiring in another life and conclude that their lives are running at a great pace because of a source of superficial security, but what isn't divulged to us is how this temporal source of happiness or contentment has evolved or "at what cost" it has been obtained.

There's an old adage that says" everything that glitter isn't gold " this too can be said for the pleasures we or others make happen for ourselves. Jesus asked "will a man gain the whole world and lose his soul"? It is only natural to want the finer things that life has to offer but to obtain them in a manner which is not pleasing to God puts you at a grave disadvantage; not with the thing but with the Lord; for when we sin we sin against God (Ps 51:4). The Apostle James asks "from whence comes wars and fighting among you? Come they not hence, even of your lust that war in your members (Jam 4:1)

The carnal man or his sin nature desires that we lust and covet after others resources but the spirit man knows that every good and perfect gift comes from above; therefore before you say in your heart I want that ask yourself "at what cost" was it obtained!

SCRIPTURE; 1Tim 6:10

AUGUST 5

"GOING AND COMING"

And Jacob vowed a vow saying, if God will be with me, and will keep me in this way that I go, and will give me bread to eat and raiment to put on, so that I come again to my fathers house in peace; then shall the Lord be my God (Gen 28:20-21)

There came a time when Jacob had his very own personal experience with God. As Jacob traveled on his way to his kinsman house he dreamed a dream. In this dream God spoke to him and gave him a promise (Gen 28:13); this would be the time of Jacobs going. He was going to a place unfamiliar to meet those he has never met but tied too none the less. During his first encounter with God he vowed a vow; I believe that it would be because of this vow that God would shield and make provision for his coming.

A personal experience will always be more than just a feeling; it should be the catalyst that takes your life into a new dimension, and it will direct your going and coming once you surrender to it with a vow of absolute. Jacob had many obstacles to overcome from the moment he made the vow until his return trip home, but God who is faithful and forget not honored the promise as he neared a place of transformation (Gen 32:29).

God has heard your vow as you entered into a place of unfamiliar; just as he made provision for Jacob on the return trip home; your provision has been instructed to meet you as you return to the place God has called you!

SCRIPTURE; Gen 32:1-2

AUGUST 6

"SECURITY BLANKET"

I am crucified with Christ nevertheless I live; yet not I, but Christ liveth in me (Gal 2:20a)

Before the caterpillar can transform into a beautiful butterfly it must first weave a cocoon and die to its old self with an expectation of becoming new. As God purges the believer making them a new creation there is a struggle taking place on the inside: the sin nature kicks and scream as it goes through the process of metamorphosing, and this is the reason the believer clings to what is known as the "security blanket"

Before Christ some were accustomed to providing for self; the angry, hurt or hostile may have used their fist or tongues as weapons; the insecure delighted in the approval of another, whereas the docile and weak may have hid behind the falsehood of security in a job or career and when things become difficult or tight, instead of going through the change it appears simpler to reach to the familiar of your security blanket. This is a farce for Satan knows that if you'll buck the process, you'll never become, and if you don't become while going through this process you'll die before you reach your full potential.

Don't hold on to the limited things you can provide for yourself when there is a limitless God who longs to provide daily for you; let go of the old and reach for the new!

SCRIPTURE; Gal 6:7-9

AUGUST 7

"ARE YOU DRUNK"

Then Eli answered and said go in peace: and the God of Israel grant thee thy petition that thou hast asked of him (1Sam 1:17)

Hanna had a longing and a desire waiting to be met; more than anything she wanted to bare a male child; therefore as per her custom she would travel to the house of the Lord and make her supplication unto him. There came a time as Hanna prayed, because of the bitterness in her soul that she began to cry to God and vowed a vow (1Sam 1:10-11): her prayer became so intense that she forgot about those in her presence. Hanna sensing the urge to be heard prayed so intently whereas the residing priest imagined her to be drunk (1Sam 1:13).

How is your prayer life? Are you radical enough to stand before God and utter your hearts desire? Or have you become intimidated by the lack or the place of reserve you've adjusted too? Hanna was desperate enough to hold fast to her confession year after year; when no child was conceived; faithful in her purpose to continue to ask. Don't give up because it hasn't showed up, perseverance is what grabs the attention of God!

SCRIPTURE; 1Sam 1:19-20

AUGUST 8

"THY PRAYER IS HEARD"

But the angel said unto him, fear not Zacharias: for thy prayer is heard; and thy wife Elisabeth shall bare thee a son, and thou shalt call his name John (Luke 1:13)

Before the birth of John the Baptist an angel of the Lord visited his father Zacharias and made this declaration "fear not Zacharias; for thy prayer is heard" (Luke 1:13). What is most profound concerning this statement is there is no indication that a prayer was ever prayed; the bible makes no mention of this fact: what can be derived is this, this had to have been a private prayer resounding in Zacharias heart! The implication is simple; Proverbs 3:5 says,"Delight thyself in the Lord and he shall give you the desires of your heart"; the promise of John is a clear demonstration of this truth.

Some view prayer as being in a prostrate position with your face to the floor, or on bended knee uttering many words however what God shows us through this is "I'll take the secret prayer; that longed for desire you've been afraid to ask anyone to touch and agree with you on and make it public. Is there something you've not shared with another but have secretly been asking God to provide? Be encouraged "thy prayer is heard"!

SCRIPTURE; Col 4:12

AUGUST 9

"PRAY FOR CHANGE IN YOU"

Or how wilt thou say to thine brother, let me pull out the mote out of thy eye; and behold a beam is in thine own eye (Mt 7:4)

Daily we encounter others and situations which cause us to think or maybe even vocalize that in which another could or should be doing differently. It becomes simple to point out the faults of someone else and suggest that they're in need of prayer; but what happens when you begin to search yourself and find that today scripture applies to you? Does it remain or become expedient for the prayer to change?

Those who have labored long and hard to find their place in God should change the direction of their prayers; instead of being snared by a sneaky critical spirit, introvert and pray for change in you. Others you can never change therefore of its change you seek let it start with you.

SCRIPTURE; Col 3:17

AUGUST 10

"EVERY STAIR COUNT"

For consider him that endured such contradiction of sinners against himself, lest ye be weary and faint in your mind (Heb 12:3)

As you scale the ladder of life it's expedient to never begrudge the unstable moments or episodes you encounter. During your trek upward there shall arise periods of stability when everything you aspire to accomplish appears to be in automation; then there will come a time when you'll brace for the next step and it prove to be unstable; it's unsteady and requires sure footing. This has the capability to hinder your progress but it's designed to push you pass this point onto the next leg of your journey.

Surely God could have destined your climb to the top to be one smooth transition after another, however He knew that you'd need the experience of shaky situations too establish within you the where withal to maintain your position once you reach the top. Don't frown on the unbalanced steps you tread upon they're there for cultivation; so when you make it you can pass along to your counterparts that "every stair count" not only the ones that remain stable.

SCRIPTURE; Heb 12:1

AUGUST 11

"SEALED THE DEAL"

And the Lord said unto him what is that in thine hand? And he said a rod (Exo 4:2)

There came a time when God would call Moses forth into his divine purpose; could Moses have missed this opportunity? Sure he could have. In Exo4:1 Moses responds to the call of God by way of excuse. In his carnal state he couldn't comprehend how the people would receive him or if they would believe him but to exemplify his Sovereignty God ask Moses "what is that I thine hand"? The statement is rhetorical it's posed with the intent to demonstrate that God will use what He has already provided you with and produce a miracle. The miracle can't take place unless Moses does his part; he must simply cast it on the ground and have the courage to pick it up again once instructed.

Your miracle is within your grasp, to be exact it's in your hand but you will never come into completeness unless you follow protocol, you must cast it down; you can't hold onto what has to be done, it has to be relinquished over to God who will change its natural intent into the supernatural support you need!

When Moses grabbed the snake by the tail it immediately conformed itself back into the rod he'd used for assistance in his life: remember had he not cast the rod down it would have remained a rod but because of obedience he would later use the same rod to part a sea and "seal the deal".
SCRIPTURE; Exo 14:21-22

AUGUST 12

"HOW DID SHE KNOW?"
God is our refuge and strength, a very present help in trouble (Ps 46:1)

When Elijah made it to his destination he used no small talk nor did he make introductions; he saw therefore he spoke; he was commanded therefore he went, he received instructions and followed through; his obedience would release the power and provision in his life and the lives of those he was sent to. How would this be possible when the scripture speaks not of a previous acquaintance, in essence "how did she know"? The bible says as Elijah instructed the woman she replied "as the Lord thy God liveth" 1Kings 17:12a); how was this seemingly stranger able to decipher that the one in which she now spoke with was a man of God, a servant of the living God? We know that God had promised that he had commanded a woman to provide for him (1Kings 17:9), but what took place within the woman which made her recognize that this was he? The answer can be none other than "deep speaking to deep". God was at work connecting the perfect lives during the right season too address everyone needs; she knew because something on the inside stirred within her leading to obedience, it came because as the Lord prompted she moved.

If there is a stirring in the inside of you pulling at your resolve, prompting you to go forward; consult with the power that is at work within you and heed to the spirit of God: what's drawing you isn't sex appeal or anything of the fleshly nature, it is the power of God at work for you!

SCRIPTURE; 1Kings 17:8-14

AUGUST 13

"CHECK YOUR PROGRESS"

If thou run with the footmen and they have wearied thee, then how can thou contend with horses? (Jer 12:5)

God told the prophet Jeremiah "before I formed thee in the belly, I knew thee; and before thou camest forth out of the womb I sanctified thee a prophet unto the nations" (Jer 1:5); this was related to him when he was but a child, it appeared to be a great order but we know if God said it that settles it. Some think you have to believe it but needless to say, rather you believe it or not it shall come to pass.

Jeremiah would suffer many things due to the calling on his life he would also go on to become a great prophet to the nations as God declared. How would Jeremiah make it from prison to the house of every believer today? Perseverance is the answer. I'm certain as the roads were not easy, when discouragement set in; when he proclaimed he wouldn't speak (Jer20:9) he would look back over his life; check his progress and become encouraged enough to go on when he wanted to quit.

When you believe life has reached a stale mate and progress appears to be slow this is the time to consult the accomplishments of yesterday, peruse and check the progress you've made and you'll find that where you started far exceed what's left too be done.

SCRIPTURE; Lam 3:22-23

AUGUST 14

"SILENCE"

Therefore say unto them, thus saith the Lord God; there shall none of my words be prolonged anymore, but the word which I have spoken shall be done, saith the Lord God (Ezek 12:28)

In every believer life there will come a time when you think that God has ceased speaking to you; not because you've committed sin or gone astray, not even for a lack of not trying; it is however a time of silence. When Elijah went on the mount to hear from God he first had to encounter a series of illusional elements before he would tune in to the still small voice speaking to him; he would suffer through the distractions before God would break his silence.

Often times we miss what God has said when nothing has been said; even in his silence he's speaking volumes n your life. He's exhibiting his ability to lead and guide your life through the word of knowledge he has already engrafted within. You must lean on what has already been divulged and recall that the spirit of the living God is prevalent enough whereas when there is silence his glory will continue to guide!

SCRIPTURE; 1 Kings 19:10-15

AUGUST 15

"PUSH, PUSH, PUSH"

And Naomi said unto her two daughter-in- law, go return each to her mothers house: the Lord deal kindly with you, as you have dealth with the dead and with me (Ruth 1:8)

A time arose when Naomi deemed it necessary to return to her kinsman. Her decision to leave would affect her daughter in laws

Ruth and Orpah. Ruth the more loyal of the two would not take heed to the advice of her mother in law she would stay the course and refuse to go back to her father house; instead of taking the road of least resistance she would push, push, push while being encouraged to go the other way. In the end her steadfastness would pay off, because of her persistence she would go on to marry Boaz and become the great grandmother of King David.

Whenever you're faced with dilemmas that can decide the course of your life; take upon the spirit of Ruth. Don't settle for the out push your way into a destiny you would otherwise miss; take on the mind of a warrior, who knows if you're next in line to birth a King!

SCRIPTURE; Ruth 1:10-14

AUGUST 16

"LET THE WORD MOVE YOU"

Study to show thyself approved unto God, a workman that needeth not to be ashamed, rightly dividing the word of truth (1Tim 2:15)

Because we live in a world that consist of much theatrics we've become a people who's moved by the antics or performances of those set before us to deliver a message, so much so that we've roped ourselves into feeding the ego or conscious as they ply us with dramatics and not simply the word.

When Satan launched his attack on mankind he was in rare form perverting the word of God; he enticed Eve, not with truth, instead he used his eloquent words to misappropriate what was already established (Gen 3). Paul warns us in 1Tim 2:16 "to shun profane and vain babblings: for they will increase unto more ungodliness; in other words "stay away from any appearance of evil". Theatrics will entertain you temporary but it has no root producing power; the word doesn't require a lot of shimmer and glimmer to be, it already is! Therefore allow the word to move you and not the antics of those that minister; you'll learn more this way and what is acquired will always produce!

SCRIPTURE; 1Tim4:3-4

AUGUST 17

"HE NEVER WENT BACK"

And, the Lord God formed man of the dust of the ground and breathed into his nostrils the breath of life; and man became a living soul. (Gen 2:7)

In the beginning when God created man the Bible says that he made him from the dust of the ground (Gen 2:7), however as God purposed that man needed a helpmate he made the woman; not from the dust of the ground but he took her from the rib of man (Gen 2:22). God in his infinite wisdom found it unnecessary to go back to the soil to create the woman for in his making he had already created the perfect specimen; therefore He would not revisit a place of creation to re-create, instead He would delve into what was and reproduce.

If you are at the initial place of increase when you first came into miracle territory waiting on the next one you're out of place, for God doesn't have to go back to where it all began too make it reproduce! He'll meet you where you are and rain down what is needed for completion. Check your spiritual compass and once you detect the problem make the adjustment and watch God make what's expedient materialize from what's available to meet the need!

SCRIPTURE; Isa 59:21

AUGUST 18

"CALCULATED DECISIONS"

Then shalt thou delight thyself in the Lord; and I will cause thee to walk upon the high places of the earth... (Isa 58:14)

Every opportunity rather gained or aborted reeks of what can be termed as a "calculated decision". Knowing this it becomes crucial for us to always consult God before we embark on any type of life changing courses, for to do otherwise can prove to be disastrous and it has the potential to pervert or prevent that which is beneficial.

When God spoke to Joshua he instructed him to do what he had never done before in the face of war; instead of setting themselves in battle array with staves and other instruments of war they were told to compass the city and shout (Joshua 6:16) and it was in following these instructions that they would conquer Jericho. Some may think that the battle was a cinch because God fought it for them, but let us be reminded that the calculated decision to step out on faith required faith. The battle could have swung in the other direction had Joshua made the wrong decision; but God. Don't exchange your Jericho because it seems easier to stay in the boat: as you're faced with your next obstacle be certain to make a calculated decision, it's the one destined to up hold rather you like the outcome or not!

SCRIPTURE; Joshua 6:20-21

AUGUST 19

"YOUR INNER ABILITY"

And Adam gave names to all cattle, and to the fowl of the air: and to every beat of the field... (Gen 2:20)

Some think they can't when God has said you can for I have equipped you. Others believe not me, but the Lord has declared "no not just you but me working through you! When God formed Adam and breathed into his nostrils the breath of life (Gen 2:7) he not only endowed him with life, but wisdom, knowledge and understanding was uniquely instilled in that moment as well. How can we tell? The word says as God determined that Adam needed a helpmate he formed every beast of the field and the fowl of the air, brought them to Adam to see what he would call them, and whatsoever Adam called every living creature that was the name thereof (Gen 2:19).

Unbeknown to the recipient (Adam, us, you) God has equipped us with an "inner ability" to do what has never been done before; Adam spoke and it was; we who are direct descendants of Adam has been given the ability to "speak those things which be not as though they were" (Rom 4:17). You have an inner strength, an inner resolve and an inner intuition that's available for use whenever you come into an uncommon situation, don't panic just tap into your "inner ability"!

SCRIPTURE; 2Co 4:13

AUGUST 20

"DID YOU LAUGH?"

Therefore Sarah laughed within herself, saying, after I am waxed old shall I have pleasure, my lord being old also? (Gen 18:12)

Has God spoken something great or even un-imaginary over your life and even though you know its God will for your life, and it was God who has spoken it, you find yourself not totally believing it? Has your mannerism spoken what you've never had the courage to vocalize? Is your order so great whereas you've inadvertently laughed in disbelief? If this is you or someone you know it's probably time to search out the heart of Sarah; how when she counted the saying of the Lord as propaganda, inwardly she hoped; not because she had the strength to bring forth, instead she believed that in-spite of her complexities the God of her heritage would cause her to become the mother of many Nations.

If your situation is one that is easily managed by you then it's not a job for God: but if you see the circumstance as impossible; know that the same God who called something out of nothing remains available and willing to defy all human capabilities; don't laugh only believe!

SCRIPTURE; Gen 18:13-14

AUGUST 21

"THE SECOND TIME AROUND"

And for that the dream was doubled unto Pharaoh twice; it is because the thing is established by God, and God will shortly bring it to pass (Gen 41:32)

According to the word of God spoken by Joseph when God show you a thing twice it is because he has already established it with a maturity date. When Pharaoh was being instructed by God concerning the future of Egypt God spoke to him through his dream: without interpretation the meaning and the provision to provide in a time of dire straits would have gone astray.

What is it that God has shown you and it has a way of repeating itself? Don't just pass it off the Lord is speaking, making plain what is to be done for the keeping of, not only your immediate family, but those who are destined to come after you or within your circle of influence. My friend it isn't just a fluke God is trying to tell you something so pay attention and listen up; it's your turn!

SCRIPTURE; Pro 4:20-22

AUGUST 22

"THE BAD REPORT"

They that sow in tears shall reap in joy (Ps 126:5)

The day came when I heard what I never expected to hear; I was summoned to the doctor office and informed that a spot was discovered in my right breast. In the midst of the bad report I tried to be optimistic; I summoned up all of my resolve to be strong, but I found within myself that I couldn't ward off the spirit of worry or even fear. I was left to consider rather or not I'd cling to the "bad report" or step out of the spirit of doom and gloom and grab a hold to the word of truth that declares "by his stripes I'm healed" (1Peter 2:26): the latter appealed to me therefore I stepped out of the funk Satan wanted me in and little by little began to declare the word of God over my life. As of August 21, 2009 I still wasn't certain of the results in mans lingo; I am however positive of this very fact "He who has begun a good work in me shall complete it until the day of Christ Jesus". I wasn't delivered and saved from the world to be eaten by it; I will live; I will become what was spoken of me in the heavenly.

If you're faced with a bad report ask yourself "whose report should I believe". Now that you've come to yourself you'll find that you were not brought this far to be left; before the problem ever occurred God had provided you a solution: so lift up your head oh ye gates; and be ye lifted up ye everlasting doors; and the king of glory shall come in (Ps 24:7); refuse to give way too sorrow knowing that he who trust in the Lord shall never be ashamed!

(At the time of publication I am cancer free and was never diagnosed with it; look at God!!!!!)

SCRIPTURE; Ps 121:1-3

AUGUST 23

"SAY SO"

We're called to be living Epistles, living sacrifices, and the image of Christ this is how we win a world who would otherwise miss the magnitude of the perfect sacrifice Jesus offered up for us when he went to the cross. How do we "say so"? Not by persuasion of many words but by actions because what a person is will always speak so loud that it will drown out whatever rhetoric used to draw or push away.

When John was exiled to the island of Patmos through divine revelation he's shown a glimpse of things which are to be. In Revelation22:10-11 he's shown this fundamental truth "for the time is at hand, he that is unjust, let him be unjust still; and he which is filthy, let him be filthy still: and he that is righteous, let him be righteous still; and he that is Holy, let him be Holy still". What is being implied? There shall come a time when what you are will resound, and in whatever state you find yourself in you shall remain; therefore while it is called today walk in the love of God and let your life "say so".

SCRIPTURE; Ps 34:22

AUGUST 24

"DRY AND THIRSTY"

For he satisfieth the longing soul, and filleth the hungry soul with goodness (Ps 107:9)

There is a famous song that says "when your heart is dry and thirsty pray for rain; if your life is void and empty pray for rain". This song oftentimes speaks of the condition we as believers find ourselves in whenever there's turmoil in our lives. We're also brought to this brink when God has orchestrated a proving place for us in life; one designed to take us into a higher dimension in God.

David understood this principle as he hid out in caves running from his enemies: not at liberty to have clarity concerning his plight he's encouraged as he writes "I had fainted, unless I believed to see the goodness of the Lord in the land of the living" (Ps 27:13). His predicament was dramatically changed at this juncture; what happened is in the midst of a void David defocused on the drought and refocused on the promised rain! If you're feeling the pinch and your prayers seem to echo back at you; it could be that it's time too re-calculate your position and pray for rain!

SCRIPTURE; Ps 34:17

AUGUST 25

"GODS BEST FOR YOU"

For it is better, if the will of God be so, that you suffer for well doing, than for evil doing (1Peter 3:17)

Being in a place of complexities allows for thoughtful consideration of ones life; why am I here, how did my life come to this, what have I done that requires this? Are some of the thoughts that bombard ones thinking during a time of perplexity and disorder? As I faced one of the toughest things I ever had to endure in my life I heard God speak to my spirit and say "even when things don't appear to be all that you'd desire; and you would rather change your circumstances instead of going through them, it's still my best for you; for I've ordained them also". It was then that I began to understand that even in my worst moment Gods best for me will always supersede; being confident of this very fact I am therefore comforted.

Some may ask "how is losing a job, being in bondage, suffering through an illness, losing a loved one or facing any type of personal or professional ruin Gods best for me? Allow me to answer with the word: when Paul was suffering through shipwreck (Acts 27), thrown into prison (Acts 26) and beaten for naming the name of Christ; Gods best was not the situation, his best would be what was instilled to bring him out of his plight and where he would go and grow in God from there. Therefore think it not strange concerning the fiery trail which is to try you as though some strange thing happened (1Peter 4:12); Gods best for you is oftentimes manifested as you're purified through the fire!

SCRPTURE; 1Peter 5:10

AUGUST 26

"DEGREES OF CLOSENESS"

And He said my presence shall go with thee, and I shall give thee rest (Exo 33:14)

If you're one who have experienced what I term as an overwhelming sense of Gods presence which eventually transitioned into what can be named as opaque or elusive know that you don't stand alone. I find that during a Christian journey that closeness is established in degrees; not because you've done something displeasing to God, and He in turn has withdrawn his hand (which does happen), what's transpired is, during the most difficult times of your life the presence of God becomes overwhelming because he becomes the only source allocated to provide the strength needed to get you through; when you're at your worst Gods presence becomes your guide. However as you matured God knew that he could trust you with your pain, trust that regardless of how you felt that you would remain rooted and grounded in truth. While you were a babe He stayed near to nurture but as you grew, going from one level to the next you became an entrusted ambassador. Therefore the next time you're feeling as if you don't feel the presence of God thank him knowing that you've been entrusted too grow into a new dimension in God.

SCRIPTURE; Exo 40:37-38

AUGUST 27

"OH YE OF LITTLE FAITH"

And immediately Jesus stretched forth his hand, and caught him, and said unto him, o thou of little faith, wherefore didst thou doubt? (Mt 14:31)

When the story of Peter is mentioned concerning his walk on water it's widely thought that he failed because once the opportunity arose he subsequently looked away and began to sink. What isn't duly noted is this point; Peter had the audacity to get out of the boat while all others remained seated: as long as he believed he stayed afloat but the moment fear set in he started to sink. Fear will pull you or drag you down, but faith is designed to keep you abreast of or on top of every situation.

Choices and decisions should be considered the core of what we anticipate from life, so let us have the faith to get out of the boat while others choose to sit around. Refuse to allow another golden opportunity pass you by because you've failed to choose correctly. Faith has to be progressive and not stagnant therefore mix your faith with the word and prepare yourself to be blessed.

SCRIPTURE; Mt 17:20

AUGUST 28

"DON'T STAY IN A PLACE OF ONLY DAILY PROVISION"

Then said the Lord unto Moses, behold I will rain bread from heaven for you, and the people shall go out and gather a certain rate everyday... (Exo 16:4)

As Moses led the Israelites trough the wilderness God is always present meeting every need. When they thirst he gives water from a rock (Exo 17:6); when they hunger He supernaturally, daily makes provision for them by sending them what some would call angel food, but the bible calls it manna (Exo 16:14): with their daily provision instructions are given but to stay in a place of recipient obedience is required.

There came a time when God was ready to make good on the promise he'd promised to Abraham. He instruct Moses to send out 12 spies and bring back a report (Num 13:17-18), they obliged but faltered at the promise and continued to suffer through the wilderness. They were sent into the promise land, touched the fruit, examined it in their hands and found that there was none like it, how did they miss it? Simple, they preferred to hold onto what was within their grasp; they had become comfortable with only daily provision and balked at the promise of more than enough, even when it appeared at their fingertips (Num 13:27)

God chose to spoon feed you while you remained a babe and that is why daily provision was plausible, He now requires more from you in order to get more to you. Don't look to be spoon fed forever, you can't be productive in that state. Don't stay in a pace of only daily provision when God has orchestrated the resources of a life time to overtake you!

SCRIPTURE; Jos 5:9-12

AUGUST 29

"YOU SHALL HAVE WHAT YOU SAY"

For by thy words you shall be justified, and by thy words thou shalt be condemned (Mt 12:37)

In a moment of panic during adverse situations; even if you're only a little bit indecisive concerning a particular something it's easy to rush judgment and allow what one is feeling to spring forth life by prematurely or impulsively speaking what you're thinking or feeling. The Israelites faced this problem when told to go and spy out the land that would be theirs. All but two gave a bad report they knew that their fate was in the hands of God (Num 13:20-33) however once the bad report was uttered they immediately began to murmur and complain against God; they spoke words that would ultimately come to pass. They questioned "wherefore hath the Lord brought us into this land to fall by the sword, that our wives and our children should be a prey (Num 14:3); even unto his day the nation of Israel continue to fight for their land: the children became a prey; they and their wives died along the way without ever entering into the promise land.

God used words to frame the world, Adams words named what God created and our lives are able to claim what our live will entail: Matthew says "we shall give an account for every idle word (12:36) therefore it's vital that we realize that our words are foundations and once built upon we create either life or death, because "you shall have what you say"!

SCRIPTURE; Mt 12:34-35

AUGUST 30

"PASS WHERE YOU'VE BEEN"

And I will bless them that bless thee, and curse him that curseth thee... (Gen 12:3)

Looking back is probably one of the things that plague the Christian believer and oftentimes the unbeliever as well. We consider our youth and what could have been, think about lost loves, or even the bodies we once had before the children; too many take outs without bodily exercise: thinking back won't render you defensive less but camping out there will. In God your journey will always be a progressive one; meaning, He's daring to take you pass where you've been.

When Abraham was called God spoke and directed him to get thee out thy country, and from thy kindred, and from thy father's house, unto a land that I will show thee: and I will make of thee a great nation... (Gen 12:1-2). Surely Abraham could have turned back as he thought about what he'd left behind; he could have made a half hearted attempt at doing what God deemed necessary, however to obtain the promise he had to be willing to forsake all and follow after God.

As you strive for hearts desires know that it is God who is able to take you pass where you've been, and able to establish you once you get there; for we can do nothing of or within ourselves but with God nothing shall be impossible!

SCRIPTURE; Mt 10:37-39

AUGUST 31

"BATTLE SCARS"

That this may be a sign among you, that when your children ask their fathers in time to come, saying what mean ye by these stones? (Jos 4:6)

Behind every testimony lies a type of monument or reminder of what was involved in overcoming or arriving at this point. My struggles were not just for me and neither is yours; some will travel roads they'd rather by-pass, not knowing that to do so would deprive God of his intended glory tied to the struggle.

The scars you receive along life's road; rather physical or emotional is destined to glorify the Lord; if we never fought a fight we wouldn't know if we were capable of winning one. Be not ashamed of the bumps and bruises you've received instead allow them to put the adversary to shame as you magnify your God. Refuse to complain even if the complaint appears logical; in doing so your scars become banners of victory and not reminders of disgrace!

SCRIPTURE; Rom 14:7-8

SEPTEMBER 1

"WHEN IN THE PRESENCE OF GOD"

And it came to pass, when Moses came down from Mount Sinai with the two tablets of testimony in Moses hand, when he came down from the mount the skin of his face shown while he talked with him (Exo 34:29)

Hesitate not to believe that there will never be a time, an occasion when someone is in the presence of God and there is no change. When Moses went on the mount to speak with God when he returned to the camp the glory of God was so prevalent upon him that he had to wear a veil before he could minister what God had instituted (Exo 34:29-33). As Jacob stood in need of a transformation God would send a representative; it would be that as Jacob prevailed in Gods chosen presence that his life would ultimately change.

It is utterly impossible for us to assume that we've been in the presence of God if our lives reek of what it's always been; not only are we to experience change but those we come in contact with daily should notice his wondrous working power evolving from our lives as well. If you believe you know what the power of God entails and where you worship or your personal worship gives you an audience with the king; why not be sure and check your change gauge to be certain, it'll determine whether or not you have been in his presence or only believe you have!

SCRIPTURE; Gen 32:28-30

SEPTEMBER 2

"COMMITTED"

Naked came I out of my mothers womb, and naked shall I return thither: the Lord gave and the Lord hath taken away: blessed be the name of the Lord (Job 1:21)

Before Christ and the knowledge of his truth I lived a life that consisted of gambling; during this phase I sort of termed or coined the phrase "I'm committed to the pot", this meant that I had put a substantial amount of money into that hand and I felt compelled to stick with it win, lose, or draw; I was committed.

Uriah experienced this same type of commitment with King David therefore when the king sent for him Uriah refused to go into his house and enjoy himself while others were still at war, instead he would sleep on the kings doorstep because of his commitment (2Sam 11:9).

Oftentimes the simple seem strange when we fail to completely process every fact. One symbolic truth or fact is rather we acknowledge the preferred paths we take; inadvertently or consciously we make the commitment with our choices. The word tells us to commit thy ways unto the Lord; trust also in him and he shall bring it to pass. What's it? It's whatever you're trusting God to do for you; what you've diligently been seeking the Lord for concerning your future. Jesus said "seek ye first the kingdom of god and his righteousness and all these things shall be added unto you" (Mt 6:33).

I once committed my livelihood too chance in a game of poker, while Uriah made a commitment to the king; some commitments are temporal and could bore lasting results while others can prove to be more noteworthy because they are life changing with eternal results; therefore chose ye this day whom ye shall serve (Jos 24:15), make the commitment you've been running from; do it now for the day is well spent and the hour is at hand.

SCRIPTURE; 2Sam 11:8-11

SEPTEMBER 3

"SEPARATED WITH A CAUSE"

Also I heard the voice of the Lord, saying, whom shall I send, and who will go for us? Then said I, here am I; send me (Isa 6:8)

During the making of or the defining of the early church God spoke and declared those he wanted set aside to establish in the earth the work He'd foreordained. As we live in the dispensation of grace the very same God has called and "separated you with a cause". Everyone has not been called with the same calling. The word says "he called some apostles, and some prophets.... (1Co 12:21), one member is as important as all others for we make up the entire body of Christ. Paul was separated with Barnabas for the work of the church (Acts 13:2); Jesus was separated to bring redemption, John the Baptist was separated because he was named the forerunner of Christ: you to have been "separated with a cause", big or small great or indifferent it remains the reason in which you've been called and separated. Are you walking in the calling in which you've been called? Paul instructed the church in Romans that the gifts and calling of God are without repentance (Rom 11:29); meaning regardless of you tapping into them, walking n them or centering your life in God and around them, on the judgment day you will still have to give an account for what you've done with them.

If you're unaware of why God has separated you I decree today as your day of awakening. You shall come into the knowledge of your purpose; God will overshadow you and reveal what and why so be made wise in the name of Jesus!

SCRIPTURE; John 15:16

SEPTEMBER 4

"DON'T WORRY PRAY"

.... Said I not unto thee, if thou wouldest believe, thou shouldest see the glory of God (John 11:40)

I awoke this morning thinking about my next to the eldest child Lionel. Being a long way away from my children and family right now oftentimes arouse a sense of edginess, however as my mind drifted to Lionel welfare I heard the Holy Spirit say "he's okay because you haven't worried you've prayed". Many days I long for my children and my family, but almost none of the time do I worry about them.

If you're far away from your loved ones and your home right now and those you love have left your area of care, don't worry pray, for God who is omnipresent is well able to hear a prayer prayed in Chicago and manifest the results of it over in Germany: sometimes the distance isn't the problem and the breakdown resides in the home, in this instance God is able to bridge the gap from room to room; fear says worry, but Jesus commands us to pray (John 16:24); remember in everything prayer is the antidote that designed to get the attention of God, who will then destroy the yoke!

SCRIPTURE; Jam 5:13-16

SEPTEMBER 5

"SECOND CHANCE"

Go and say to Hezekiah thus saith the Lord, the God of David thy father, I have heard thy prayer, I have seen thy tears: behold I will add unto thy days fifteen years (Isa 38:5)

In Jan 09 what's described as the" miracle on the Hudson" took place. A pilot whose plane flew through a flock of birds was able to not panic and partake in what's considered the miracle because he landed a passenger plane on the Hudson River, and no one aboard the flight was injured or maimed. For those aboard this aircraft God in his mercy would afford them (saved or unsaved, I don't know) a second chance at life and an opportunity to right what had previously been wrong.

Your miracle may not have happened on the Hudson; it maybe that you've never experienced a near death situation nevertheless as you have been given the space and the grace to repent and to be engrafted in the kingdom you too were given a second chance. Paul second chance came as he was in the midst of mischief (Acts 9); David experienced a second chance after he encountered a night of folly (2Sam 11); Hezekiah second chance came after he received a

death sentence (Isa 38). What transpired in the producing of your second chance isn't as important as you receiving one, or making the father proud as you minister unto him with your faithfulness while you monopolize it, remember to make the most of it for third ones are not always promised to us!
SCRIPTURE; Luke 7:37-50

SEPTEMBER 6

"THE LORD HEARD IT"

And they said, hath the Lord indeed spoken only by Moses? Hath he not spoken by us? And the Lord heard it (Num 12:2)

It's easy to become engrossed or even preoccupied with what others think or say. To take the time to answer every innuendo, dispute every indiscretion or even address each supposition could take up the better part of ones life. The simplest thing which often proves to be the hardest thing to do is to allow God to fight your battle for you.

When Aaron and Miriam had a gripe concerning Moses, even though they thought they were in private quarters the bible says and the Lord heard it" (Num 12:2), negative feelings had crept into their hearts that was designed to come up against the man of God, but again the Lord heard it; not only did he hear it but he would expose it as well.

Before you allow yourself to get into a battle of words which could lead to more ungodliness consider that God has already decreed that the battle is not yours, but Gods (2Cron 20:15). Refuse to allow anothers words or thoughts to become your to become your truth; for vengeance is mine saith the Lord, I will repay (Heb 10:30), instead do as Moses did and pray knowing that when the Lord heard it, he also took care of it!

SCRIPTURE; Pro 25:21-22

SEPTEMBER 7

"HE PROMISED"

For when God made a promise to Abraham, because he could swear by no greater he sware by himself (Heb 6:13)

We've been left with an innumerable amount of promises within the word of God. How many of us have received a clear Rhema word from the Lord which promises to move our lives from degree to another? Does your promise appear to be a long ways off or even something beyond the scope of your imagination? Whatever your situation entails, believe the truth which is, He who have promised is faithful and will hasten to perform his word!

The promise of a deliverer as the Israelites suffered through hard bondage appeared bleak; the promise of a perfect sacrifice to redeem us from death and the law was long coming but He came (John 3:16). Don't let doubt or disappointment rob you of the joy available to you as you embark upon a new day; yesterday nothing transpired for you however today could very well be that day, why? Because he promised!

SCRIPTURE; Rom 10:1

SEPTEMBER 8

"PROVISION"

This book of the law shall not depart out of thy mouth: but thou shall meditate day and night, that thou mayest observe to do according to all that is written therein: for then shalt thou make thy way prosperous, and then thou shalt have good success (Jos 1:8)

Being self sufficient isn't a bad thing unless of course you've become so dependent upon one self, that you've pushed the theory of god being your provider to the back and have programmed yourself to believe that you're the source of what's being provided to you.

To become puffed up in pride and flirt with the idea that your job, your career or your expertise can and will sustain you in life is to become blindside with propaganda and not fact; the word says for it is God who gives us the power to get wealth (Duet 8:18), not to mention that real provision, complete provision, unhinged provision comes down from the father of light in whom there is no variableness nor shadow of turning (Jas1:17). God expects you to do what's he's equipped you to do, he does however expect you to cease from self reliance so that you can experience his sole provision.

SCRIPTURE; Ps 23

SEPTEMBER 9

"NOTHING IS TOO SMALL"

And the man of God said, where fell it? And he shewed him the place, and he cut down a stick and cast it in thither; and the iron did swim (2Kings 6:6

To dispel the theory that God isn't actually concerned about the small matters in our lives he leaves us an example through his word. As Elisha and the sons of the prophets prepare to rebuild and enlarge their territory they found it necessary to borrow an axe; during preparation the axe head falls into the River Jordan (2Kings 6:1-3): what could have been a tedious matter is now the opportunity for God to impress upon us that "nothing is too small" to grab his attention, produce his power or request is assistance. In the face of this misfortune God, through divine wisdom instructs the man of god of what's expedient for him to retrieve the lost and borrowed article.

God wants you to know that He's just as concerned about your paper cut as He is about the miracle you need to purchase your dream house, or the favor you're in need of to help advance your children education. Wherever you find yourself in life know that the Lord will use what is already available to get the job done. If you stand in faith and go to the correct source you'll find that "nothing is too small", because with our father the little things do count!

SCRIPTURE; 2Kings 6:1-7

SEPTEMBER 10

"NEW MANAGEMENT"

If any man be in Christ he is a new creation old things have passed away, behold all things have become new (2Co 5:17)

Usually whenever a business is failing those who have the ability to make prevalent changes in the advancement of said business are forced to make pertinent decisions, fast; in doing so the quality of the business is taken into consideration as well as the growth, and what can be salvaged; the recourse of getting to his point becomes crucial. Whenever possible the business may exchange hands and the consumer will often see an advertisement declaring "under new management", this is designed to draw the old, inspire the curious, and captivate the onlooker.

The same is true of the Christian life; once we have been cleansed from all unrighteousness and our sins forgiven (1John 1:9) no longer should our lives which have been invested in by God and our Lord Jesus Christ continue to fail. Through the word we can reconstruct our lives as the Holy Spirit use his demolition ability to refurbish the broken structures we once were.

God who is now the head of your life is speaking to your spirit. He has called you out of poverty to enjoy the fullness of his joy;

what you once were won't compare to what you will become, you were brought with a price (1Co 6:20) you are now under new management, when Jesus paid the price he paid it in full: your old landlord is angry but don't fail to read the end of the book because you've won (Rev 21:6)!

SCRIPTURE; Ps 24:1-6

SEPTEMBER 11

"BELIEVING RIGHT"

So then they which be of faith are blessed with faithful Abraham (Gal 3:9)

Tearing down the enemy first line of defense is not an option, but how does one complete this task? It's simple; only believe; you must believe what God has already stated concerning his will, his word and his way. The word says "he who comes to God must believe that he is and a rewarder of those who diligently seek him" (Heb 11:6).

Anytime you come to God in prayer it's imperative to know that God who is faithful is not only willing to answer prayer, but he delights in doing so, if prayer is done in unbelief expect nothing; your words become rhetoric or sounding brass.

Satan attempts to paralyze the saints by selling the lie that God doesn't hear your prayer, won't answer them; suggest that you're unworthy because of some past mishap; the devil is a lie; what's standing between you and everything you need to become established in your purpose is within you: what's needed is to believe right. Once this is done you'll have reached inside of the enemies' camp and taken back the victory that has previously been handed over through an act of intimidation. If you stand your ground and keep believing right you'll begin to see miracles unfold once you apply this principle.

SCRIPTURE; Heb 10:23

SEPTEMBER 12

"MISSED OPPORTUNITIES"

Be not forgetful to entertain strangers: for thereby some have entertained strangers unawares (Heb 13:2)

As we embark on life often we become entangled in those things that cling close to our hearts desire; preoccupation could prove to be a snare, not because it's sinful or shameful to strive for that in which we desire, it is however crucial that along each path we take that we stop the voices in our heads long enough to make certain that we won't look back and realize that we've missed opportunities to step outside of ourselves long enough to minister to the needs of those we come in contact with daily.

Too often we look back and find a place where we've missed opportunities designed to take our lives or the lives of another on a different course; good or bad who knows? However lets make a conscious decision to take advantage of every opportunity presented to act and allow our lives to speak of the hope we have in Christ Jesus, therefore put away procrastination, put away preoccupation and every weight and the sin that can easily beset you and let us run with endurance the race that is set before us (Heb 12:1).

SCRIPTURE; Jam 1:25

SEPTEMBER 13

"IF THAT HAD BEEN TO LITTLE"

And let us not be weary in well doing: for in due season we shall reap if we faint not (Gal 6:9)

There came a time when the chosen leader of God committed a sin which caused God to send forth the prophet to reprove him of his faults. As Nathan depicts a picture of a man who has everything and another who has nothing accept one little ewe lamb he inquires of the king what should be done to the fellow who has taken all that the man has; David answers "as the Lord live this man shall surely die" it is then that Nathan says to David "thou art the man" (2Sam 12:7). Nathan who is standing proxy for God goes on to say to David "I gave thee thy masters house and thy masters wives into thy bosom, and gave thee the house of Israel and of Judah: and had that been too little, I would have given thee such and such things (2Sam 12:8)

Because we are children of promise God wants us to always wait upon the Lord. No circumstance, no situation, no need will ever come upon you without Gods provision. Now is not the time to look upon your neighbors goods and presume to want them; this is the hour of manifestation. As long as you're willing and obedient you shall eat the good of he land; we serve an unlimited God so why not take the limits off of him and begin to ask him for the things you have need of and even those you desire!

SCRIPTURE; Ps 37:4

SEPTEMBER 14

"REVERSE THE CURSE"

Think not that I am come to destroy the law, or the prophets: I am not come to destroy, but to fulfill (Mt 5:17)

Before the life and death of Jesus we were bound by the law of sin and death. It is however through his redemptive power that we're able to live the lives appointed to us from the beginning of creation. By one man (Adam) sin entered into the world, by another man (Jesus) we were set free and reappointed unto life; in essence Jesus came and reversed the curse. Under the mosaic law by the witness of two or three a man could be stoned to death (Heb 10:28), this law places you, your children and your children, children under the curse but the blood of Jesus has removed the stumbling block and placed you at a advantage. Jesus has reversed the curse so that you might have life and that more abundantly; so stay away from the things that restrict your liberty in Christ and cling close to his grace.

Whenever an intrusive thought enters your mind bearing condemnation, sin or shame take thought of whose you are and how Jesus has "reversed the curse" too liberate you; walk in your liberty and be not entangled again with the yoke of bondage for whom Christ has freed is free indeed!

SCRIPTURE; 2Co 5:17-20

SEPTEMBER 15

"24HOUR TURN AROUND"

For thus saith the Lord ye shall not see wind neither shall you see rain: yet the valley shall be filled with water, that ye may drink both you and your cattle and beast (2Kings 3:17)

Have you ever come to a place in your life when you presumed that it surely can't get any worst than this? Has life served you a cold dish which disagrees with your plans as a parent, a teacher, a provider? Are you waiting on your divine moment of release, your breakthrough, your long awaited answer? Have you somehow continued to hold on; not actually realizing where you've gotten the added strength to continue to fight? Well there's a word for you, there once was a situation that required Gods expedient attention; during an intense famine the people in the land began to commit all that was unlawful in the sight of God too sustain, but when things got so bad that it would affect the man of God, God sent a word to restore order and alleviate the problem (2Kings 7:1). They too were in need of a right now word, bearing right now fruit and as always God would come through. As you've labored and seen no fruit know that your running hasn't been in vain; God has seen your affliction and has now released your increase. What failed to show up in your yesterday will present itself in your today and your tomorrow; no longer is help on the way for it has arrived. God has declared a 24 hour turn around in all matters that concern you: not just in the home but at the work place as well.

Don't worry about God coming through and doing what he has declared, you just make certain that you're doing the one thing he's asked of you; only believe! Now watch debt, depression, unruliness and disorder turn its back to you as you begin to thank God for your "24 hour turn around" in advance.

SCRIPTURE; Ps 1:1-3

SEPTEMBER 16

"CLOSED CAPTIONING"

I will not leave you comfortless: I will come to you (John 14:18)

The broadcasting industry has come up with a format which include everyone who has the capability to watch television broadcasting; this format is called closed captioning: it's designed to allow the hearing impaired the privilege of not only visualizing what's being broadcasted but they are now afforded a sense of normality by becoming completely in tuned to what's taking place by reading along.

We as the Christian have been equipped with a greater, the Holy Spirit; whose strength and power is enough to speak to our inner man, our consciousness and guide us into all truth; we've been equipped with a prototype of "closed captioning" to help as we face every challenge in life. Whenever trouble arise refuse to give in to the temptation to quit or stray from where God has called you, instead dig internally, press the closed captioning button connected to your spirit and get reconnected to what God is already doing in your life; the spirit is designed to guide so why not allow him to do so!

SCRIPTURE; John 17:8-9

SEPTEMBER 17

"THE POWER OF THE TONGUE"

For he that will love life and see good days let him refrain his tongue from evil, and his lips that they speak no guile (1Peter 3:10)

We've been given a heads up on what's required to experience the best in life along with good days; why then does it sometimes become difficult to do what's expected? James explains "and the tongue is a fire, a world of iniquity that defileth the whole body and setteth on fire the course of nature... (Jam 3:6), could the answer be as simple as us not using restraint in what we allow to proceed out of our mouths.

We have the wherewithal or the ability to set snares with our speech. When Satan came up against Jesus he used words to tempt (Mt 4:4); when he deceived Eve we see that the power was not within anything he possessed; it remained within his deceptive words. Words can build up or tear down either way they shall bear fruit. Again James informs "a fountain can not send forth sweet water and bitter (paraphrase Jam 3:11), neither can we. We must take control of our lives by thinking before we speak and realize that if our words aren't used to edify then it's probably best if it's unsaid.

SCRIPTURE; Jam 3:10

SEPTEMBER 18

"UNDER CONSTRUCTION"

For consider him that endured such contradiction of sinners against himself, lest ye be weary and faint in your minds (Heb 12:3)

When we come to God we bring all of the broken pieces of our lives believing that now after so long a time that we've reached the place of restoration and renewal. Oftentimes during transition we balk at the change because nothing is as uncomfortable as being "under construction"; even though we're received with all of our baggage to make it to places we've only dared imagined we can not hold on to it. Your garbage and baggage can be used, for God will cause it to be your testimony, but anything outside of being a testimony it becomes a stumbling block. Your being under construction right now isn't designed to punish, the word says "for whom the Lord loveth he chasteneth and scourgeth every son whom he receiveth" (Heb 12:6).

You are not alone what you're going through isn't about something you've done; it's about whose you are and where you're going. Scripture also declares "now no chastening for the present seemeth to be joyful, but grievous: nevertheless afterwards it yieldeth the peaceable fruit of righteousness unto them which are exercised thereby (Heb 12:11). Therefore endure what's placed in front of you; stand therein knowing that the displeasure you withstand today has the potential to give you a full return at harvest time!

SCRIPTURE; Heb 10:38-39

SEPTEMBER 19

"BOLD AS A LION"

The wicked flee when no man pursueth; but the righteous are as bold as a lion (Pro28:1)

Before our transformation in Christ, as we inspired to do things which pleased ourselves I dare to believe that even in our confused states as we lived contrary to the truth that we were yet "bold as lions". The sin that resided within us compelled us to do what was necessary too feed it and to go the extra mile, but our boldness took us there.

As we've surrendered ourselves and have made the decision to live the life of a Christian we still need to be "bold as lions". Some think to be a Christian signifies you're weak, one to be pushed over and used, however that was not the persona of Jesus: he was assertive when needed for he whipped the moneychangers out of the temple (Mt21:12), he served as servant when he washed the disciple feet (John 13:5) but he was never a push over. In all his splendor he took on the form of a servant, endured the shame of the cross so that we may live an abundant life. Refuse to become intimidated concerning your circumstances or to be manipulated by what's transpiring all around you; when God called you he intended for you to be "bold as lions"!

SCRIPTURE; Pro 16:7

SEPTEMBER 20

"CLUTTER FREE"

For to be carnally minded is death; but to be spiritually minded is life and peace (Rom 8:6)

The attack is on the mind: when the enemy comes against your life in Christ he first attacks the mind. Even as we minister to God with our gifts and calling he's still at work attacking the mind with contradictions of what's good and true.

As we engage ourselves in everyday living it's imperative that we are mindful to live a "clutter free" lifestyle. Clutter in the sense that once we've prayed about a particular something that we not allow a stagnant thought of doubt to lay dormant; clutter in the sense that while you're praising God or meditating on what God would have you to do that you allow that thought to be dismissed and another to take its place, one that is not conducive to what is necessary. Satan wants you to be a scatter brain; when Christ has already called you to wholeness and clutter free. Therefore gird up the loins of your mind (1Peter 1:13), take control of your thought life before it start to control you!

SCRIPTURE; 1Pet 1:13-16

SEPTEMBER 21

"WRITING ON THE WALL"

In the same hour came forth fingers of a mans hand; and wrote over against the candlestick upon the plaster of the wall of the king's palace: and the king saw the part of the hand that wrote (Dan 5:5)

When Jesus spoke he often used what's called a parable to get his message across. A parable is defined as a earthly demonstration with a heavenly connotation or meaning. The message wasn't always clear, the listener needed spiritual ears to hear what thus saith the Lord, or the message would fall to the wayside.

King Bel-shar-zar needed an interpreter (the prophet) to explain to him what God was speaking and decreeing (Dan 5:6-7); however because of the sacrifice of Christ we are now afforded more than a glimpse of what's being said or done, God has made the writing on the wall plain. What you've been hearing in your heart isn't an echo; there is no chance meeting with God, neither do we operate in the realm of coincidence: the posture you've taken has been orchestrated by God, you don't need a second opinion the "writing on the wall" is clear; follow the prompting of the Holy Spirit he will never lead you astray. Just do it!

SCRIPTURE; Dan 5:24-29

SEPTEMBER 22

"YOU'RE MINE"

For thus saith the Lord of host; after the glory hath he sent me unto the nations which spoiled you: for he tat toucheth you toucheth the apple of his eye (Zech 2:8)

Don't believe the hype; there's a misconception and a deception concerning the things we've previously done, past faults or failures doesn't have the ability to keep you out of the promised land; Satan conjures up lies to keep you bound, pay no attention God has called you mine: he's even ready to fight for you. He loves you so much that he has numbered the hairs on your head, and engraved your name in the palm of his hand; oh yes my friend you belong in the kingdom, your adversary is no longer just yours for God has declared he who toucheth you toucheth the apple of his eye. You're loved I mean really loved! He's loved you long and hard never willing to give up on you, always looking out for your best interest, even when it sometimes hurt.

Allow yourself to be healed as God kiss away your pain, bind up your broken heart and mend the tattered parts of your life: I love you saith the Lord for you are mine!

SCRIPTURE; Zech 3:4

SEPTEMBER 23

"STEP INTO THE NEW"

... And the Lord said, arise anoint him: for this is he (1Sam 16:12b)

On this day every year those who reside in the Midwest visually experience a change, but everyone rather admitted or indifferent has the opportunity to step into the new and enjoy this change.

Today is the first day of a new season with the new season comes life and death; death to the old and life to what's been incubating waiting on its divine time of manifestation.

This is the place where God has called you today while things are preparing to sleep for the winter, God has said not you step into the new and allow him to envelope you with the magic of his love. This season is one of change. Are you ready for advancement? If you position yourself in the path of openness you'll experience much more than you anticipated. This season won't look like your last season God has called forth those things you thought were dead and caused them to produce; today is that day.

As a young child God called the boy Samuel (1Sam 3:4); some probably thought that his season would come later in life but God knew that now would be the appropriate time. God didn't stop when he called Samuel he called you also; refuse to be afraid of what's transpiring in your life embrace it and "step into the new"!

SCRIPTURE; 1Sam 3:10-11

SEPTEMBER 24

"THE SPIRIT LEADS"

... If any man will come after me, let him deny himself, and take up his cross daily and follow me (Mk 9:23)

A similar challenge all Christians face is one of not allowing what you've been delivered of the ability to re-emerge into ones life. How is this possible? By allowing "the spirit to lead": Paul who suffered much for the gospel of Christ knew it to be expedient to overcome the flesh; he writes in Romans 7:18 "I know that in me (that is my flesh) there is no good thing: for to will is present with me; but to perform that which is good I find not". Paul struggled with a prototype of adversity, but he never wavered from the truth of who the son set free is free indeed (John 8:36).

The vises which held you bound will oftentimes re-visit you, for these are the things that the enemy uses to draw you back into a place of prediction; not Gods but his. Don't be surprised if that in which you've overcome has come knocking; Satan remembers what you once enjoyed. He's the total opposite of God who throws your sins as far as the east is from the west: he uses what worked before; only remember that when he speaketh a lie that he speak from his own resource, for he is a liar and the father of them (paraphrase John 8:44b).

If you've come to the fork in the road and what you use to be or do is appearing tempting, stand firm; don't answer the call of the flesh and "let the spirit lead", for in God there is no failure!

SCRIPTURE; John 10:27-30

SEPTEMBER 25

"VOLUNTEER PRAISE"

Thou art worthy o Lord to receive glory and honor and power: for thou hast created all things, and for thy pleasure they are and were created (Rev 4:11)

Looking back on what has been done to establish us worthy of eternal life should be enough to invoke a praise from within; when you stop and consider what life could have been if not for the blood of Jesus immediately you should begin to make a joyful noise unto the Lord.

David wrote the 23 Psalms as he faced adversity running for his life; he didn't allow what his life read to hinder him from offering up his volunteer praise unto God: not just for what he'd done, but for what he knew him to be capable of providing. You don't have to wait until Sunday, neither does it require anyone to pump or prime those who not only believe, but those who have experienced the power of the living God to honor Him because He is. Praise and worship shouldn't be forced; God receives it with gladness when it's done because we've chosen too, he loves "volunteer praise". Praising him because he's worthy is great but giving him praise because you love to is better, remember "total praise is complete surrender!

SCRIPTURE; Rev 5:11-14

SEPTEMBER 26

"NEW LEVEL NEW DEVIL"

For I will give you a mouth and wisdom which all your adversaries shall not be able to gainsay nor resist (Luke 21:15)

As I've committed myself to the writing of this book I've been under attack which is designed to stop its production. Many days I'm finding myself distracted, but I'm certain of this very fact "when God is taking you to a new level you'll encounter new devils!

Peter was destined to do a great wok for the ministry in Christ, Satan was privy of this fact; Jesus said that Satan had asked for him by name (Luke 22:31), detailing to us that where you're destined to go is no secret to the enemy, but it's already predestined that you succeed why? The bible says "Jesus declares. But I've prayed for you that your faith fail not (Luke 22:32): knowing then that Jesus sits on the right hand of the father making intercession for you the saints; we can boldly proclaim "the Lord is my helper, what can man do to me. Fear says turn back and head in the opposite direction, but faith in God screams "there maybe obstacles ahead, challenges to face, adversity I've yet to encounter, but I'm determined to reach my new level therefore I welcome those new devils!

SCRIPTUURE; Luke 21:18-19

SEPTEMBER 27

"I'LL BE THAT "

Then he questioned with him in many words; but he answered him nothing (Luke 23:9)

Jesus who's being questioned by Pilate and again by Herod gives us an example of how to treat our accusers: the bible declares and he answered him nothing, in other words: he balked not at what they said neither did he allow offence to rule his judgment to not answer; instead he would allow silence to meet their accusations.

We'll all encounter people or circumstances who will belie who we really are; sadly we live in a world which gives handles to describe individuals: those born with birth defects are called retarded, someone who is born out of wedlock is considered a bastard; the list goes on and on. At the time of this writing I'm incarcerated and daily I'm called inmate. Having time to consider my plight I'm amazed at many who are employed in corrections, because of an offence we are dehumanized. To some you're no longer human, just an inmate. God taught me through this experience to master what Jesus expressed so long ago "too answer them not a word", to tem "I'll be that, but in God I am royalty!

Don't get emotionally tied to what another say or think about you, the only opinion that actually matters is the Lord; let go of what you're feeling about what's being thought about or said about you, your silence says I'll be that while your actions prove I'll be much more than that!

SCRIPTURE; 2Tim 3:12

SEPTEMBER 28

"DON'T BUY THE BAD"

... Thus saith the Lord, set thine house in order: for thou shalt die and not live (Isa 38:1)

When Isaiah was sent to King Hezekiah to inform him to set his house in order immediately he brought what was confirmed by the prophet, he believed the report which caused him to seek the face of the Lord and request an acquittal. God in his infinite love relented and added fifteen years unto his life. When the prophet returned to relay the good news he believed yet he required a sign. Why do we often believe the bad or buy the bad and not cling to what's good? Is faith turned upside down that it's now easier to believe the report of destruction?

King Hezekiah found it easier to believe the bad report God sent not recalling that the same God sent both the bad and the good. If you're living under the shadow of guilt and shame you may find it difficult to embrace the good that's been declared over your life. You must start to visualize yourself as God has seen you: by flipping your fear upside down; causing its counterpart faith to stand up knowing that the same God who allowed it is the same God who will cause it to turn over for your good.

SCRIPTURE; Rom 8:31

SEPTEMBER 29

"AN ANCHOR"

And the Lord shall deliver me from every evil work, and will preserve me unto his heavenly kingdom: to whom be glory for ever and ever Amen (2 Tim 4:18)

In the natural when someone takes a boat or ship out into the ocean; to make certain the vessel doesn't go adrift an anchor is used to immobilize the carrier. Likewise, those of us who follow Christ also requires an immobilizer to keep us grounded and stable, we too need an anchor and that source is no other than Jesus Christ!

When the storms of life began to rage and to toss your resolve to and fro we can latch onto our greater strength Jesus. There came a time when Jesus and the 12 disciples entered into a ship to pass over unto the other side, that while Jesus lay asleep on a pillow a great storm arose (Mk 4:36-38): this could have proven to be a deadly situation but they were equipped with "an anchor". The bible says they woke Jesus who rebuked the wind and said unto the sea "peace be still" (Mk 4:39).

Whatever your plight know that you have been provided an anchor to get you through the storm; the rain may come, the storm can rage, but God has promised that "no weapon formed against you shall prosper" (Isa 54:17a). You can look adversity in the face and proclaim the words of your deliverer; speak to your situation and declare "peace be still", not because you can carry the load, but it's Jesus because Jesus is an anchor for your soul, through the hope you have in him.

SCRIPTURE; Heb 4:13-16

SEPTEMBER 30

"A LONG WAY FROM HOME"

… go home to thy friends, and tell them how great things the Lord hath done for thee, and hath had compassion on thee (Mk 5:19b)

It's often simple to look back on what's been unaccomplished or left undone and become critical of oneself. We weigh ourselves against the dreams and desires of youth and oftentimes come up lacking;

peeking back on an old life doesn't bare detriment, becoming enthralled can and will.

One of the devices Satan uses to keep the Christian in bondage is self disappointment. If he can distract you long enough and defocus you from what progress you have made then he can temporary employee you in your own destruction: the game plan is for you to become preoccupied in your life failures; that you'll fail to realize that you're "a long way from home"; you're pass where you started and even if you are not where you initially thought you'd be today, you're ahead of your yesterday, every little bit count. Don't discount the progress you've made in your walk in God; the lord can see your struggles but he also knows your expected end. If you're ready to give Satan a black eye then stop criticizing and start praising God by thanking him for your progress!

SCRIPTURE; 1Pet 4:12-13

OCTOBER 1

"EVERYTHING YOU NEED"

The Lord know how to deliver the godly out of temptations; and to reserve the unjust unto the day of judgment to be punished (2pet 2:9)

God demonstrated a great truth to me through his divine creation. As we have entered into a new season certain changes are destined to take place; the bear will go into hibernation, the squirrel will squirrel away its food, insects will die while the trees prepare to sleep until the spring.

I looked at the trees around me today and God spoke he said "when I created the tree at that precise moment I equipped it with all it would ever need; to do all that is required for it to fulfill its purpose and mankind is no different. When God called you, when he created you, he made no mistake he supplied you with everything you needed to prosper and become a success in every arena in life! You might be struggling with how to tap into it but you know you've been equipped. Just as the tree has roots that goes deep into the earth to sustain its life during a time of inactivity; so to have God fortified you. Your source of wellness and health isn't from an outside representative you have been endowed with strength and power. Whatever life lesson you're currently addressing forbid it to overshadow the Christ in you, you are not haphazardly existing inside of you is everything you need to succeed!

SCRIPTURE; 2Pet 1:19-21

OCTOBER 2

"CONTAGIOUS"

Let your moderation be known unto all men, the Lord is at hand (Phil 4:5)

There is an old adage that says "laughter is contagious", but I've found that in whatever state you find yourself in that that state can be contagious. If you're feeling downtrodden in spirit or maybe even somewhat melancholy you can't go and latch unto the friend who sees very little good coming their way; what you're experiencing will ultimately trigger what they've been repressing and you'll end up throwing a pity party. When you're in a slump run to the crowd that reeks of hope; the hope you see vested in them will begin to supersede the negative that is trying to pull you down, and before long what you've been encountering will turn upside down.

As Peter and those waiting with him waited for the day of Pentecost the bible says "they were all on one accord in one place (Acts 2:7), which says because they all waited with expectancy, their hope in what Jesus promised became so contagious that after they became filled with the Holy Spirit and spoke with other tongues (Acts 2:4), and they each sold what possessions they had to make certain that none lacked (Acts 4:32). What you put out will determine what you'll intake, therefore sidestep the viral affection being passed along by those who have no hope; get you a daily dose of hope and watch the cloud of despair disappear!

SCRIPTURFE; Phil 4:8

OCTOBER 3

"DOUBLE ANOINTING"

... and Elisha said, I pray thee let a double portion of thy spirit be upon me (2Kings 2:9b)

Whenever the double portion of Elisha is spoken of it's generally with the notion that it would be awesome to be able to have that type of anointing on ones life; what isn't foretold or even misconstrued is this fact "the double anointing wasn't without cost". Elisha was used of God Justas was Elijah but because of what he was given he was called to a much higher standard. God is willing to provide to you a double dose of what he's given to the covering he's placed you under, but are you able to endure the position? Your gifting can't supersede your character; your character or integrity is what you do when no one is looking; it's the thing that causes your life to prosper when those around you seem to stall. You must pray for the anointing but also pray that you'll become well able too utilize it properly. Elisha did double the amount of miracles but I'm certain he shared double the amount of test as well, remember be careful of what you ask for because you can certainly get it!

SCRIPTURE; 2Kings 2:10-12

OCTOBER 4

"FAITHFUL OVER FEW"

His Lord said unto him, well done thou good and faithful servant; thou hast been faithful over a few things, I will make thee ruler over many things; enter thou into the joy of the Lord (Mt 25:21)

During the course of life we all shall be given specific instructions concerning that in which we have been given charge over. We are entrusted with certain task, including that of raising children for those who are parents, but before we'll make any real advancement in this life or the one to come we must prove ourselves to be numbered among those who are considered "faithful over few".

David understood this concept when he was just a boy tending sheep in his father field. When given charge over the sheep David realized to honor the privilege given (great or small) that it would be expedient for him to entreat the task as if God himself had given the decree: this is why when the lion and the bear came and took a lamb out of the flock he went after them and prevailed (1Sam 17:34-35)

Your meager beginnings are only a test; if you'll step outside of what you believe you deserve and prove to be a good steward over that in which you've already attained you'll find yourself positioned in a place just as David was (1Sam 17:55-58). How was this established? In the beginning when no one was looking he was faithful over few therefore God made him ruler over many!

SCRIPTURE; Luke 12:48

OCTOBER 5

"BITTER WATER"

... behold I will rain bread from heaven for you (Exo 16:4a)

During the time of the Israelites exodus out of Egypt they found themselves in the wilderness; in a place where there was no sterile drinking water. To all who encamped there this was a true travesty, but to the man of God who had just witnessed the great power of God with the freeing of these people, this would be another place for God to prove his excellence.

When led to a place of provision only to find what should have been attainable was not could in every way deter the soul of those who are unstable in their faith, but to those who will diminish the mountain by exalting their God the "bitter water" becomes a conduit in which God will manifest the miracle.

Just because we come to stagnant places in our lives doesn't assure that those seemingly unproductive situations will not produce; us getting there is not to defy the possibility of fruit upon our arrival, but us becoming bitter concerning the road God has paved for will. When Moses came to Marah and found that they could not drink of the water there because it was bitter (Exo 15:23), he cried unto the Lord and the Lord provided him with a remedy (Exo 15:25). If you've been led to a place of barrenness look out, this is the opportunity appointed unto you for a miracle. God used what was available to get them what was needed and he's willing to do the same for you. Have you done as Moses? Have you cried out unto the Lord? Do so and watch you "bitter water" become sweet!

SCRIPTURE; Exo 15:22-25

OCTOBER 6

"WILL YOUR MIND TO"

'I THANK God through Jesus Christ our Lord, so then with the mind I myself serve the law of God (Rom 7:25)

A lessoned I learned is "where the mind is the body will follow". Yesterday I decided I would re-incorporate aerobics into my exercise regiment. As I followed the instructor about 15 minutes into the routine I realized that my calves were crying out for relief; instead of lowering my step I pressed my way to finish my course. How was this possible? I willed my mind to refocus off of the pain and concentrate on how I was previously able to complete this routine in times past.

There will be instances when you'll find yourself face to face with conflict, trail and tribulations; it is however during these times that that we're instructed to endure the hardship as a good soldier (2Tim 2:3) and seek what steps are necessary to overcome and become victorious! You must "will your mind to"; to what? To do and go through what's required to obtain the prize. If its not saying what's been sewing inside of you, don't say it: it could be concerning your worship time, how often you exercise, the ability to break that bad habit; in essence it's whatever your plight is. You start winning once you will your mind to!

SCRIPTURE; Rom 5:3-5

OCTOBER 7

"HAVE TO OR WANT TO"

For to be carnally minded is death; but to be spiritually minded is life and peace (Ro 8:6)

One day as I thought about my life and the route it was taking, I can recall thinking "I guess I'll just have to do thus and so if this is the way God has planned my path", as soon as the thought fully processed I could hear the Spirit speak and say "why not want to do it instead of feeling as if you have to " immediately I became convicted in my spirit knowing that what I'd been doing (some of it) has been generated out of a sense of duty and not desire; Lord forgive me I repented.

As you take a critical look around, you should find that you're blessed above most, especially above those who have yet to come into the knowledge of the truth; consequently leaving us with a sense of desire and not duty. God doesn't want you to feel obligated to praise him, worship him or serve him; because you are not! As Jesus rode in on the colt those all around him began to cry out "blessed be the king who cometh in the name of the Lord" (Luke 19:38a): the Pharisees asked him to rebuke them, but Jesus answered "I tell you that if these should hold their peace the stones would immediately cry out" (Luke 19:39-40); you see those who cried out didn't have to they wanted to!

Thinking back on what has already been done for us at Calvary should be enough to invoke more than just dedication, it should illicit a pattern of love and the determination which makes one "want to and not feel as if I have too"; the love of God is not and can not be burdensome!

SCRPTURE; Mt 21:28-30

OCTOBER 8

"BEING OPEN"

Arise therefore and get thee down, and go with them, doubting nothing: for I have sent them (Acts 10:20)

Having a one track mind or a mind that's opposed to different can prove to be fatal in the life of the believer. During the making of the church had Peter not waited in expectation of what was uncommonly anticipated (the Holy Spirit, the comforter, a sign from above); at the direction of Jesus he would have missed the opportunity to be apart of a climatic event (Acts 2:2)

As followers of Christ we can't be so entangle in our own plans; forging ahead with what pleases self and fail to operate under the conception of "Lord this is what I'd like to do, it's what's been tugging at my heart strings: is it your divine will for my life? Being open to the ways and will of God say "Lord I heard you and because have not released me I won't go"; this is what separate the mature from the carnal; the dedicated from among the selfish: being open can be painful but I guarantee that it will always produce Gods best!

SCRIPTURE; Acts 10:28-44

OCTOBER 9

"PEOPLE NOT STEEPLES"

Therefore my beloved brethren be ye steadfast, unmovable, always abounding in the work of the Lord, for as much as you know that your labor is not in vain in the Lord (1Co 15:58)

One of the greatest gifts that's been bestowed upon people is the gift of the Holy Spirit that's come to dwell within us, and too lead us into all truth. There's a misconception in the world of Christianity; some think the church consist of brick and mortar when in essence we, us, the people of the living God are the church. In the old testament, before the life of Christ there was an ARK OF THE COVENANT erected and designated as the place where those who had been consecrated would go to hear from God (Exo 25:8-22). Overtime because God in his infinite wisdom knew that he would one day redeem us from the curse of the law and sin: a plan was constructed which would eliminate the need of a sanctuary and he would choose "people and not steeples" to dwell in and among.

You are not ordinary for within you dwells the spirit of the most high; which means you are capable of creativity, your life doesn't have to be mediocre, you have the ingenuity to produce far above your potential therefore you need to know that what you purposed to do is already blessed!

SCRIPTURE; 2Co 6:16

OCTOBER 10

"LOST TWICE"

For God so loved the world that he gave his only begotten son that whosoever believeth on him should not perish but have everlasting life (John3:16)

There are those who have chosen to live their lives according to what they feel, think or know. The travesty is that they fail to believe that one day everyone will stand before the judgment seat and be judged for what they've done in this life (2Co5:10). The good news is, for those who are still alive they have yet another chance to rectify themselves with God, but those who have passed from this life and shared the mindset that they would do what they wanted and suffer the consequences later, they're condemned already. In short they've been "lost twice".

Sin is often repetitious and while one is engrossed in it, it seem sweet, the word of God says that "Moses choose rather to suffer affliction with his people than to enjoy the pleasure of sin for a season (Heb 11:25). It's called pleasure for a season meaning it's destined to change: there is no feasible reason for anyone to be "lost twice", being lost in the beginning has a regiment for restoration, but there is no answer or way of escape if anyone is lost twice.

SCRIPTURE; 1John 1:9

OCTOBER 11

"GUILT FREE"

Stand fast therefore in the liberty wherewith Christ hath made us free, and be not entangled again with the yoke of bondage (Gal 5:1)

Looking to receive a divine truth today proved to be rewarding; as I meditated on what my life entails God showed me how pondering on the three years and six months I've been incarcerated thus far adds nothing to my portfolio, for it is certain that I can never do, say, think, or imagine anything that will change what has already been; I'm therefore reminded to focus on my today. This analogy can serve as a propeller in the lives of those who have been unable to push pass what travesties or mistakes they've made long enough to take on a "guilt free" posture.

Paul exclaims that "there is therefore no condemnation to them which are in Christ Jesus (Rom 8:1a); declaring by the will of God that what you've done in times past has not the authority or the ability to hold you in bondage because the Lord is that Spirit and where the Spirit of the Lord is there is liberty (2Co 3:16). Liberty in the Lord allows the unjust the right to become just; it makes way for the guilty to live "guilt free". If you'll meditate on what freedom in Christ has erased in your life you'll leave behind the falsehood of needing to make amends for the rest of your life and begin to enjoy what remains of the life you now have.

SCRIPTURE; 2Co 10:4-5

OCTOBER 12

"ALREADY WON"

The Lord shall fight for you, and you shall hold your peace (Exo 14:14)

In terms of fighting to win it is clearly understood that there is never a battle, a fight, a war that God has not won; a simple truth is this "whenever we take up the mantle of going out to conquer our own foes, we have just relinquished our grip on allowing Jesus the opportunity to fight for us".

What we oftentimes call a fight is what we should now refer to as "already won" for there has never been an instance when the Father, the Son or the Holy Spirit has inserted themselves into a situation and not prevailed! Why then do we take the posture of contending with a competitor who has already been defeated? We're instructed in the word to "cast all of our cares upon him for he cares for us (1Pet 5:7). Believing that you have to fight this battle alone is not biblical: looking back you'll find that it was always the hand of God that assisted with victories; some he even sent strong delusions to assure the win (see 2 Kings 7:5-6).

As you retire your fighting gear you'll witness the Lord get in hot pursuit of what's been pursuing you and utterly destroy it, remember "it's already won"!

SCRIPTURE; 2Cron 20:17)

OCTOBER 13

"TRUIMPH IN TROUBLED TIMES"

God is not man that he should lie; nor the son of man that he should repent: hath he said, and shall not do it? Or hath he spoken, and shall he not make it good? (Num 23:19)

As life throws opposition in our path one of the common things for us to do is to forget the first directive that was given before the storm. In Mark 4 Jesus and the disciple has entered a ship heading for the other side when turmoil hit and the ship is now full of water;

this causes them to awake Jesus who immediately puts to flight the disturbance and creates a great calm (Mk 4:37-40).

During this event the disciple has forgotten the first directive that Jesus has given before the crisis; he states "let us pass over to the other side (Mk 4:35). The storm could not prevent the declaration, it would transpire; not because of stature or privilege; it would happen because he has already spoken this truth and his word would never return unto him void (Isa 55).

Whatever you're dealing with today has not the ability to hurt you, what has been exposed in times past is destined to come too past; when the Lord spoke it nothing pressed him to speak, it wasn't declared for a lack of something to say; it was uttered in love and in truth. Hang on to your resolve and when you feel as if you can't stand the word says "....and having done all to stand, stand therefore..." (Eph 6:13b-14a), therefore hold onto your word for you are destined to "triumph in troubled times"
SCRIPTURE; Ps 40

OCTOBER 14

"ALL AROUND WORSHIP"

Giving thanks always for all things unto God and the Father in the name of the Lord Jesus Christ (Eph 5:20)

To describe what's being said in this hour would be to explain the simplicity of today's' title. "All around worship" is a concept not a command, it's a process contemplated and perceived from a heart of love and the willingness to be a doer and not a hearer only.

Paul instructs the church in Thessalonica "in everything give thanks: for this is the will of God in Christ Jesus concerning you (1Thess 5:18). How does one incorporate this into their everyday affairs? You do so when you fail to complain as you persevere through hardship;

it's implicated each time you restrain yourself from sinning with your mouth; it's portrayed as your soul cry out to the father for assistance and he verdict remains the same "my grace is sufficient for thee: for my strength is made perfect in weakness" (2Co12:9); and through it all you suffer not your feet to fail, this is the epitome of "all around worship"; it's not an experience it's a lifestyle!! SCRIPTURE; 2Co 4:8-9

OCTOBER 15

"PRATICE WHAT YOU EAT"

These were more noble than those in Thessalonica, in that they received the word with all readiness of mind, and searched the scriptures daily (Acts 17:11)

The Apostle Paul gives us two descriptions of the word as it pertains to food and drink. (1Co 3:2) gives us an example, however it is much more defined by the author of Hebrews (see chapter 5:12-14). Why do you suppose we're instructed to intake the word or to consume it? Could it be that mere reading won't sustain you in your walk? Are Paul and the unknown author implying that "the word of God is a vital substance used for the up keep or the nurturing of a life? We're often told that the life is in the blood and this is correct however spiritual life is in the word! In the natural if you eat healthy, exercise properly and get plenty of rest you should be able to pass a physical with high remarks: the same apply with your intake of the word! You must practice what you eat. When you on purpose sit down your novels and pick up your bible you'll find that what you couldn't endure is now doable and you're less apt to miss the mark because discerning the voice of the Lord becomes easier. On every page in each sentence the Lord has sent you an encrypted message that only you can decode; don't become complacent with just milk delve into the main course and begin to enjoy all that's named yours..

Remember milk is the substance all babies need to grow but once they begin to grow no longer does milk satisfy; something within cries for solid food. As it is in the natural so to be it in the spiritual, so, "practice what you eat"!

SCRIPTURE; Heb 5:12-14

OCTOBER 16

"I DECLARE WAR"

Wherefore take unto you the whole armor of God that ye may be able to withstand in the evil day, and having done all to stand, stand thereof... (Eph 6:13)

Growing up as I learned to play card games I can recall being taught to play the game called war. Both players would play a card and the highest card would win but if you both played the same card someone would say "I declare war"; which would lead to a procession of other cards being played and whoever played the best cards would win the round.

This concept can be implemented into the battle we encounter in our minds. Daily the enemy assumes the posture of attack with hopes of manipulating us onto the other side. 1Peter 1:13a explains that we should "grid up the loins of our minds, be sober and hope to the end" which says regardless of what's being thrown your way you can reach back for who you are in Christ, never wavering from the truth that God dwells within you and will strengthen you. Being sober doesn't suggest abstaining from intoxicating substances it gives you the rite of passage to remain cognizant of what is truth as you hope to the end.

As you're being bombarded with thoughts of failure, unworthiness, or anything that would lead you down a path of questions or bewilderment, use your tools, declare war! The scripture says to bring every thought into the obedience of Christ (2Co 10:5b); once you've done that begin to speak the word: exchange the lie for the truth and show the adversary that you're prepared to fight in order to contain your stability and obtain the blessing. Be vigilant endorse your dream by protecting our mind. Thought will either mature there or they'll die there; God has given you a voice in this now use it.

SCRIPTURE; 2Co 10:3-5

OCTOBER 17

"FRIEND OF MAMMON"

No servant can serve two masters; for he will hate the one, and love the other; or else he will hold to the one and despise the other, ye can not serve God and mammon (Luke 16:13)

Scripture dictates that there are only two types of people, the righteous and the wicked; those who do well, and those who practice evil; which are you? Now consider those that's within your circle of influence: Jesus exclaims that there's only one reason to make to yourselves friends of the mammon of unrighteousness; and that is when ye fail (Luke 16:9): in essence it's more like just in case, or I may have need of that because I'm not completely committed or convinced that my walk will be a productive one therefore "I'll make me a friend of mammon"

Be not deceived or persuaded by what the world has to offer, for all that is in the world is the lust of the flesh, the lust of the eye, and the pride of life and this is not of the father but of the world (1John 2:16). Everything which pertains to this life is temporal, destined to pass away. Your intended possessions should be eternal for God has promised you "the eyes have not seen, nor ear have heard type of blessings" (1Co 2:9), so don't pass up a sure thing and settle for a temporary fix because what God does he does forever and this includes making you a friend of God and not "a friend of mammon"!

SCRIPTURE; 1John 5:4

OCTOBER 18

"YOU HAVE SOMETHING TO DO"

The name of the Lord is a strong tower the righteous run into it and are safe (Pro 18:10)

A terrible place to find oneself in, is in a state of not doing anything. When God gives the decree to "be still and know that I'm God" (Ps 46:10), he's suggesting that you come to a place of rest, patience and fearlessness; it's not a command or request that you idly sit by and do nothing because "you have something to do". It takes assurance, trust and confidence to get to the place of being still: again "you have something to do"!

Elijah couldn't operate under the anointing of God without first believing; therefore the first thing you must do is believe. Hebrews 11:6 says "for without faith it is impossible to please him, for he that come to God must believe that he is….; believing entails standing sure of the word regardless of what's being thrown your way. Peter believed that when Jesus bid him to come that he would walk on water and he did (Mt14:29), however believing it still required physical action. What are you believing God too perform for you? Have you written the vision down and made it plain (Habakkuk 2:4-5)? Or have you become complacent as Eli; who failed to rebuke his sons for the evil they performed in the house of God (1Sam 3:13). Whatever your position remember that while you're waiting on God he's waiting on you because "you have something to do"!

SCRIPTURE; Pro 24:30-34

OCTOBER 19

"YOU CAN'T AFFORD IT"

But put ye on the Lord Jesus Christ, and make not provision for the flesh to fulfill the lust thereof (Rom 13:14)

Irrational decisions lead to consequences we're often not able to afford for when trouble comes it becomes hard for us to divvy up. If we were given the option to mete out our own prescription for punishment I'm certain that everyone would choose the proverbial slap on the wrist, but what happens when you're not considered when it's time to pay up? Is that the moment you discover that "you can't afford it"?

In the midst of a trail I realized what was my burden too bare was simply more than I could handle in and of myself but during this I was shown that if it had not been for the Lord who was on my side I would have cracked under this pressure. David experienced enormous pressure when he realized that the consequence for his sin would be the death of his son (2Sam 12:14), thank God for mercy!

At decision time make certain that you count up the cost, consider the whole picture and not just the temporary relief: temporary relief brings right now answers, but its fruit usually bears lasting, irreversible changes and "you can't afford it"!

SCRIPTURE; Rom 11:21-22

OCTOBER 20

"THE LORD HAS NEED OF YOU"

Come now and let us reason together, saith the Lord: though your sins be as scarlet, they shall be as snow; though they be as crimson, they shall be as wool. If you be willing and obedient you shall eat the good of the land (Isa 1:18-19)

As Jesus prepared to make his triumphed entry into Jerusalem he knew that this would be the time to make use of a particular colt that was born or breed for this cause. Others (especially the owner) may have thought the colt would be used in another fashion; they never imagined that theirs would be the one summoned to make history and employ a service for Jesus.

Just as the colts destiny was tied into the masters' plan, so too has yours been predestined. Yes you may have stumbled, making little or no use of your talents; considered an underdog or maybe even hopeless according to some standards, but you can disregard all negativity as you realize "the Lord has need of you". No it may not have come as or when you expected but the great news is "your new beginning is here, it has arrived! The Lord has sent forth a word which declares "loose them and let them go for the Lord has need of them (Mk11:2-3): hesitate not to come, make the journey; this is the movement and assignment designed to liberate you and allow your God to receive the glory, come now!

SCRIPTURE; Mk11:2-3

OCTOBER 21

"WHAT'S KILLING YOU"

Casting all your care upon him, for he careth for you (1Pet 5:7)

Peter encourage us he informs us to think it not strange concerning the fiery trails which is to try us as though some strange thing happen unto you (1Pet 2:12); the pivotal point being made here is "trails will happen": your station in Christ does not deter the turbulence of the trail but it will place you on the winning side of the trail because you're in Christ.

On Saturday as I struggled in my flesh with where God had allowed me to be positioned, in my spirit I poured out my complaint before God (I prayed in the spirit): as I cried unto to God I began to say Lord this is killing me; immediately I heard him say "that's what I want to happen" it was then that I understood that he spoke not of a physical death but referred to me dying to myself, you see God can't completely use us when we're in the way. There is a process called death that must manifest so that we can freely live, so, what's killing you? Is it a burden you're trying to come from under? Or could it be the ministrations you're using to win the soul of a loved one for Christ? Whatever your plight know that as you die out to the Lord he'll begin to resurrect your desire, it might be killing you but it's for your best!

SCRIPTURE; 1PET 4:19

OCTOBER 22

"HOT PURSUIT"

Fight the good fight of faith, lay hold of eternal life: whereunto thou art also called... (1Tim 6:12)

Does it seem as if your fire has gone out and you're no longer as diligent as you were when you were first saved? Have the sparkle sort of diminished and you can't quiet grab a hold of the oomph which lead you from one service to another? Maybe that isn't you and you're still running on full and haven't encountered any distractions, but if this is you and you're wondering how to put the zeal back into your walk consider past relationships you've had. When you first fell in love you romanced the person, you spent time alone, enjoyed each others company and this is what kept your motor running; it's no different with the Lord. It's time to romance God with his word, sing psalms and hymns as you share the intimate details of your day with him. As you begin to recapture the moment you'll see that what you thought lost was never gone, you just couldn't see it because your attention was elsewhere, God has never moved!

To re-establish acquaintance you need to get in "hot pursuit"; he's not running away from you, he's trying to get to you; pray that God will give you your drive back, now all that's required is for you to take the needed steps to obtain it!

SCRIPTURE; Heb 6:4-6

OCTOBER 23

"TEETERING"

For you have not received the spirit of bondage again to fear: but you have received the spirit of adoption, whereby we cry, Abba, father (Rom 8:15)

Being on the brink of a discovery which pans out will lead to a place of celebration and positive change for those it directly affect, but what happens when you're teetering on the brink and it's an unproductive experience for all intended parties? What do you do when your life flash before you and you realize you've begun to teeter slightly backwards; in the opposite direction in which you've been called? First you must come to the realization that yours is not the first life that has been affected in this capacity and neither will it be the last. This mindset will steer you away from guilt and condemnation: now it's time to focus, focus on what caused you to nibble away; ponder in your heart how and why this happened and why you, lastly you must use corrective measures. Begin to casually remove yourself from opposition, ease back into a place of safety, and as fast as you can, head in the direction you were initially called too. Refuse to be like Jonah who knew and understood he Lords will for his life but decided to ignore it and run from his presence instead (Jonah 1:2-3). Reposition yourself, now walk it out; just when you thought you couldn't along comes God who'll show up, strengthens you and proves yes you can!

SCRIPTURE; Rom 8:26-27

OCTOBER 24

"ARE YOU IN MOAB"?

If we judge ourselves, we should not be judged (1Co 11:31)

The next verse too today's scripture reads "but when we are judged, we are chastened of the Lord, that we should not be condemned with the world (1Co 11:32). The implication is this; periodically it's important that we take self examination lest we be deceived, believing ourselves to be something when we are not.

As the Israelites came to their last destination before crossing over to enter into the promise land; they became engrossed in the pit stop and began to commit whoredom with the daughters of Moab, sacrificed to their gods and joined themselves unto their gods (Num25:1-3) (paraphrase). What happened? Had they become preoccupied with the length of the passage and not the manner of provision and love generated during this passage?

If you're facing a situation and your Moab is beginning to entice you consider what the Israelites failed to overview; the last stop signifies you're almost there and the next stop takes you to the promise. You can cancel the assignment of the adversary by taking precautions to see and understand what the will of God is for your life; don't become flustered and frustrated because of the ride: remember your Moab is only a portion of what is named yours, now you decide.

SCRIPTURE; Isa 60:11

OCTOBER 25

"IN THE SIMLITUDE OF GOD"

And when he had called unto his twelve disciples, he gave them power against unclean spirits, to cast them out, and to heal all manner of spirits, and all manner of disease (Mt 10:1)

Genesis 1:26 states "so God created man in his own images, in the image of God created he him; male and female created he them". Looking at the natural man its safe to assume that he spoke not of the appearance of man but of what he had empowered man to do. We were made in the similitude of God which enables us to operate in the power of God.

It was never intended that we become victims of our circumstances, nor did God desire us to not have dominion over the work of his hands (Isa 45:11b); you may not look like God but you have been equipped, not by man or any other entity, but by God to say, create, and demonstrate in the exact manner as God has and does. It's unnecessary to primp and preen attempting to redress who you are they'll no who you are as they witness the results in your life.

When man fell the ability bestowed upon him became ineffective, he inadvertently relinquished his power, but God who is longsuffering with man re-established man and power with the death, burial and resurrection of Christ Acts 1:8). Begin to conquer and create, you have the ability to call those things which be not as though they were (Rom 4:17), it's in the word!

SCRIPTURE; Mk 16:17-18

OCTOBER 26

"IT DEPENDS ON WHAT YOU DO IN IT"!

Now thanks be to God, which always causeth us to triumph in Christ, and maketh manifest the savour of his knowledge by us in every place (2Co 2:14)

Helplessness is not what God has called you to be; no matter the situation, bond or free, you have been given liberty! Yes even in the midst of a seemingly powerless situation there is an answer and the answer is "it depends what you do in it"!

Goliath was a prototype of storm for young David (1Sam 17:1-51), prison was a format that could have deterred Peter (Acts 12:1-7), Steven at the threat of death failed not to proclaim Jesus (Acts 7:56-60): these are just a few examples of those who faltered not at the chaos surrounding them but knew the outcome would bare witness of what they did while they were in them.

Your situation might not call for a sling and five smooth stones (1Sam 17:40), it does however require that you utilize the hidden resources you've acquired in God too overcome that in which is threatening to overtake you. Your victory isn't completely tied up in just making it through, that's half the battle the other half is perched upon what you do while you're in it!

SCRIPTURE; Rom 8:35-37

OCTOBER 27

"OUCH"

If you endure chastening, God dealeth with you as with sons; for what son is he whom the father chasteneth not? (Heb 12:7)

You're probably examining your perplexities and all that you're up against and no feasible answers are surfacing which would explain your pain; well the truth is "what you're experiencing is for your good. Yes, that's correct you're being pruned for greater. Jesus said "every branch that beareth fruit, he purgeth it, that it may bring forth more fruit (John 15:1b): again the word says "for whom the Lord loveth he chasteneth, and scourgeth every son whom he receiveth (Heb 12:6).

Your light affliction is but for a season and we know in God seasons have temperament and aren't apt to last long; neither will they produce above what you are able to bare; the process is never painless however the results are life changing. Consider the great men and women of God who suffered lest you become discouraged and faint in your mind. In John 10:10 Jesus exclaims "the thief cometh not but to steal, kill and destroy"; if he can get you to focus on the pain and or the process he can steal your fruit. So "ouch", it maybe a little uncomfortable but if you'll allow it to have its perfect work they'll soon call you the planting of the Lord!

SCRIPTURE; Heb 12:11-13

OCTOBER 28

"RE-CALIBRATE"

For thus saith the Lord God, the Holy one of Israel; in returning and rest ye shall be saved; in quite and confidence shall be your strength (Isa 30:15a)

We're admonished in the word to "be ye transformed by the renewing of your minds (Rom 12:2b) to insure that the old us or the former conditions we once operated in will no longer guide or lead us during the course of living. But what happens when you've sat up under the word, meditated on the word and know beyond a doubt that the word has transformed your mind along with those things you previously surrendered, but you've found yourself becoming somewhat sluggish in your actions or deeds? The simple truth is this is the time that you must "re-calibrate": taking the time to make the needed adjustments to bring you into alignment with that in which you've already attained!

Don't allow your focus to drift or your focus to diminish "recalibrate". When the enemy says "you've not changed you're still the same" realize that he's doing his job, he's doing what he's done from the beginning, he's lying; the word has transformed your mind you just have to make certain that you continue therein!

SCRIPTURE; Isa 43:16-18

OCTOBER 29

"WHEN GOD SAYS YES,SATAN WILL TELL YOU NO"

I have spoken it, I will also bring it to pass: I have purposed it, I will also do it (Isa 46:11b)

The concept or the principle of having eyes and see not, or ears and hear not (Mk 8:18)is one that has interrupted the lives of many; it signifies and under scores the ability to misconstrue what is being administered or spoken in ones life. Clearly it is the will of God for each of us to understand his divine will for our lives. We fit into a designated pattern that the enemy works diligently at trying to redirect. You heard correctly, God did tell you yes, but when the pain strikes or the deadline is fast approaching Satan will send someone to be about their fathers business; the spirit of fear will show up, the spirit of doubt will begin to interject and tell you it isn't so; attempting to annul the yes you heard in your spirit. To doubt the word is to undermine God, hold on to your first word for God hasn't changed his mind his yes is yes!

SCRIPTURE; Isa 44:2-3

OCTOBER 30

"DON'T WORRY ABOUT THE PROCESS, MEDITATE ON THE OUTCOME"

If they obey and serve him, they shall spend their days in prosperity, and their years in pleasures (Job 36:11)

To overlook current dilemmas isn't always an easy feat to accomplish: they usually come loaded down with grievous burdens, equipped with heart piercing questions and with what appears to be an endless timetable. The truth is all that has been described may be factual but it is never to become a focal point if you intend to make it through successfully.

Moses was given the task of leading the chosen people of God into a place called promise. This eleven day journey would become a forty year excursion. In the face of opposition Moses understood this "he couldn't allow himself to worry about the process, instead he would meditate on the outcome! Moses wouldn't be allowed passage but he would do what no other had been esteemed to accomplish. Stop looking at your natural situation, it isn't about the process but about what is destined to yield later, now meditate on that!

SCRIPTURE; Pro 21:1

OCTOBER 31

"GODS LOVE IS A CONSTANT"

Greater love hath no man than this, that a man would lay down his life for his friends (John 15:13)

I heard a slogan while growing up that says "there's nothing constant but change" and for many years I believed that. One day I came into the knowledge of whom and what God meant to me and realized that change isn't the only constant, so is the love of God! David understood this concept as he composes the 139th Psalm: in the 7-8 verse he writes "whither shall I go from thy presence, if I ascend up into heaven, thou art there, if I make my bed in hell, behold thou art there". God himself won't reside in hell but what's ascribed is the notion that everything that is anything was fashioned through God and when he created he did so in love: those who make their beds in hell shouldn't look to see God; they will however visualize the works of his hands!

When everything around you appears to be crumbling and you can't tell your left from your right, know that you have not been abandoned. The love of God will show up in your life in an embrace, and chase away the façade of emptiness. How will you identify it? You'll recognize it in the smile of a stranger, with the touch of a concerned someone; its shown when you receive mercy and not judgment and in the fact that you are allowed to live, move and have your being (Acts 17:28) along with knowing that you are fearfully and wonderfully made (Ps 139:14a): the next time that you're feeling unloved do a review of your life and be reminded that "Gods love is a constant" and your being alive proves it!

SCRIPTURE; 1John 4:15-19

NOVEMBER 1

"HE'LL BRING YOU THROUGH IT ALL"

Come unto me, all ye that labor and are heavy laden, and I will give you rest (Mty11:28)

Sometimes it's crucial that we stop and acknowledge that even when hardships are upon us and the drama won't seem to stop; if we lean on the rock called Jesus, hold onto our profession for that in which we have declared and decreed according to the word that we will enlist the truth which is "he'll bring us through it all".

Becoming distracted is a reality that each of us face. What is needed is for us to invoke extra time in concentrating on the way maker, and not the way. The word never said that it would be easy in fact Jesus states the opposite in saying "in this world you shall have many tribulations: but be of good cheer; I have overcome the world (John 16:33b); in short he's saying, oh yes you'll encounter turmoil, disappointments and trails but know this "I'll bring you through them all" as long as you don't quit.

SCRIPTURE; Isa 61:4

NOVEMBER 2

"DON'T QUIT"

...let us lay aside every weight and the sin which doth so easily beset us, and let us run with endurance the race that is set before us (Heb 12:1b)

Some may think it totally necessary to abort a plan or stop an action before it considered quitting but this is far from factual. Before a person ever quit or stop they actually stop in their hearts before the mind and body follow.

Today someone is thinking about giving up, some have already quit in their heart, while others are possibly straddling the fence questioning their level of commitment; allow me to encourage you, "if you're at the point of quitting that means you're at the point of breakthrough", this is why the enemy has turned up the heat. He wants you to become fed up and stop: stop believing that it will happen, stop looking forward to it happening and stop waiting for it to happen, but don't quit, he may not come when you want him but he's never late!

For those who have said oh that isn't me I haven't stopped, I'm just as dedicated today as I was when I first started, remember repetition isn't the formula that says you're okay. When Jesus spoke of the Pharisees he said "these people honor me with their lips but their hearts are far from me; they had long ago stopped in their hearts but continued to go through the motions; but again that isn't you therefore do me a favor and let your friend or neighbor read today's devotion, it's for them; wink, wink!

SCRIPTURE; 2PETER 3:8-9

NOVEMBER 3

"THE LORD HAS A REASON"

Let us hold fast the profession of our faith without wavering: for he is faithful that promised (Heb 10:23)

Consider all that the Lord instructed Moses to do in reference to consecrating and anointing Aaron and his sons before the Lord: even as we read and begin to understand the book of the laws there is no practical reason (within man's reasoning) why this formality would be necessary, needless to say, "the Lord had a reason". In the natural we deal in reason and logic and when a particular something makes no sense we dismiss it as frivolous but there is nothing frivolous or unnecessary in the ways of God; just because you aren't completely privy to all of the facts doesn't declare it as illogical.

When the Lord sent Moses to Pharaoh to free the Israelites the word says that the Lord declared "and I will harden Pharaohs heart and multiply my signs and wonders in the land of Egypt. To the minds eye this seems like a contradiction of what God has spoken, but in the spirit God was creating what had never been done before; again the Lord has a reason: for in the end it says that Pharaoh released them and they left with the wealth of Egypt (Exo 12:36). If you're up against something in your life and its baffling to the natural eye, trust that "the Lord has a reason". Joseph had to go through the prison to get to the palace and you must go through the struggle to obtain your promise, your dream, your vision so be encouraged "the Lord has a reason"!

SCRIPTURE; 2Thess 2:15

NOVEMBER 4

"WARDING OFF BITTERNESS"

Follow peace with all men, and holiness, without which no man shall see the Lord (Heb 12:14)

Any adverse situation can be a breeding ground for bitterness, for in them strife can generate along with its negative counterparts called rivalry, anger, and wrath which will and can lead one onto the path of bitterness. The Lord showed me a truth this morning he opened my understanding and enlightened me with how the enemy has launched an attack on my mind, my life, yes through bitterness. Lately I've been preoccupied with the unfairness of the judicial system and inadvertently allowed a root of bitterness to spring up causing a temporary disconnection to the reason God allowed me to be here. He said "the system is man made and devised upon the reasoning of human thinking; it comes with flaws and it will fail: me on the other hand "I can do anything but fail", don't allow yourself to become bitter with an entity that is anything but absolute; either your hope is in the Lord or the worlds system but it can't be in both!

Hebrews 12:15 says looking diligently lest any man fail of the grace of God: lest any root of bitterness springing up trouble you, and thereby many be defiled, the operative phrase in this verse is "trouble you" meaning any bitterness you become enamored with troubles you; it puts your life in disarray and creates havoc for you. Therefore as much as is possible; live peaceably with all men as you ward off bitterness for in doing so you shall reap where another has planted, and receive the former and latter rain (Joel 2:23).

SCRIPTURE; Heb 13:1-2

NOVEMBER 5

"HOW YOU APPROACH GOD"

Let us therefore come boldly to the throne of grace, that we may obtain mercy, and find grace to help in time of need (Heb 4:16)

Here is a great truth that affects the way most people perceive and or communicate with God. Generally when we are born into the kingdom of God we have what I refer to as a spiritual defect: because our relationship is new and it must blossom our approach to god is usually done in the same manner as our approach to man; in doing so this stifles the hand of God and limits what could be transpiring for you.

Many of us have suffered at the hand of man, leaving us somewhat leery and distrustful and if this has become a pattern the after effect has the propensity to cause a lasting affect, but here's the good news the spiritual defect mentioned earlier is curable. As you become washed in the word you'll grow out of seeing God through mans eye, eventually you'll begin to witness that the only lasting effects that the father leaves behind are those bathed in love; he'll never treat you as others have. When this is unfolding you'll begin to visualize the father differently, making your approach to God more direct, without skepticism, open and honest: then you'll go boldly to the throne of grace believing that you'll receive that in which you've decreed and then it will begin to come to pass.

If there is a lack in your life that has failed to be met I implore you, reevaluate "how you approach God"; for when you approach him with confidence and faith you'll envision your desired help, but not until then.

SCRIPTURE; John 4:24

NOVEMBER 6

"HE'LL TRY WHAT TRIPPED YOU UP LAST TIME"

Behold I give unto you power to tread upon serpents and scorpions, and over all the power of the enemy: and nothing shall by any means hurt you (Luke 10:19)

As a believer it's impetrative that we understand one pertinent fact; just because you're saved, has declined the life you once participated in and now allow your life to speak of that in which you believe doesn't mean you're safe from the wiles of the devil. In fact and I can attest to this through personal experience "he'll try what tripped you up last time". In essence the vise you've been set free of given the power too overcome will be the exact instrument Satan will use to recommit the bondage you've been delivered of. The addict may suffer from dreams which involves drugs and alcohol, a cheat will be shown a way to get involved in a liaison; theses are just a couple of examples. If you're suffering through a bout of rather or not you've been completely healed and delivered disregard the thought because when God started the work he completed it in the very same act.

Philippians 1:6 says "being confident of this very thing, that he which hath begun a good work in you shall complete it until the day of Jesus Christ" subscribing that your deliverance has already been made eternal; therefore when the enemy attempts to trip you up again you must remember its completeness: no one can take it away, only you can lay it down!

SCRIPTURE; Rom 5:13-14

NOVEMBER 7

"BEEN THERE, DONE THAT, NEVER AGAIN"!

Stand fast therefore in the liberty wherewith Christ hath made us free, and be not entangled again with the yoke of bondage (Gal 5:1)

One of the most effectual tools we've been fortunate to have in our arsenal of weapons is the tool of experience: nothing is of more value than the learned lesson you've already obtained. Yesterdays devotional spoke of Satan launching the weapon of duplication too re-entangle you into a place of bondage; his disadvantage is that we've been equipped with a recall and at any given moment we're able to consult the trash can of our memories and recall any hardships or pain we've suffered; we can no w proclaim "been there done that never again". Why? Because we have the battle scars to prove the intensity of the battle, plus we remember the pain.

Don't allow anyone to tell you that it's not good to say never; I've learned therefore I share with you that never is a choice that you make and regardless of what's taking place in your life you must stand behind your choice. With that said I implore you to declare you're never: I'll never have another unfortunate year, I'll never be entangled with the yoke of bondage (Gal 5:1), I'll never go through what I've already encountered, why? Because I've been there, done that and never again, besides the Lord is your helper, what can man do to you, and if the Lord be for you, it's more than the world against you (Rom 8:31).

SCRIPTURE; Gal 5:16-17

NOVEMBER 8

"THRIFT STORE MENTALITY"

For when we were yet without strength, in due time Christ died for the ungodly (Rom 5:6)

Imagine being offered the opportunity to go on an all inclusive 21 day cruise at no expense, but being afraid to except the offer because you feel somehow that you're unworthy. You probably can't imagine something of this magnitude actually happening right? But I tell you of a greater, there are those who suffer from a bout of guilt, unforgiveness and self condemnation that they have refused to believe that God in all his splendor will or can forgive them; only because they have not the wherewithal to forgive themselves. They're living under a façade that they've done too much, and asked for forgiveness only to revert back to what they've been forgiven of and this now has made them unworthy, not so. God has offered you a mansion in the kingdom: he established this order through the blood of Jesus. You can't allow a "thrift store mentality" tell you that you can't spend your money else where, that you're unworthy of the riches in glory because of your past. When God created you he had a divine purpose in mind the word says that even the hair on your head is numbered. He didn't make you like another and neither is another made like you; stop believing that you don't when you do, you can't allow a thrift store mentality keep you out of the finest establishments, they were made for you also. The word tells us that "the kingdom of heaven suffereth violence, and the violent taketh by force (Mt 11:12) therefore you must stand up and say something!

SCRIPTURE; Rom 10:11-13

NOVEMBER 9

"NOT AS GOD INTENDED"

For he that soweth to his flesh shall of his flesh reap corruption: but he that soweth to the spirit shall of the spirit reap life everlasting (Gal 6:8)

I took a hard look around me today and what I noticed was disturbing. On the news I heard of sudden destruction ; as I watched Trinity Broadcasting Network I witnessed the fatalities of small children, men and women lost or caught up in the snare of hunger and disease and it was at that moment that I realized that all was "not as God intended". When God began creation, after each pronounced action became a reality God declared "and God saw that it was good (Gen 1:10b).

We're living in the time of the prophetic. Jesus spoke of this day when he declared "and nation shall rise against nation, and kingdom against kingdom, and there shall be famines and pestilences and earthquakes in divers' places. All these are the beginning of sorrows (Mt 24:7-8). Even though it's of a truth that we must transition into such a phase it's also factual that initially this was not Gods plan for mankind. When the divine plan was aborted we were left with the consequences of having to discern good and evil; this is why our lives reek of the choices we've made: some inherit chaos, but most created it.

Maybe you're on a road that has veered off course and you've found yourself becoming distracted with prior mishaps, or maybe you're simply meandering around in where you see yourself on the body of Christ or you may not be physically going through anything but if one member suffer than all members suffer (1Co 12:26a) (paraphrase); the thing God wants you to know is this "everything may not be as intended but he has made provision to bring everything full circle and place it into to its intended purpose. Weeping may endure for a night but joy cometh with the morning!

SCRIPTURE; Gal 3:13-14

NOVEMBER 10

"A WORD IN DUE SEASON"

The Lord God hath given me the tongue of the learned, that I should know how to speak a word in due season to him that is weary (Isa 50:4)

Battling or fighting can be a tiresome ordeal; so much so that it'll cause those who have not been rooted and grounded to reconsider their stance (I know I've been there, thank God for second chances). It's also true that even those who have built their houses upon the rock can at some juncture become weary of the fight or the wait.

Those who have been walking this path the Lord wants you to know that just as he sent Isaiah unto those who were held in captivity in Babylon to ease their minds and bring peace to their hearts, so has he provided for you. You might be looking for a person to personally deliver you a word in due season but when God wants to speak to you he'll speak through the pages of this book! He'll amplify his word to you using a method that will insure that it was the Lord delivering you a word in due season.

You may have thought that you couldn't last another day if the answer didn't show up soon; that you'd faint along the way but God is saying "hearken unto my voice and know how to hear me in spite of what's going on around you; it isn't as it appear, what you went through yesterday was for your tomorrows". It may have hurt a little it but it can't kill you. If you're sick in your body you can speak life where disease abounds and it has to obey. "Be ye not weary in well doing, for in due season you shall reap if you faint not" (Gal 6:7); in other words your harvest depends on you making it out. Solomon said if ye faint in the day of adversity thy strength is small (Pro 24:10); it's not as bad as it look you must stop giving your situation a once over and begin to examine it with the mind of Christ: it's not getting worse because it's destined to get better. Now declare I believe God because there's power in the spoken word!

SCRIPTURE; Isa 26:3

NOVEMBER 11

"THE LORD WALKS WITH YOU"

When thou passes through the waters, I will be with thee: and through the rivers, they shall not overflow thee, when thou walkest through the fire, thou shalt not be burned: and neither shall the flame kindle upon thee (Isa 43:2)

When the king gave the decree to throw the three Hebrew boys into the fire the scripture says "when he looked in he saw four men loose, walking in the midst of the fire and they had no hurt: and the fourth is like the son of God" (Dan 3:25). I dare to believe that as they were being bound and readied for travesty that they thought that God would show up in such magnitude: tat he'd not only deliver , but he'd also stand in the midst of the fire to insure no hurt. This would speak to the heart of those faced with dilemmas and difficulties saying whatever your plight "the Lord walks with you", he's only a prayer, a word away!

Be reminded that anything that's been demonstrated previously that God is fair enough to duplicate in your life. A need will never arise in your life that has not already been addressed through the life of another. Find your word and stay right there until deliverance comes; until then be reminded that you are not alone, "the Lord walks with you"; you may look to the ft or to the right and not see those you assumed would stand with you but be assured "the Lord walks with you"!

SCRIPTURE; Dan 1:9-15

NOVEMBER 12

"A CERTAIN SOMEONE"

And the Lord God said it is not good that man should be alone; I will make him an help meet for him (Gen 1:18)

This date will always be an important day in my life. Today my oldest sister was born; not to say that the dates of my other siblings aren't special, that's far from true; however this sister is that "certain someone" for me. Unlike my other two siblings we grew up in the same household and being a younger sister I always thought that she would compliment my life in a way that no other could or would and inadvertently she has. God allows us a "certain someone" in our life time rather their siblings, husbands, friends or wives; he knows that eventually we'll compliment one another; their lives are designed to enhance yours and visa-versa.

In 1kings 19:l9 Elijah would find Elisha that "certain someone" God had predestined he'd come in contact with too tutor and pass his mantle on to. Paul life would be intertwined with young Timothy, Peters with John and each of ours would intersect with Jesus! You may still be on the look out for that "certain someone" in your life, or maybe you've come across them but have not understood that this is their position, either way know this "you won't accomplish a lifetime without first making proper acquaintances. You're on the brink of a new discovery that's orchestrated by God and it's called to realign not just one household but two!

SCRIPTURE; Gen 1:21-25

NOVEMBER 13

"NOT SUPPOSE TO BE LIKE THIS"

And it shall come to pass, that as I watched over them, to pluck up, and to break down and to throw down and to destroy, and to afflict: so will I watch over them to build , and to plant, saith the Lord (Jer 31:28)

Often we look at our lives and adhere to the point that this is what God intended; if God wanted different he would have incorporated different into the genetics of my destiny, not so. We have different because we lusted and wavered against perfection: either we refused to be boggled down with rules and regulations or we instinctively decided that fast and easy surpassed the norm.

One day I saw myself as I were; here I was at 44 in the top bunk of a prison cell, away from loved ones with a few meager possessions finally realizing that my life was "not suppose to be like this": not simply because I desired more but understanding an insurmountable truth "my God who shall supply all of my needs according to his riches in glory" wanted to give me more!

David was satisfied with tending his fathers sheep but God had greater therefore he sent Samuel to anoint him king of Israel (1Sam 16:13). You may be like me today, you've had an epiphany and realized that "it's not suppose to be like this": don't just sit there start now, begin to take control of your situation; do what you can and watch the Lord do what you can't!

SCRIPTURE; Isa 42:6-7

NOVEMBER 14

"LIVING UNDER AN OPENED HEAVEN"

The Lord shall preserve thy going out and thy coming in from this time forth, and even for ever more (Ps 121:8)

What does living under an opened heaven means? It implies that you'll begin to reap the "in earth as it is in heaven" (Mt 6:10), you'll benefit from being able to ascend into the heavenly, take what has already been manifested there and descend with that foreknowledge into the earth and become established: therefore bringing about the perfect will of God in your life and in the lives of those closely knitted to you and around you. This gives you the resources needed to establish the perfected life destined yours. It entitles you to an all the time audience with God! With that said who doesn't want to live under an opened heaven right? But the truth is, not everyone will. This privilege will be for those selected to be selected by God. The word says "many are called but few are chosen", in other words you must recognize that you're called and answers.

Jacob understood this concept as he visualized the opened heaven in his life (Gen28:12), this would be the catalyst that would cause his soul to make a commitment unto the Lord (Gen 28:20-21). I imagine he saw all of the possibilities awaiting him if he'd position himself to be the recipient of an opened heaven and delighted himself in the opportunity.

You're meant to enjoy the knowledge, the fruitfulness and the goodness of heaven here on earth: this is why the scripture says "thy kingdom come, thy will be done, in earth as it is in heaven" (Mt 6:9). Don't miss what's meant to be yours because you've deflected the hand of God and walked away from "living under an opened heaven". God may be asking you to slow down, or the request could be for you to pick up the pace; either way it's expedient that you comply, you know where you are, now make the adjustment!

SCRIPTURE; Ezek 37:5-6

NOVEMBER 15

"EXTRA BAGGAGE"

...but the Lord will be the hope of his people, and the strength of the children of Israel (Joel 3:16b)

Aren't you glad that God isn't like the airline companies that charge a surcharge for any extra baggage you carry unto a flight? To be exact God welcomes you and all of the extra baggage that you have. It's his desire to alleviate you of the grievous burdens you've picked up along life's road. Understanding this we can never reach our full potential unless we dispose of the "extra baggage". Baggage comes in the form of hurts and disappointment; it'll weave itself into ones life during a time of waywardness and disobedience. It really isn't important how you acquire baggage it is however necessary that you rid yourself of it, for it has the ability to hold back and stagnate growth.

Today let us assume the posture of the man who lay by the pool waiting on the troubling of the water (Johnb5:1-8). He had no idea that Jesus would come by and bestow upon him what he'd waited long and diligently for; his faithfulness paid off. If you'll let down your guard, eliminate all pretense, let bygones be bygones and stop censuring those around you with a critical eye, the extra baggage you brought into your relationship with Christ will stop and desist. He never asked you to carry the load, he said "casting all your care upon him for he careth for you (1Pet 5:7)

SCRIPTURE; Joel 2:27

NOVEMBER 16

"HINDRANCES"

Wherefore we would have come unto you, even I Paul, once and again, but Satan hindered us (Thes 2:18)

While in the waiting room you must always consider this truth, if you believe that the Lord has spoken the word to wait Satan himself will use the elements available to hinder the work in your life.

The titled scripture gives us a fore look into the possibilities of delays producing itself within a consecutive manner. Paul declares "once and again", which is to profess an attempt of at least twice that he Paul made to come to the aid or assistance of those in Thessalonica. When the Lord speaks a word to wait he'll never place a stumbling block in your path to hinder! "Hindrances" derives from the work of the enemy, created to steal the believers hope, faith and ultimately an eternal life within the kingdom of heaven.

As you're in the waiting room of expectation refuse to become confused or even manipulated out of your place. The wait my seem long with the distractions happening at break neck pace, but you're in the right place diligence always proceed due season; therefore if you'll stand fast, press forward and trust in whom you have always believed you'll find that "hindrances" only hinder or stop temporarily they don't have the quality to undo what God has said will be!

SCRIPTURE; Habakkuk 2:3

NOVEMBER 17

"THE MIND; A WEAPON"

And be not conformed to this world. But be ye transformed by the renewing of your mind, that you may prove what is that good, and acceptable, and perfect will of God (Rom 12:2)

To misunderstand the concept of taking control of your thought life and your mind could render the believer helpless. The mind is a weapon and to make certain it's always operable you must take the necessary precautions to make certain that you're caring for it in a manner that will assure it remains in top working form. When or if we allow our minds to become cluttered with thoughts that run contrary to the word then we have failed to keep our weapon (the mind) in a working condition that will work for us and not against us. Isaiah 26:3 declares "thou will keep him in perfect peace, whose mind is stayed on thee, because thou trusteth in him". This is the formula designed to keep the believer in a place of clarity; when the mind is clear of debris the enemy can't hold you hostage or captive in relation to what was or what is to be. He desires to disarm you therefore he attacks the mind by sending leading and intrusive thoughts just remember that Jesus said "I have come that they may have life and it more abundantly (John 10:10), take hold of the word.

Paul told the church in Corinth to cast down imaginations or any high thing that would exalt itself against the knowledge of God and bringing into captivity every thought to the obedience of Christ (2Co 10:5). You do likewise, don't allow your mind to control you, you control your mind; it's your weapon for success!

SCRIPTURE; 1Tim 4:15-16

NOVEMBER 18

"YIELDED VESSELS"

No man can serve two masters; for either he will hate the one, and love the other, or else he will hold to the one, and despise the other. Ye can not serve God and mammon (Mt6:24)

Unbeknownst to each of us we have been and will always be "yielded vessels" at the quick disposal of either the Lord or Satan, our lifestyles will reflect which.

In Paul's second epistle to Timothy he teaches "but in a great house there are not only vessels of gold and silver, but also of wood and of earth; and some to honor, and some to dishonor", if a man therefore purge himself from these, he shall be a vessel of honor, sanctified, and meet for the master's use, and prepared unto every good work (2Tim 2:20-21): he speaks of us as children of the kingdom in and before our changed states. Is it possible to be converted from a lowly state? Sure, the word says "if we purge ourselves, meaning you must do the express opposite of what you've become accustomed too; no longer practicing nor walking in a manner which belies what is now professed, for that in which you've yielded your members too will ultimately rule: for it is written " ye can not drink the cup of the Lord, and the cup of devils: ye can not be partakers of the Lord's table, and of the table of devil's (1Co 10:21). You cannot serve God and mammon (Mt 6:24b)

Today is a time of reflection, the hour to look over ones life and evaluate the type of vessel you are as opposed to the type of vessel you're striving to become. If you're not where you thought you were now is the time to make the adjustments. Or maybe you've made the adjustment but find yourself falling short to often; be encouraged we strive for perfection however the word says "but we know that when he shall appear, then we shall be like him" (1John 3:2), rejoice the day of the Lord is at hand.

SCRIPTURE; Ps 139:23-24

NOVEMBER 19

"QUENCH NOT THE SPIRIT"

Verily, verily, I say unto you, he that believeth on me, the works that I do shall he do also; and greater works than these shall he do: because I go unto my father (John 14:12)

In times past I thought I knew exactly what "quench not the spirit entailed", but God who is faithful to revolutionalize your life through revelation downloaded into my spirit "when we shun our obligation to work and operate in the power of the Holy Ghost we inadvertently "quench the spirit". We've been endowed with an irrefutable gift of power that demands our attention: it's relevant so that we can operate in the earth as direct conduits of God to accomplish healings, miracles and wonders; to embellish our lives and the lives of our loved ones. Why then do we fail to comply? Could it be that we simply don't believe? Have we dismissed the power which lay within because we consider it something done in biblical times, not necessarily for this age; something mystifying, or above our comprehension?

When the word was written it wasn't designed to fail, Jesus said "till heaven and earth pass away one jot or tittle shall in no wise pass from the law, till all be fulfilled (Mt 5:18). You are a speaking spirit that has the propensity to turn the world upside down as Paul did; "quench not the spirit". Actively submit yourself to the power within you, refuse to live beneath your potential: God has already created what you need, for he has given you the spirit of power (2Tim 1:7b) now operate therein.

SCRIPTURE; Acts 1:8

NOVEMBER 20

"A PLACE OF ILL REPUTE"

Who hath saved us and called us with a Holy calling, not according to our works, but according to his own purpose and grace, which was given us in Christ Jesus before the world began (2Tim 1:9)

Everyone has been saved from something; we each share a common ground, we each are saved by grace! If you delved into my meager beginnings you may find that we frequented some of the same bad choices, and entertained almost identical heartaches: subsequently these things won't define us they'll only serve as a testament of the awesomeness of God! Take Rahab for instance she ran and operated a place of ill repute, but God would use these same quarters to provide a way of escape for those who were sent in to spy out the land (Jos 2:4). In the natural one would think that nothing good would come out of a place like that, however God wants to impress upon you this "you're discounting your situation because it appears hopeless, but when faith in self fails, trust in the Lord should abound"! You're not qualified to bring yourself out but with God nothing shall be impossible; your demons are destined to become your doormat and the places you thought would hold you back were designed to prosper you. Stop looking back on where you were; you can't see your future with you head in that direction; don't despise your small beginnings!

SCRIPTURE; Jos 1:2-6

NOVEMBER 21

"NOT EVEN A LITTLE BIT"

When I walk through the valley of the shadow of death I will fear no evil, for thou art with me, thy rod thy staff, thou comforts me (Ps 23:4)

Lets face it none of us would sign up for adversity of any type. To be brutally honest I believe we'd even appreciate when trouble comes our way if we had the option of eluding it all together. I was employed with this important truth as I sat begrudging myself of all that I'd endured from childhood until now. In my heart I began to cry out to God saying "Lord maybe things would have been different and I wouldn't be going through what I'm enduring now if you hadn't allowed thus and thus; this is when God spoke back and said "what you went through was for what you were destined to receive and become; relief from past hurts or pain would have stunted your growth, therefore "not even a little bit": if I would have changed one thing you wouldn't be headed in the direction you're headed in now; you wouldn't be able to distinguish my voice, understand my purpose, walk in my stature or heed my word! Your pain was destined to produce power. Stop focusing on your pain and look unto the hills from wench come your help (Ps 121:1).

Don't become convinced that you must exchange your pain for a temporary fix called immediate relief, you were built to do "all things through Christ who strengths you" (Phil 4:13), and yes God is talking about you!

SCRIPTURE; 1Tim 4:12

NOVEMBER 22

"WHAT'S THE DIFFERENCE"?

And Mary said behold the handmaid of the Lord; be it unto me according to thy word... (Luke 1:38)

Whenever you get into a quite place with God he'll begin to open unto you mysteries. You aren't obligated to take my word for it, but I implore you to try it and see don't you leave his presence more knowledgeable.

One evening as I entered into my quite place in my spirit I asked "why did everything Jesus spoke and all he put his hands to do prosper", since I was asking I inquired "why did it seem polar opposite for us as a people today"? God immediately replied "the only difference is; when Jesus operated he did so in complete confidence", we know this because he states "I know my father always hear me" (John 11).

You not having compete confidence in the word or in what you've asked the Lord to do in your life will ultimately become the tool used to hinder your progress. Of a certainty you will never promote 100% of due diligence to what you don't fully trust, and a lack of confidence is on the same rung of the ladder as a lack of trust. If you're seeing no real progress in your life and your growth appears to be at a standstill; check your confidence level, for it's what makes the difference between obtaining and always trying to acquire.

SCRIPTURE; Luke 1:45

NOVEMBER 23

"THAT DOESN'T BELONG TO YOU"

... forgetting those things which are behind and reaching forth unto those things which are before (Phil 3:13b)

How often have you found yourself looking back over your life pondering on how you could have done this or that differently? We cur 'see with the notion of if I could have, would have or should have without fully comprehending that "your past doesn't belong to you". 2Corinthains 5:17 says "therefore if any man be in Christ Jesus he is a new creature, old things are past away, behold all things have become new". Your new life in Christ doesn't come equipped with your past failures or faults; it does however allow for you to embark upon new endeavors as you strive to embellish what God has freely given you, a future , your future.

When those who were delivered out of Egypt came face to face with fear they would attempt to forfeit the future as they thought it better to return to the known than to face the unknown. They didn't realize that what God brought them out of no longer belonged to them, for he had already paid the debt when he paved the way. Attempting to rehash or reconstruct yesterday is not what you've been called to do; lay aside every weight and the sin which so easily beset you (Heb 12:1) what didn't happen for you was not destined to happen. Arrest your yesterday and go forth with your life; it probably doesn't look like it but something good is purposed to come your way. Don't miss your opportunity to grab it due to your hands being full of past yesterdays!

SCRIPTURE; Phil 3:14-15

NOVEMBER 24

"THE GIFT OF DISCERNMENT PLUS THE ADVANTAGE OF EXPERIENCE"

We have the same spirit of faith, according as it is written, I believe, and therefore have I spoken; we also believe and therefore speak (2Co 4:13)

A song writer once sang "experience is a good teacher"; now visualize experience coupled with discernment: what you should see is a person living in victory as they move from glory to glory. In the world we relied on a gut feeling to lead or prompt us. How often have you said "I don't know how I knew I just knew"? What you considered as your gut speaking was never really that at all. When God breathed into the nostrils of man the breath of life (Gen 2:7), transference was made that would cause us to intuitively know the heart of God: you've been endued with power. Taking what you know and coupling it with what God is speaking makes for the perfect combination to create the successful life you're seeking here in the earth.

Think about this; when Adam begun the task of naming what God created to populate the earth he didn't have to ponder nor confirm his choices with God, why? Because the God in him spoke and he just knew (Gen2:19)! What about you? Are you allowing the God in you to lead you and establish you in your going out and coming in? Have you coupled your experience with your ability to discern what's expedient for you? It's time, time to push pass the barriers and eliminate the excuses because you can do all things through Christ which strengths you!

SCRIPTURE; Ezek 37:9

NOVEMBER 25

"LIKE CHAFF IN THE WIND"

Whose fan is in his hand, and he will thoroughly purge his floor, and gather his wheat into the garner; but he will burn up the chaff with unquenchable fire (Mt 3:12)

In 2006 during a difficult season in my life the Lord showed me a vision. In the middle of a park I saw mountains spring up, but as I nudged the person sitting next to me to show them the mountains were no longer, they were trees swaying from side to side in the wind. I sought God for the interpretation and was led too "the problem present in your life showed up as a mountain. But as you survey it again you'll see that it becomes "chaff in the wind"!

That maybe your position today an unexpected expense or an unexpected event has shown up and it could mean disaster, however God wants you to know that "what look as if it's a mountain is but chaff in the wind and what appeared to have the strength to harm you or hold you back shall not come near thy dwelling. Why? Because the word says "blessed is the man (woman) that walketh not in the counsel of the ungodly, nor standeth in the way of the sinner, nor sitteth in the seat of the scornful; but his delight is in the law of the Lord (Ps 1:1-2), and whom God has blessed cannot be cursed. Therefore stop attempting to climb the mountain, you were never told to do so: Jesus said "whosoever say unto the mountain, be thou removed, and shall not doubt in his heart, but shall believe that those things shall come to pass: he shall have whatsoever he saith (Mk 11:23). Remember whenever mountains show up as obstacles God always show up as a mighty rushing wind.

SCRIPTURE; Ps 1:1-4

NOVEMBER 26

"ELIMINATION"

Let not then your good be evil spoken of (Rom 14:16)

We were designed in a fashion which makes elimination necessary. Daily we intake substances in our natural bodies and to continue in form we must eliminate these toxins before any unforeseen danger arise: now let us switch lanes. If the possibility of contamination is present within our natural bodies imagine the grave danger which lay ahead when we fail to consider what need to be eliminated in our spiritual lives. We look for spiritual promotion and have not the character to withstand it. We can't expect to be forgiven if we cannot forgive (Mt6:12), neither should we look for a harvest if we have not sown: Jesus said "give and it shall be given unto you; good measure, pressed down, and shaken together, and running over (Luke 6:38).

Is there something you need to get rid of? Are you holding a grudge? Or dealing with bitterness? Whatever you're dealing with know that the process of "elimination" has to take place before you can move forward; 1John 1:9 says "if we confess our sins he is faithful and just to forgive us our sins, and to cleanse us from all unrighteousness". Confession brings wholeness, for what is uncovered is no longer hid from the possibility of being made whole. Are you waiting on a turn around? If you'll get turned around spiritually you'll begin to see the hand of God move on your behalf, it's the word!

SCRIPTURE; Rom 14:19

NOVEMBER 27

"PRAY LEST YOU ENTER INTO TEMPTATION"

And he said unto them, why sleep ye? Rise and pray, lest ye enter into temptation (Luke 22:46)

Prayer isn't just dialogue! It consist of more than a one sided conversation that we have with God expressing those things that we're grateful for or the things that we have desire of. Prayer is also designed to build up the sluggish in spirit so that they may become rejuvenated. It's one of the most important tools available to the believer enabling them to ward off future failures.

When Jesus was on his way to the cross he instructed the disciples to "pray lest they enter into temptation" because he knew the time would come and he would no longer be as close to them as he was previously, and during this time the tempter would readily avail himself of an opportunity to wreck havoc in their lives. Luke 22:41 says that he was about a stones cast away: he wasn't in their direct line of vision but he remained within ear shot.

There may come a time when the presence of God isn't as near as in times past but we are not to fret as though we have no hope. During those times you're admonished to "pray lest you enter into temptation". If you're thinking why would the Lord permit himself to stand off while you're striving to stand, the answer is simple; he's attempting to move you unto higher ground: you're the toddler with unsteady steps and he's the father who beckons you to come with opened arms. Prayer is the conduit used to bring forth what' needed to get us to the next leg of our journey: it's when we fail to tap into what's been meted out to accommodate us during difficult periods that we become prey and do fall. Don't become the disciple who because of sorrow fell asleep on the job (Luke 22:45-46), didn't pray and eventually fell into temptation (see Luke 22:54-62); instead pray without ceasing (1Thes 5:17) which will keep you abreast of Satan who wishes to devour and steal.

SCRIPTURE; Philemon 1:4

NOVEMBER 28

"EXAMINATION BRINGS REVELATION"

Examine yourselves, whether ye be in the faith; prove your own selves (2Co 13:5a)

It doesn't matter why you visit a doctors office there are still customary procedures that will precede the doctors examination. A ritual is performed regardless of the symptoms; your vitals are assessed which helps to eliminate certain possibilities or shine light on other probabilities. "Examination will always bring revelation".

When we take the time to examine our motives, our intents, and our hearts we'll then come to a place where we're no longer impoverished concerning the tings of God; spiritual breakthroughs generally follow new revelations.

Before communion Paul admonish the church in Corinth to "let a man examine himself for to drink or eat of the sacraments in an unworthy manner would lead to damnation (1Co 11:28); he further say "if we judge ourselves, we should not be judged (1Co 11:31); in essence, search yourself to see if there be any wicked way in you; don't allow anything defiled to reside within. You must examine the thoughts and intent of your heart in doing so the "examination will bring revelation" that's destined to overturn judgment and produce lasting provision!

SCRIPTURE; 1Co 11:31-32

NOVEMBER 29

"INCREASE"

A good name is rather to be chosen than great riches, and loving favor than silver and gold (Pro 22:1)

In the year of the microwave generation and among those who are from the baby boomer decade; we hear a lot about increase. Increase has become so popular that some ministers will attempt to sell you a blessing from God by suggesting "if you give a particular monetary gift it will move the heart of God thereby prompting him into action concerning the need in your life; not so, God can't be bribed and increase isn't always about substance. 2John 1:2 says "beloved I wish above all things that thou mayest prosper and be in health even as thou soul prospereth "this declares that increase will address you in a well rounded manner. That Lord doesn't want you wealthy but unable to enjoy the fruit of your labor: for if you all things but have not love or a sound mind you'll be above all men most miserable. Gods' desire is for you to increase but it has to start from the inside out which will allow you to maintain it. Proverbs 15:27a says "he that is greedy for gain troubleth his own house". Take your time don't get in a rush, the Lord of the breakthrough has appointed unto you a daily increase and what God does he does it forever.

SCRIPTURE; Pro 30:7-9

NOVEMBER 30

"THEIR THOUGHTS"

Blessed is the man that endureth temptation; for when he is tried he shall receive the crown of life, which the Lord hath promised to them that love him (Jam 1:12)

During the life and times of Jesus Christ amongst his biggest critics were those who kept the law; they were called the Pharisees and the Sadducees. Oftentimes they would contemplate a thing within their heart against Jesus, but it would be during these occasions that Jesus would admonish them for their wicked thoughts and behavior (see Luke 11:37-53). Even when Jesus was faced with trepidation on every side he never allowed what others thought about or said about him to deter his actions. I would like to suggest to you that instead of him becoming engrossed in the thoughts of another he operated under this principal "what you think about me has not the decorum nor the ability to effect my life: it's what I think about you that will ultimately effect me! We should choose likewise.

We spend countless hours examining our lives through the eyes of others thereby becoming slighted or cheated. Don't allow the inane thoughts of another to become your reality, oftentimes they are either shortsighted or nearsighted either way you lose. A grave mistake would be to never figure out who you are, the answer lies within your grasp. Psalm 139:14 says "you are fearfully and wonderfully made". God called you his beloved (3John 1:2), Paul informs us that we are more than conquers (Rom 8:37): God isn't calling you to work at changing their mind he does however expect your walk of life to ultimately change their thinking!

SCRIPTURE; 1Peter 3:1-2

DECEMBER 1

"UNTAPPED RESOURCES"

As it is written I have made thee a father of many nations, before him whom he believed, even God , who quickeneth the dead, and calleth those things that be not as those they were (Rom 4:17)

We're designed with wells of living water the problem is, we decline to tap into the source and it therefore goes unused. Consider the rites and the extraordinary power Adam was given in the garden; Gen 2:19 says "out of the ground God formed every beast of the field, and every fowl of the air: and brought them to Adam to see what he would call them: and whatsoever Adam called them that was the name thereof", now meditate on this fact; Adam had the capability before he ever used it, it resided on the inside and when it became necessary he tapped into this unchallenged resource thereby declaring what would become an established truth now and forever!

Just as God initiated and supplied the essential source that would speak and call forth Adams untapped resource he has obligated himself to you as well. Inside of you the dexterity to create and attain has been instilled and at the precise moment you'll begin to operate in it.

You might be thinking that God hasn't called you for anything extraordinary because it hasn't showed up before now, but I challenge you to think outside of the norm and begin to tap into your untapped resource. Remember, one moment Adam was only a resident in the garden but when called upon he began to rule and name what would become a part of that same garden; you too have all that you need within to take dominion!

SCRIPTURE; Gen 2:22-25

DECEMBER 2

"NEEDING A TOUCH"

Can a woman forget her suckling child, that she should not have compassion on the son of her womb? Yea, they may forget, yet will I not forget thee (Isa 49:15)

In every believers life there will come a time when you believe that your strength is being depleted and you're not suitably equipped to handle what you're currently facing. You may begin to question whether or not the Holy Spirit guided you or if you made a wrong turn because of the havoc in your life: it's during an episode with this type of magnitude that you'll find that what you actually need is a touch from the Lord.

When Elijah strength was ebbing he went into the wilderness sat under a juniper tree and requested of himself that he might die (1Kings 19:4): God overlooked the request and instead he sent him a touch from above; Gods love commanded provision where Elijah lack demanded payment.

If you're "needing a touch" do like Elijah and go off into your own secluded space, get as comfortable as possible and begin to cry unto the Lord, your help is only a touch away; stay focused, be encouraged and be ready!

SCRIPTURE; 1Kings 19:4-8

DECEMBER 3

"LIFE IS GIVEN"

By the breath of God frost is given; and the breadth of the waters is straitened (Job 37:10)

For those who have no depth or insight into the workings of the supernatural it would be a small feat to believe that life is given once conception is established within the womb of a female. However in Genesis 1:27 the word of God declares "so God created man in his own image, in the image of God created he him, male and female created he them, therefore life was given before you were formed (cross reference with Gen 2:7).

Are you nursing a dream or in the transition phase of your dream becoming a reality, but nothing is lining up as it should? Could it be that you've deviated some and began to look for life from a source that has not proven itself, and therefore can never produce? Our featured scripture declares "by the breath of God frost is given" which exemplifies life only comes through God! Consider this; ice is made up of two chemical components water and a freezing temperature. The ingredients needed to compute ice is available but until God shows up and draw the life out of it it'll remain just water and cold. Don't allow your dream to die in the birthing process; forsake all forms of cultivating the dream and look unto the only source with the innate ability to bring what has been established into its natural state. It hasn't worked previously because you've been willing it to work and have decline God ability to breathe life into it. Through the breath of God ice is given and trough the same breath life is given to what's necessary to complete you.

SCRIPTURE; Job 37:23

DECEMBER 4

"A WINDOW OF OPPORTUNITY"

Then she came and told the man of God, and he said ,go, sell the oil, and pay thy debt, and live thou and thou children of the rest (2Kings 4:7)

Each day we are afforded the opportunity to embark and encroach upon new opportunities. Although realizing this we must also confirm this fact "with certain people, in certain instances, dealing with particular circumstances we're only given "a window of opportunity" to profess and proclaim that in which will be ours.

2Kings 4:4 speaks of a woman whose sons were being demanded of for the payment of a debt owed even in her distraught state she realized her "window of opportunity" had drawn near. She then would cry unto the prophet of God who gave her instructions concerning what was to be done and it would be through her obedience that she would get the provision she needed in spite of her lack. She took what she had in her hand and allowed God to multiply it.

What you don't have should not speak so loud that you close "windows of opportunities" under the presumption" I'm just not sure that this is God". John10:3 say "and the sheep hear his voice and a stranger they will not follow, but will flee from him: for they know not the voice of strangers". Even as Satan has the ability to transform himself into an angel of light (2Co 11:14) he could never be mistaken as the voice of God. Be encouraged if your "window of opportunity" hasn't presented itself it's on the way, and for those who've been starring at their chance but have been faulted between two opinions move now it really is happening!

SCRIPTURE; John 10:1-5

DECEMBER 5

"IT SHALL BE WELL"

When the enemy shall come in like a flood, the spirit of the Lord shall lift up a standard against him (Isa 59:19)

The miracle of the Shunammite woman is a verse of scripture that each of us can learn and grow from. It speaks of a mothers unfailing faith and the wisdom she portrayed as she regulated what she would allow herself to proclaim when faced with the death of her only child (paraphrase 2Kings4:18-37). When asked on two separate occasions the welfare of her child her reply would remain the same "it shall be well"; she spoke of what was to be, her hearts desire and not her reality; she refused to allow what was to remain what would be!

You may be dealing with a situation right now that belies everything you've hoped to maintain, or maybe an unexpected health issue, lay off or some other type of financial burden has arisen which threatens your resolve; worry not, you can take your cue from an old ancestor and begin to declare "it shall be well", for it's when you press pass the obvious and set your face like flint to obtain the necessary that you'll witness the miraculous change you need. Therefore instead of speaking what you feel utter words of life remembering that Jesus promised "you shall have what you say" (Mk 11:22)

SCRIPTURE; STUDY 2Kings 4:18-37

DECEMBER 6

"DEALING WITH DISAPPOINTMENT"

Looking unto Jesus the author and finisher of our faith: who for the joy that was set before him endured the cross, despising the shame, and is set down at the right hand of the throne of God (Heb 12:2)

Disappointment is a road that has many tunnels. You could be heading in what you assumed to be a progressive direction with insolvable plans and without prior warning you can find yourself in a full blown situation, nursing a bruised ego, a broken heart or a mountain of emotions you thought you conquered but there's only one way to deal with disappointment and that is to just do it! You deal with it and you get over it but while you deal with these two attributes you must learn from them.

When Moses defied God he lost his rites to enter into the Promised Land (Num20:12), however this set back or disappointment would not deter the promise or purpose for his life; instead of giving up, gripping or throwing a pity party he continued the journey set before him. Yes the same God that lead him along the way, instructed him step by step also commanded him access denied, but in Moses understanding this he considered it better to continue in the Lord and envision the promise land than to turn back with nothing leading to no where. When man disappoints the word says to forgive (Mt 6:12) and if you become disappointed concerning that in which you've inquired of the Lord; consider that you may have "asked and received not because you've asked a miss" (Jam

4:3), either way we deal with disappointment in love because love never fails (1Co 13:8a).

SCRIPTURE; 1Co 13:4-7

DECEMBER 7

"GOD IS UP TO SOMETHING"

… fear ye not, stand still and see the salvation of the Lord, which he will shew you today: for the Egyptians whom ye have seen to day, ye shall see them again no more for ever (Exo 14:13)

We often come to a place in our lives where everything seems to be out of control; we're feeling discombobulated and it seems as if we're running out of steam. No one desires to find themselves here but whenever we do we can rest assure that as we're depleted of the energy to continue to rise above our circumstances and we are down to nothing that "God is up to something".

During the great exodus out of Egypt Moses met a different type of adversary, the Red Sea. He had nothing within himself, no prior experience parting seas, but when he was down to nothing God was up to something (Exo 14:15-16) and to dispel Israel of any further attacks from these Egyptians the Lord utterly destroyed them (Exo 14:28). This would be a catalyst that would help to declare the greatness of God and cohesively bless his people.

Every trail isn't directly about you but each of them is designed to elevate you as they bring God the glory for getting you, taking you or carrying you through them all. God knows your weaknesses, your frailties; he's aware of your glitches and each one of your hang ups. Your hard place is of no surprise to the Lord he knew you'd be there. There's one other thing that the Lord knew as well, he knew you wouldn't be able to make it on your own therefore he met you there! Get into the presence of the Lord, now tarry there until you get your second wind; remember "God is up to something, especially if you're down to nothing!

SCRIPTURE; Exo 16:12-13

DECEMBER 8

"INVAULABLE"
I must work the works of him that sent me, while it is day; the night cometh when no man can work (John 9:4)

As I breezed past my past week I recognized one fact that stuck out most, I had failed to do what I knew to do: I didn't do what I said I would. I told myself that I would get up in the morning and run instead of hitting the gym after work I did neither. The next morning I got up and ran and realized that I had missed something "invaluable"; the time to do something that would alter and make a difference in my well being. I had time and space to make a change but failed to monopolize it!

Time is a privilege that each of us presume we have the truth is that we must rethink our position because time is a substance that we are running out of. Scripture says "the day of the Lord comes as a thief in the night" (1Thes 5:2) and if today is that day are we ready? Have you tied up your loose ends and done what's expected of by God? Have we made amends and forgiven those who have violated us in one fashion or another? What about being good stewards, have we utilized our gifts and talents to the fullest degree? Have we made a difference in at least one life? Will you stand before the Lord and find yourself lacking because you misused the precious commodity called time while it was yours to handle? Isn't it wonderful that this doesn't have to be your plight? God is so concerned about what you do with your time here in the earth that he sent you a friendly reminder; so get up and get moving life is waiting on you to happen.

SCRIPTURE; Eccles 8:6-7

DECEMBER 9

"VANITY"

A good name is better than precious ointment; and the day of death than the day of ones birth (Eccles 7:1)

In the book of Ecclesiastes Solomon shares that he's searched many devices under the sun and surmised that all is vanity and vexation of spirit (paraphrase). Previously I glanced at a talk show and I saw the host and a guest going from one food station to another taste testing samples of fine cuisine and giving reviews and was struck with how meaningless a life is if it gives God no glory.

We put our hands to many inventions and at the end of the day we've made no indent or imprint in the world if we have not done so for Christ. I firmly believe "only those things you do for Christ will last". Paul writes "every mans work shall be made manifest: for the day shall declare it, because it shall be revealed by fire; and the fire shall try every mans work of what sort it is" (1Co 3:13).

Life consist not of obtaining stature or wealth and living a carefree life; rather you're defined by the needs you meet for another, the joy you bring to a life, and what you do to edify the life of someone other than yourself. Solomon said it best in Ecclesiastes 12:13 when he wrote "let us hear the conclusion of the matter; fear God and keep his commandments; for this is the whole duty of man". When we follow this protocol we'll live productive, blessed lives, for all else is "vanity and vexation of spirit".

SCRIPTURE; Eccles 7:13-14

DECEMBER 10

"SO LET IT BE"

Then said he unto me, prophesy unto the wind, prophesy son of man, and say unto the wind, thus saith the Lord God; come from the four winds o breath and breathe upon these slain, that they shall live (Ezek 37:9)

We live beneath our potential whenever there is no clarity identifying the principles in which our Lord implemented that are intended to make ones life prosperous. When God took Ezekiel up in he spirit he showed him an analogy of his people, how they were lost, destitute and without hope. During this God also commanded a word of restoration to bring his chosen back into their natural order. In the ninth verse of the 31 chapter God instructs the prophet to prophesy to the wind so that it may come forth and bring life (paraphrase). He was given permission to speak to the unseen and call it what it never was (see Ezekiel 37:9). In this text Ezekiel operates under the principal of calling those things which be not as though they were (Rom 4:17).

It's time to come up a level, we want Gods best but yet we speak words contrary to acquiring it. That which is seen is not of faith; we must step up and walk in obedience to the entire word and not just the portions easy to digest; we must eat the entire stroll. Within lies the power to change the atmosphere around you, what's needed is the courage to by pass criticism and proceed with declaring what has already been spoken to your spirit: God would never place you in what's considered an impossible position without making available to you impossible provision. In your voice, in your speech lays the answer to what ails you; speak to that thing and declare "so let it be" which is defined as Amen or it is done!

SCRIPTURE; Ps 89:34

DECEMBER 11

"GIVE WHEN YOU DON'T HAVE IT"

He that have pity upon the poor, lendeth to the Lord; and that which he have given that will he pay him again (Pro 19:17)

Whenever we make a sacrifice unto the Lord; if it is done in humility it automatically transfers itself into a sweet smelling aroma pleasurable unto God: whatever you do that it thought or known to be a real sacrifice will always be accepted and never go un-repaid or unrewarded. If your spirits are low give a smile anyway, when finances are short pay your tithes and give an offering; "giving when you don't have it" is a sure way of receiving what you don't deserve.

As Moses saw to the constructing of the ark, the word says "and all the women who were wise hearted did spin with their hands, and all the women whose heart stirred them up in wisdom spun goats' hair (Exo 35:35-36). It makes no notation of them being asked; it clear that from deep within them came a tugging which steered their hearts to want to partake in the constructing of a temporary place for God who would be a permanent fixture in their lives: love compelled them forward, it superseded over selfishness, self centeredness and even stinginess.

It's never foretold of what transpired in the lives of those who made this sacrifice, however we learn of it daily when we understand that this act went on to alter the lives of generations to come; their bloodline is still blessed because they had the gumption to "give when they didn't have it"! When what you already have falls below what you need why not relinquish it over unto the Lord who'll give you double for your trouble plus a triple investment designed to exceed the need; you gotta believe God and "give when you don't have it!

SCRIPTURE; Mt 10:7-8

DECEMBER 12

"LOST FOR WORDS"

Wherefore he is able also to save them to the uttermost that come unto God by him, seeing he ever liveth to make intercession for them (Heb 7:25)

I've had days when I've come before God in prayer and found that I'm sort of stymied or "lost for words". It was during those times that I could forget about eloquent speech or proper pronunciation and give God the highest praise; I'd sit in his presence, magnify his name and cry out alleluia.

We deceive ourselves if we think it proper or necessary to always have a voice before God, there comes a time when we ought to be "slow to speak and swift to hear(Jam 1:19) for during theses times it's us who'll find themselves ministered too. Being "lost for words" isn't a curse the word says "likewise the spirit also helpeth our infirmities: for we know not what we should pray for as we ought: but the spirit itself maketh intercession for us with groaning which cannot be uttered" (Rom 8:26). Words aren't always prescribed to get the attention of God: if you're facing a situation that has you "lost for words" go before the throne of grace and bellow out a groan; your father is diverse enough, knowledgeable enough and God enough to decode this coded message and supply the need!

SCRIPTURE; Isa 55:1

DECEMBER 13

"NO DRESS REHEARSAL"

For yourselves know that the day of the Lord so cometh as a thief in the night (1Thes 5:2)

There are events that we plan or attend which allows for the participants to participate in what some would call an informal practice run or dress rehearsal to assure minimal or no complications will hinder the said event. Our lives are a prototype of dress rehearsal as we are generously given the opportunity to delve into what our father has said our lives should entail; we have a manuscript that we can follow, live our best years yet and also make preparations for the day we are called to the wedding (Rev 19:7-9). The only time available for us to make adjustments is now, today. In the moment we are called we will cease from decision making; no hidden opportunities are squandered away that will enable us to try again; there will be "no dress rehearsal".

Consider your position in life don't just breeze past those small hang-ups believing the lie "it's just the way I am"; the only hang-up you were born with is sin and if you have been born again in Christ than you no longer live under sin but grace (paraphrase Eph 2:5). Take advantage of what has been provide for you and positioned to you for the day will come when we all shall stand before the judgment seat and the word says" he that unjust, let him be unjust still: and he that is filthy; let him be filthy still; and he that is righteous, let him be righteous still; and he that is Holy let him be Holy still (Rev 22:11); signifying your life now will determine your status later!

SCRIPTURE; Mt 22:9-14

DECEMBER 14

"NOT PROPERLY PREPARED"

And when the king came in to see the guest he saw a man which had not on a wedding garment (Mt 22:11)

In Matthew 22:1-4 Jesus speaks in a parable concerning what the Kingdom of heaven is like; he likens it to a wedding and the guest who will attend. In verse 11 it says "and when the king (God) came to see the guest he saw a man which had not on a wedding garment". What has transpired is the man who came to the wedding was an invited guest, but he failed to come "properly prepared": he had an invitation he wasn't a party crasher; however he lacked the adequate garments to be an honored guest. What Jesus makes clear is this "he has come that we may have life and it more abundantly nevertheless we cannot obtain this life unless we wear the blood of Jesus as our official garment". Everyone has been invited but not everyone will attend or be seated; for again the scripture say"for many are called but few are chosen" (Mt22:14).

Don't be just another church member, one who settles in their favorite seat Sunday after Sunday to hear the man or woman of God but never actually apply what's being taught to their lives; or one who has done what you thought you should but has never done all that you could thereby still lacking and not "properly prepared". Think on this: when the Lord takes roll call on that day if you're not there an excused absence won't apply so be prepared!

SCRIPTURE; Mt 13:12

DECEMBER 15

"HAPPINESS IS A CHOICE"

A good name is rather to be chosen than great riches, and loving favor that silver and gold (Pro 22:1)

Oftentimes we are left with the stigma that happiness is weighed or attributed to what we have obtained in life, what neighborhood we reside in, or the monetary assets at our quick disposal. We delude ourselves when we believe that true happiness will transform in any outside force beside oneself; regardless of past or present circumstances "happiness is a choice". You choose your path in life by not allowing what's taking place around you to interfere with your ability to be happy in spite of it!

During a time of adversity I would often elaborate on how happy I would be when the era or season passed: one day when I uttered these words to myself I could heard the Holy Spirit say "why wait until your situation change, what's preventing you from being happy now, in your present position, right where you are", after a quick perusal the answer was clear, nothing but me and my perception of where I was along with every negative thought the enemy would attempt to introduce into my mind could navigate me away from the happiness I sought!

We'll never have the complete happiness we seek after if we take our eyes off of the cross for in his presence is fullness of joy and at his right hand is pleasure evermore (Ps 16:11). Don't magnify your problem magnify your God: if it were meant for you to be doing otherwise, residing elsewhere, with other people you'd be there already. Don't allow the happiness allotted for you in today slip away; embrace and celebrate where you are remembering that it was God who allowed it!

SCRIPTURE; Phil 4:11-12

DECEMBER 16

"HIGHLY FAVORED"

And the angel came in unto her and said, hail, thou that art highly favored, the Lord is with thee: blessed art thou among women (Luke 1:28)

Surely Mary was not feeling "highly favored" as she was being told the plight her life would take, for it was contradictory to the plans she previously made, it ran perpendicular to mans wisdom and denied the logic of rationale thinking: why then was her salutation mimicked in this fashion? Could it be that through this God would demonstrate "your current station in life will in no wise nullify the thoughts God think toward you, nor the plans he has for you (Jer 29:11)?

Mary was instructed by the angel to fear not: for thou hast found favor with God (Luke 1:30); today God echo these words to you. You can't allow fear to come in and paralyze you and rob you of your favor. Why is that important? Because where fear is faith isn't, and if you have not the faith to believe that you are highly favored, you cannot receive it. Push pass any anxiety or befuddlement you maybe experiencing and begin to utter words that will expedient to re-develop your position "be it unto me according to thy word" (Luke 1:38b), God is faithful enough to oblige!

SCRIPTURE; Luke 1:29-38

DECEMBER 17

"BLURRED VISION"

Every way of a man is right in his own eyes: but the Lord pondereth the heart (Pro 21:2)

In the natural when the eyes are no longer working properly or as per the norm it is then customary to go see the eye doctor: an exam is completed and usually a prescription is given which is believed to make the necessary adjustment for normality. Well the truth is as it is in the natural so too is it in the spiritual and we can become of those who suffer from "blurred vision", it usually occurs during the times we are unable to hear or feel God as per the norm; what has happened is we've inadvertently nibbled ourselves away from the relationship: the cares of this world has begun to take precedence in our lives and our relationship with Christ has suffered somewhat. We think God isn't listening when in fact we aren't saying much, we've become short with our waiting and have developed the symptoms of "blurred vision"; not because the Lord has moved, we have; unbeknown to ourselves we have taken small steps backwards which has caused us to lose sight of the intended goal. This doesn't mean that we love the Lord any less, it means we have faltered somewhere in our walk.

Now that the problem has been identified allow me to forecast a speedy recovery along with the prescription which brings healing. Identify where you've become lax, confess that fault and turn away from it: now as you apply the adjustments you'll begin to experience the closeness of the relationship you once had plus the victory you've been attempting to acquire; remember the righteous fall seven times but he gets back up again (Pro 24:16).

SCRIPTURE; Pro 20:27

DECEMBER 18

"WHAT'S YOUR PROBLEM"?

For I am with thee, saith the Lord to save thee... (Jer 30:11a)

Talking to God is a wonderful thing. It was during one of my many conversations (as I lodged my complaint) that I could hear God answer the complaint as it was still on my lips; before I could fully release every word the answer came; he said "your situation (prison) isn't your problem what you think about it is". Oftentimes we think changing our position or making substitutes with the situation will bring the satisfaction we so desire, but the truth is "you can have a most favorable life with everything going our way, but if your thoughts or your mind isn't functioning up to par you have nothing, no peace, no stability and no joy.

Consider Paul who suffered through much affliction yet during the affliction was victorious in what Christ proclaimed he would accomplish (2Co 6:4-5). The wicked one would rather you fight against the place you're in by murmuring and complaining; which shows a lack of faith and trust, but think on this "the weapons of your warfare are not carnal, but mighty through God" (2Co 10:4); in other words; you have no problem, you're involved in a situation that's destined by God to bring forth increase for the edifying of your life. Satan wants you to believe you have a problem but the Lord is saying "that's not a problem that's a situation for a miracle", now whose report will you believe? To relinquish the hold that Satan is attempting in your life you can think on these things "whatever is true, honest, just, pure, and lovely and of a good report and if it has virtue or praise (paraphrase Phil 4:8).

SCRIPTURE; Jer 30:17

DECEMBER 19

"TAKING THE GRAVES CLOTHES OFF"

And he that was dead came forth, bound hand and foot with grave clothes: and his face was bound with a napkin, Jesus saith unto them, loose him and let him go (John 11:44)

One day Lazarus died and those who were next of kin to him thought that his was his end, his final resting place. In their hearts they settled on seeing him on the other side, in the resurrection (see John 11:1-24), but God had other plans; he would do with Lazarus what others thought preposterous ; he would take what he wasn't and make him what he was to be. This would require something first, he would have to be loosed of his graves clothes.

We to are modern day Lazarus; we've heard Jesus call us forth, we've answered the call and come out of the tomb (the world) which had us encapsulated nevertheless we're left with something else to do. Us coming forth means little if we remain in our grave clothes. We must disentangle ourselves from the worry, the lust, the distrust, the restlessness, the strife and other situations or emotions that bound us and buried us initially: we must take the grave clothes of low self esteem, brokenness or pity and do away with them. If it's your desire to live past your potential or become resurrected out of your past free yourself from restrictions: even if you do so little by little. Remember a little leaven leavens the whole lump.

SCRIPTURE; 2Co 3:18

DECEMBER 20

"HOW TO WAIT"

And his inward affection is more abundant toward you, whilst he remembered the obedience of you all, how with fear and trembling you received him (2Co 7:15)

Many make the confession that they are waiting on God, but how many know that it's not that you wait, instead its how you wait! Joseph in all his afflictions understood this concept; for even though he was sold into slavery, betrayed by his brothers, lied on by Potiphors wife, thrown into prison, he remained the same in his faith (see Gen 37-41 for the life of Joseph), he counted him worthy who would deliver him and he waited patiently until his appointed time knowing that regardless of the circumstance the same God who had given him the power to interpret dreams and dream dreams would bring to pass what was already declared.

As you wait on the Lord to make good what he promised wait declaring the word of the Lord. Wait in expectation, wait knowing that he called you to endure hardship as a good soldier, wait never wavering, always patient, being longsuffering toward others, but most importantly wait in love, without dissimulation, not walking in strife or bitterness because this will get the attention of God!

SCRIPTURE; Heb 10:36

DECEMBER 21

"NOTHING TRADITIONAL"

So then brethren, we are not children of the barren woman, but of the free (Gal 4:31)

Traditions are restraints which are oftentimes placed upon us when we believe the way that we've learned, the things we've been taught or the way we take has to be fitted or formatted as the way excluding all else. However God has not called us unto bondage but has given us freedom from every ordinance, every restraint, all things that bind, and anything that would contain or restrain our freedom in Christ. We're told to "stand fast therefore (this means to stay there) in the liberty where with Christ hast made us free, and be not entangled again with the yoke of bondage" (Gal 5:1).

The traditions of a family member, the traditions of a church, the traditions we've been taught as children which has filtered into adulthood are just that, traditions: never learn traditions learn and understand what the will of the Lord is for your life. We are all called to be the sons and daughters of God, it is his will that we prosper and be in health (3John 1:2); we're not instructed to lay hold of traditions, but liberty. Don't allow anything to harness you for Christ has come that you may have life, life should not have you; instead traditionally love the Lord thy God with all thy heart, soul, and strength, and thy neighbor as thyself (Lev 19:18) and you'll be doing well, this is what the Lord expect of you!

SCRIPTURE; Gal 3:23-29

DECEMBER 22

"IT'S IN THE OVERFLOW"

Then she came and told the man of God and he said, go, sell the oil, and pay thy debt, and live thou and thy children of the rest (2Kings 4:7)

Whenever your cup begins to fill up and it seem impossible to get to the next leg of your journey getting into the presence of the Lord is designed to sustain you but basking in the overflow is a guarantee that you'll become replenished in the spirit. David must have followed this precept when he fled from the Saul and hid himself in a cave (Ps 57); he knew and believed that "thou they slay me, yet will I trust him".

Relief isn't always on the surface sometimes it'll become expedient that you move beyond your normal flair for getting things done, for when it's not right there it's in the overflow. Your breakthrough maybe intertwined with a fellow sister or brother in Christ, it could come via the wicked: the word says "the wealth of the sinner is laid up for the righteous (Pro 13:22); however you won't obtain it without tenacity! Have the courage to step out and do what you normally wouldn't, consider this; who would have thought the walls of Jericho would tumble down with just a shout (Jos 6:17), likewise shall you obtain!

SCRIPTURE; Job 5:19-21

DECEMBER 23

"BREAKING BARRIERS"

... the Lord hath his way in the whirlwind and in the storm, and the clouds are the dust of his feet (Nahum 1:3)

Taking a look back in history we see that barriers were broken when Lincoln freed the slaves, Dr king marched for equality, women were afforded the right to vote, men walked on the moon and when President Obama became the Americas first black to be voted into the White House; just to name a few; how then do we surmise that we too are not or won't become barrier breakers? Hebrews 13:8 say "Jesus Christ the same yesterday, and today, and forever, so then we've been called to break barriers in our life time!

Your barrier won't be that of Nelson Mandela, or even the family next door; it could be something as simple as you actively destroying the yoke or the generational curse of drug abuse, molestation, incest, dysfunction or alcoholism. Maybe none of these describe your position but the truth is "we all have barriers that have been erected in our lives by Satan designed to destroy us that we must break through, breakdown, and breakout of. It won't be without cost but consider this, the price has been paid, the way have been paid and the victory has been claimed: at Golgotha Jesus declared it is finished (John 19:30) and this gave you the authority over every barrier, any stumbling block, and the wiles of the devil; all that is left is for you to realize that it's in your genetic makeup to win and move forward!

SCRIPTURE; Isa 45:11

DECEMBER 24

"GODS PLAN WAS ALWAYS PERFECT"

For he performeth the things that is appointed unto for me: and many such things are with him (Job 23:14)

You can be certain of this very thing "God is not sitting in heaven, drumming his fingers, scratching his head attempting to piece together way this or that happened in your life. He isn't surprised at your standings, he knew you'd be right where you are doing exactly what you're doing, suppressing thoughts of why me or failure. What you need to know is Gods plan for your life was always perfect! You may have been in some unpleasant situations, experiencing what wouldn't be considered or justified as perfect, but they too were necessary; life can't give you a rainbow without first relinquishing a little rain.

When Satan thought he won after he enticed Eve to eat of the forbidden fruit what actually transpired is he set in motion the active plan for mans redemption (Gen 3). Gods plan to reside with man forever has not changed, when he made man he did so knowing that he would be an eternal relationship; there fore the question isn't how much you've done but rather what you've done in changing your position from death to life (see Rom 10:9-10). Jesus has paid the price for you so that you can have everything you need: healing, salvation, and prosperity; also know this, whenever your circumstances dictate impossible the angels in heaven are chanting "it's possible with God, for God's plan was always perfect, mistakes included".

SCRIPTURE; Ps 84:11

DECEMBER 25

"NOT NEEDING NOTHING TRUIMPHS OVER NOT GETTING NOTHING"

And he saw that there was no man,, and wondered that there was no intercessor, therefore his arm brought salvation unto him, and his righteousness, it sustained him (Isa 59:16)

Christmas has become a season in which the exchange of gifts and presents oftentimes rule. Some think themselves less fortunate than those who are able to give beyond measure; then too there are those who bask in the season waiting in expectation of that perfect present, needless to say disappointment ensues.

During this Christmas season refuse to get engrossed in the hustle and bustle of a commercialized holiday; you don't need to do above what you are able. If you take a critical look at your surroundings at what has been provided to you you'll surmise that "not needing nothing triumphs over not getting nothing". Don't settle for being down on yourself if a desire to do more goes unmet; God never etched in stone notes to determine what a successful Christmas would entail, instead make today a day of gratitude for that perfect gift of salvation that was orchestrated with the blood of Jesus but offered to each of us free of charge; thankfulness unto God far exceed thankfulness for material possessions!

SCRIPTURE; Luke 2:7-14

DECEMBER 26

"BEWARE OF PRIDE"

Pride goeth before destruction and a haughty spirit before a fall (Pro 16:18)

What's the big deal, King Hezekiah is only showing the King of Babylon his riches, his jewels, the things he has aspired to obtain right? There's no harm done, it's not as if he's stolen these possessions or obtained them by illegal gain, right? (See 2 Kings 20:12-13). So why then does God send the prophet to rebuke him along with the message of losing everything? To be frank it isn't as simple as you may have first believed; it's not that he has shown them that cause Gods anger to kindle, but that he has somehow taken the credit for what God has allowed and placed within his grasp. Hezekiah has fallen prey to the spirit of pride which dictates I and not God (see 2 Kings 20:15). The pride is so prevalent that he fails to repent and even as he's being forewarned of the grave lost he and those of his lineage would suffer he still think it's okay as long as it doesn't happen in his day. (paraphrase 2Kings 20:19)

There is no sure way to know when King Hezekiah began to walk in pride it's only evident that he does, however what's exceptionally clear is "God will never allow you to retain what he has provided if or when you conveniently forget that it is the Lord that gives us the power to get wealth, that he may establish his covenant (Deut 8:18b), what you have or will attain in this life isn't designed just to elevate you, but to promote the awesomeness of God himself. Scripture declare "God resisteth the proud but give grace to the humble (Jam 4:6b) therefore don't allow your I and my replace your God has or through Christ, for if God would hold back his strength you wouldn't have the energy nor the resource to accomplish anything in life!

SCRIPTURE; Jam 4:10

DECEMBER 27

"ACCORDING TO THE TIME OF LIFE"

And he said, about this season, according to the time of life, thou shalt embrace a son... (2Kings 4:16a)

Whenever there is a word of prophesy being spoken over your life you must take in more than what's been promised it's imperative that you regard in what timetable the vision is purposed to come to pass. In the featured scripture the prophet Elisha has confirmed that this woman who has made provision for him will in turn bare a son; so too is it with concerning all things which pertain to you. When you're thinking t it'll be too late, you'll witness it happen right on time. As you wait stay focused on what was promised, instead of how long ago it was promised. Don't attempt to give   birth to a premature dream with thoughts of helping your promise along; you'd rather wait than to abort the dream! Faithful is he that has called you, who will also do it (1Thes 5:24), but it's according to the time of life and not mans time!

SCRIPTURE; Isa 49:23b

DECEMBER 28

"TUNE IT DOWN"

A mans heart deviseth his way; but the Lord directeth his steps (Pro 16:9)

Being a minister I must be careful that I never say what the Lord has not directed me to speak. Everyday I must purposely tune down my heart so that I never say something false about a loved one, a friend or someone I believe to be waiting on a word from God; you see what you feel about a person can distort the truth as you know or believe it to be. To be successful in whatever you put your hands to do requires the inner ability to decipher what you feel apart from what is factual. Sometimes we miss it but when we do there remain a way of reconciliation. Consider Abraham and Sarah who were promised a child in their old age: when it appeared as if the promise would not materialize they listened to the prompting of their hearts and created an Ishmael (see Gen 16). Abraham missed it because he was unable to tune down his heart but God being unable to lie made him a father of many nations as promised in Genesis 12:1-3.

Your heart maybe prompting you in the opposite direction of where God has called you and you're tempted because you think it's beneficial to go, but hear ye the word of the Lord "be still and know that I'm God (Ps 46:10): stand still and see the salvation of the Lord (Exo 14:13); don't allow your heart to sound off louder than your God because sometimes he'll show up in a still small voice "1Kings 19:12) therefore pay attention!

SCRIPTURE; Pro 21:5

DECEMBER 29

"UNTO A PLACE I WILL SHOW YOU"

Commit thy way unto the Lord, trust also in him and he shall bring it to pass (Ps 37:5)

Before Abraham became the father of any nations God visited him and instructed him to "get thee out of thy country, and from thy kindred, and from thy fathers house, unto a land that I will show thee" (Gen 12:1). Nothing miraculously appeared that would sway Abraham to obey; God didn't show him a vision of what he would encounter along life's path but what he had was the word of God and the faith to believe that he would obtain what was promised.

Are you being led to an unfamiliar place? Have the course of your life changed suddenly and you find yourself turned north when you started out going south? Could it be that the Lord has spoken and wants to take you "unto a place that he will show you"? You can't hold unto yesterday's wishes hoping to obtain tomorrows promises! You're comfortable with where you are but you don't realize you've become complacent and real soon the hum drum of a familiar pattern will ensnare you if you refuse to move now! You're not too old for school, no it's not to late to transfer jobs, yes you can start all over again: if God has called you out don't hesitate move now; this is your appointed time, your approved hour. The well is destined to dry up there because the source of all resources has distributed it elsewhere: what are you waiting on, "go unto the place that he has shown you "and reap the benefits of a loving father!

SCRIPTURE; Pro 16:3-7

DECEMBER 30

"HE'LL BRING YOU THROUGH IT ALL"

... To give unto them beauty for ashes, the oil of joy for mourning, the garment of praise for the spirit of heaviness... (Isa 61:3)

Being on the verge of bankruptcy, foreclosure, joblessness, a type of illness, or any form of loss is enough to drive one to the brink of distraction and or discouragement, the truth is in our life times we'll each face different dilemmas that can cause us to choose to walk away from, attempt to correct them on our own or we'll stand regardless of what's taking place believing "he'll bring us through it all". Not every choice you make will be easy but each of them will be necessary and they each will produce a harvest.

It matters not what comes your way because we each have a promise of victory and safety, the word declares" when the enemy shall comes in like a flood, the spirit of the Lord shall raise up a standard against him" (Isa 59:19). The standard God uses is his word and we know that "Heaven and earth shall pass away before one jote or tittle of the word fail" (Mt 5:18): so if you feel pressure today remain strong, be encouraged knowing hat "he'll bring you through it all"!

SCRIPTURE; Isa 58:8

DECEMBER 31

"SECRETS"

Confess your faults one to another, and pray one for another, that ye may be healed. The effectual fervent prayer of a righteous man availeth much (Jam 5:16)

A secret has the propensity and the ability to ensnare and entangle so why then is it considered fashionable amongst the mass population to keep them? Could it be that some are unlearned as to the detriments caused by them, therefore we hold fast to them? God being faithful has decided that this is a day of liberation; the time to pull back the covers and reveal the true intent of secrets because with them comes shame and shame bring along its friend guilt and where these components are fear is there: where fear is faith isn't and what isn't born of faith is established in fear or sin!

When the servant of Elisha, Gehazi accosted Naaman and received goods from him on the account of his master he assumed that no one would know; for he manifested his doings and hid the proceeds all in secret not realizing that your sins will find you out: his consequences was to become the leper Naaman once was (2Kings 6:21-27).

Anytime we pamper or blanket unfavorable incidents or situations from our past we inadvertently douse our chances of complete recovery; for what is hid cannot be treated and likewise that which is exposed is destined to be made whole! Take advantage of what's being presented, find you someone reliable and confess your faults one to another and pray ye one for another that ye may be healed; refuse to be another Gehazi and allow your secrets to become a form of leprosy which can lead to contamination and an estranged life.

SCRIPTURE; Ps 147:3

DAY 366 (LEAP YEAR)

"IN LEAPS AND BOUNDS"

For every house is built by some man, but he that built all things is God (Heb 3:4)

As you're reading this page sit and wonder how your life has been transformed from what it was three years prior. Did you have to dissect your life or were you able to immediately gravitate toward what drastically changed? If you experienced drastic change that means you should have learned something about you that you've previously missed: taking your cue from there and instantly monopolized the opportunity to enhance your life and those connected to you; in other words you've grown "in leaps and bounds". Expecting your life to be forever changed you've taken off the can't do mentality and replaced it with "I can do all things through Christ which strengthens me" (Phil 4:13).

Don't become despaired if you find that you were one of those who had to dissect their minds to come up with anything slightly remote to change; chances are you worked long and hard at improvement but it never really got off of the ground; things just didn't intersect as you thought they would. The good news is "God is still faithful", he gives grace to the humble (2Pet 5:5b) and seed to the sower (Isa 55:10), this is not the time to give up you're on the brink of a new year with new fortitude, ask the Holy Spirit to lead and guide you into all truth while this is manifesting and the Lord will provide you with the resource for provision. Your change won't be in vain for with it comes love, life and liberty: expect it for it's destined to show up "in leaps and bounds"!

SCRIPTURE; Heb 2:6-7

www.ingramcontent.com/pod-product-compliance
Lightning Source LLC
Chambersburg PA
CBHW021217090426
42740CB00006B/262